W9-AEJ-248

CARMELITE MONASTERY
GUNHILL ROAD, BRONX, N.Y.

GREAT PENITENTS

THE MACMILLAN COMPANY
NEW YORK · BOSTON · CHICAGO · DALLAS
ATLANTA · SAN FRANCISCO

MACMILLAN & CO., LIMITED
LONDON · BOMBAY · CALCUTTA
MELBOURNE

THE MACMILLAN CO. OF CANADA, LTD.
TORONTO

GREAT PENITENTS

By REVEREND HUGH FRANCIS BLUNT, LL.D.

New York
THE MACMILLAN COMPANY
1921

All rights reserved

PRINTED IN THE UNITED STATES OF AMERICA

Copyright, 1921

BY THE MACMILLAN COMPANY

Set up and printed. Published October, 1921

FERRIS PRINTING COMPANY
NEW YORK

Nihil Obstat

REV. PATRICK J. WATERS, PH.D.,

Censor Librorum.

Imprimatur

WILLIAM CARDINAL O'CONNELL,

Archbishop of Boston.

August 23, 1921.

Ah! is Thy love indeed
A weed, albeit an amaranthine weed,
Suffering no flowers except its own to mount?
Ah! must—
Designer infinite!—
Ah! must Thou char the wood ere Thou canst limn with it?
—*The Hound of Heaven.*

PREFACE

Christianity is a religion of hope. It was one of the bitter reproaches against Jesus Christ by some of His Pharisaic contemporaries that He received sinners and even ate with them. They affected to be scandalized at the teaching that it was possible for one who had sinned to be redeemed. The parable of the prodigal son, of the lost sheep, and other stories, told for the purpose of bringing home to men the knowledge of the mercy of God, were lost upon them. To them there could be but one treatment for fallen women, for instance,—stone them to death.

The reclamation of Magdalen is a glorious argument for the divinity of Christianity. It is only God that could work such a change in the human heart. Her example has ever been an inspiration in the Christian Church. After Magdalen, why despair? Hers is the deathless story of hope. And for that reason she has ever been chosen as the patroness of the houses (never wanting, where the religion of Christ has been preached) whose doors are open to those who wish to imitate the great penitent in her penance as they had imitated her in her sin. One such house in the Italy of the sixteenth century was aptly called, "OF THE ILLUMINATED AND CONVERTED WOMEN". There is a wonderful beauty in the word "illuminated" as applied to the penitent. It is as expressive as that definition of penitence given by St. Clement of Alexandria. He called it "tardy knowledge", which has something of the ring of the cry of the converted Augustine—"Too late have I loved Thee, O Beauty so ancient and so new!"

PREFACE

The Middle Ages are justly called "The Ages of Faith". It is not that the faith has failed in other times; but so great were the accomplishments of those days in every field of endeavor, all due to the fact that the whole of Europe was filled with the spirit of religion, that they are best described as "ages of faith", par excellence. In like manner the third and fourth centuries may be called the ages of penance. It was then those great exemplars of the penitential life, the Fathers of the Desert, flourished. There is no more romantic reading than the lives of these men, and women, too, who fled from the riches and the pleasures of the world, some of them sacrificing rich estates and positions of power, to give themselves to the practice of austerities, the very relation of which makes us weaker ones quail.

Those were days of glorified penance, when the world was amazed at the sufferings of these "holy criminals", as St. John Climacus calls them. Many a book of great penitents could be compiled from the Lives of the Saints. We have passed over most of those whose lives are readily accessible, who may be called the traditional penitents, like St. Mary of Egypt, St. Augustine, St. Thais, and St. Pelagia.

In this selection of penitents there is the design to show that every age is the age of penitence; that every day the Prodigal Son is coming back home to his Father, in the twentieth century as well as in the third, joyfully testifying to the old truth that it profiteth a man nothing to gain the whole world and suffer the loss of his own soul. These men whose stories are told here are witnesses to the wisdom and the beauty of the penitential life. Their sacrifices were heroic. Possessed of the genius or the wealth that got for them the flattery of the world, their one care, once they were "illuminated", was to atone for past sin and die well. Yesterday their lives a scandal, today an inspiration to all who, like St. Teresa, see in the penitent sinner an incentive to renewed searching for the mercy of God.

PREFACE

The author hopes that these stories of "GREAT PENI-TENTS" will be of service in providing spiritual reading to the individual and to communities; that priests may find therein many hints for addresses to sodalities and other societies; and finally, that the book may find a place on the "mission table" to help in the great work of re-claiming souls to god.

CONTENTS

GREAT PENITENTS

THE FOOL OF GOD

IT is not by that name that this great man is known in
history. His intercession is sought under the beautiful, God-given name of St. John of God. But somehow
we like to think of him as the mad penitent, wandering
through the streets as a poor fool, the sport of a sneering
populace. The proud world of John's day, time of Spain's
glory when new worlds were being discovered every day
and men had the lust for power and money, considered him
a poor harmless sort of creature, if not a burden to society.
Public penance for sin! Who ever heard of such vulgarity,
such utter simplicity? Why, of course, he must be a fool.
A fool, indeed! Yet he was God's own fool, Heaven's
court jester; he had learned the folly of the Cross If he
went through the streets of our own cities today he would
be locked up as a vagrant, and learned boards would be
called upon to pass upon his mental powers. But the fool
became a very wise man. It was just because he found out
what a fool he had been in following the wisdom of his
very wise contemporaries that he was able to establish his
great work of charity and finally win the gratitude of those
who once had laughed at him. The man who considers
himself the worst of sinners, who offends the sensibilities
of the dainty with the sound of his self-scourgings, is always the one that has the gentlest touch for others. The
greater the penance, the greater the charity. The greater
the realization of sin, the greater the effort to atone by getting nearer to Christ. And the nearest way to Christ
leads through the alleys of the poor and the sick. The fool
of God became St. John of God by following that path.

John was born at Montemor o Novo in Portugal in the

year 1495. The day of his birth was March the eighth, and by a strange coincidence March the eighth was also the day of his death. It was not a high position in the world to which he was born. He who later on was to be the friend of kings and nobility was of the poorest of the poor. His parents had nothing of the world's goods. They belonged to a low peasant class. But poverty was no burden to them. It did not prevent them from being especially devout in their service of God and in sharing their little with those who had less. His biographers tell us that there were signs at his birth indicating the future greatness of the child. However that may be, the little John was brought up by his sainted mother as one who was particularly favored by God. He might never be great, but he must be good. So his boyhood years up to the age of nine were lived under her watchful eye in innocence and great piety.

It may have been this very piety which was the cause of the beginning of his wanderings. For some reason which we do not know the boy one day left his home and followed a Spanish priest to Oropeza in Spain. It may have been with the knowledge of the mother or it may have been without it. We rather believe that neither the priest nor the good mother knew of the lad's plans, for the biographers speak of his "mysterious" disappearance. She was heartbroken anyway at his absence and died shortly after he had gone from her.

Why the priest did not send the lad home at once when he came to him at Oropeza it is useless now to seek to discover. What he did was to find a home for him as a servant in the house of the mayor of the place. It was a good home for the boy. The mayor was exceedingly kind to him and gave him every opportunity to advance, being won to the lad by his fine manly character, his devotedness to duty, and above all his great piety. John spent his boyhood there and grew into manhood. So fond did the mayor become of him that he was willing that John should marry his daughter. Willing? He even insisted. But John could not see things that way. Why he turned down the offer of the lady's hand we cannot guess. It was very likely for the very good reason that he did not love the girl; or it may have been that deep in his heart he felt that he was called to other things in God's good time. But the more he tried to put off the match the more the mayor insisted. It speaks well for the character of John in those days that he was considered such a desirable catch. But he was not going to be caught that way, and, thinking to settle the matter, he enlisted in the army of Charles V.

That did not settle the matter, however. John was now more appealing as a soldier. The young lady's infatuation increased at sight of the military grandeur of the man she loved and the eager father again came to him with the proposal which meant position and money. John was sick of the importunities. If he was going to marry he would marry the girl of his choice; he would not have his wife picked out for him, even if that wife was the daughter of the mayor. He determined to get away from the man who wished to make him his son-in-law, and put miles between him and the grieving lady by going to Hungary to fight against the Turks.

That act was the undoing of John. It was a far cry from the quiet life of the mayor's house to that of the camp. He was then twenty-seven years of age in the full vigor of manhood. He had come into a school which did not make for sanctity. Many of his new companions in the army were youths to whom licentiousness was as the air they breathed. It was a corrupted society where a youth with pretence to piety and morality was a strange being. The evil examples daily before his eyes did their work. In time John's piety wore off and he became as easy a liver as the rest of the soldiers.

During those thirteen or fourteen years that he served

in the army there was little good in his life. He was a
soldier of fortune, wandering about from country to
country, filled with the restless spirit which characterized
those days of great discoveries. Yet we can well believe
that all the while his conscience was bothering him as he
sought to find his pleasures in this free and easy life. He
got tired of the army life eventually and left it. It was
the beginning of his conversion. He knew well the destruction which the army had worked in his soul; his piety
gone, his morality gone, the great things for which as a
lad he had had ambition impossible now of attainment.
He was over forty years of age, the best part of his life
had been lived, and it was all wasted.

To one in distress the first thought is that of home. Out
of the mists of his evil years there came the face of the
mother who had instilled her piety into his soul. He
would go back to her and seek to atone for the long years
of suffering which he had caused her. But there are
some things a man never can restore. The ex-soldier came
back to Montemor; she was not there waiting for him to
make good all the years of neglect. The grass had been
growing on her grave for more than a quarter of a century.

John did not remain long in his home town. There
was nothing there to keep him. Every day brought him
fresh memories and more bitter tears for his rank ingratitude, his forgetfulness of her. So he set off again, back
to Spain, and next we find him working as a shepherd for
a rich lady near Seville. It was a menial position for
the once gallant soldier, but he felt in his heart that it
was better than he deserved. The thoughts of his youth,
of the mother he had treated so shamefully, burned into
his soul. He saw himself as he was—a wastrel. His
sins rose up in all their enormity before him there as he
tended his sheep, and he wept bitterly for them. The realization of his wasted life made him determine to do penance. He lost no time in making plans. He set about

the work at once, and gave most of his time both day and night to prayer and acts of mortification. Ever before his eyes was his past ingratitude to God, and he lamented it from the bottom of his heart, wondering how best he might show God that he wished to make up for the wasted years. To do something for God; that was his desire. The years of service in the army had made known to John what misery there was in the world. In his continual travels for those twelve years or more he had witnessed the sufferings of others. One class of afflicted that appealed strongly to his tender heart were the slaves who were carried off into Africa by the Moors. He immediately made the resolution that he would leave his place as shepherd and go into Africa to attend to those afflicted ones, and in so doing win, perhaps, the crown of martyrdom.

But God had other work for him to do. When he arrived at Gibraltar, from which place he was to take passage for Africa, he fell in with a Portuguese gentleman who was being exiled with his wife and children to Barbary after his estate had been confiscated by King John III. What the man's offense had been we do not know, but whatever the cause the only thing that John knew was that here was a fellow being in distress. His new idea of the service of others was strong within him and he insisted on serving the man and his family without any remuneration during the voyage to Africa. So earnest was he in that charity that when on landing in the country of his exile the gentleman became very ill and was obliged to dispose of what property he had remaining in order to care for his family, John went out to work as a daylaborer in order to support them, and even sold whatever he himself possessed to help in the work of charity. It was, though he knew it not, a prophecy of the days to come when he would take the very clothes off his back to give to the needy.

But John did not win his crown of martyrdom. His confessor, to whom he opened his heart, assured him that his desire to lay down his life in this way was an illusion. Perhaps he was not over-impressed with this ex-soldier who at forty years of age yearned to lay down his life. Go back to Spain, was the common sense advice of the priest, and John immediately went back, disappointed no doubt that God had not accepted the offer of his life.

John was in earnest in his wish to help in God's work, but what that work was to be he had not yet discovered. He wasted no time in useless pining, however. As soon as he arrived at Gibraltar he became a pedlar. He canvassed the towns about Gibraltar selling pious pictures and books of devotion. He was thus one of the earliest apostles of the press. There was very little profit on his wares, but the new avocation brought him in contact with people and gave him a chance to do missionary work by exhorting his customers to virtue, confessing to them very likely the miserable defection of which he himself had been guilty. But though there was next to no profit in his small line of business, he saw the demand for his wares increase so much that he decided to open a small shop in Gibraltar. Perhaps he thought himself settled for life, content in this small way—for the humility of the man did not permit him to aspire to big things—to help the cause. Meanwhile he had time to give to prayer and to the works of penance begun when he was a poor shepherd. Up to this time John was what may be called an ordinary penitent. He became a great penitent in this way:

One day while he was engaged in this work of apostleship the Infant Jesus appeared to him and affectionately called him "John of God," and directed him to repair to the city of Granada. Without knowing why, John closed his little shop and set out for that city.

The celebrated Father John of Avila, now known as the Blessed John of Avila, was at that time preaching in the city of Granada. One of the most eloquent preachers of all times, burning with zeal for the salvation of souls, his sermons were known to convert whole congregations. It was the feast of St. Sebastian, the beautiful soldier-saint, and John who had been a soldier, too, but in a manner far different from the martyred Sebastian, listened to the great orator as if the occasion were for his special benefit. His eyes were now fully opened. He saw himself in all his misery; saw that the penance with which up to now he had been satisfied was but a life of luxury compared with that which his sins demanded. At the melting words of the great preacher he could not restrain himself. He burst into tears, raised his voice in lamentations, beat his breast in sign of his sorrow, and begged God for mercy to him a sinner.

The congregation was amazed at this exhibition and pitied the poor fellow as a bit touched. But John cared little for their commiseration. He knew only that he was a great sinner and that it was necessary for him to atone. Out of the church he came and, carried away by his sentiments of self-humiliation, ran through the streets like a madman, tearing his hair and crying out what a sinner he was. It was a strange sight, the man running wild with a crowd at his heels throwing sticks and stones at him and abusing him in such a way that he came home covered with blood and dirt. To the crowd he was nothing but a poor fool. John did not resent that; rather it was music in his ears to hear himself called a madman. The occurrence gave him a hint as to how he might do penance. He immediately gave away all he had, reduced himself to absolute poverty, and then went running through the streets again confessing his life of sin and begging God to have mercy upon him. Surely he must be mad, thought the onlookers, and some of them, taking pity on him and wishing to protect him from the abuse of the rabble, brought him covered with blood and dirt to the

preacher whose words had stirred him to this strange
method of doing penance. At once the holy man saw that
in this strange penitent there were extraordinary signs of
virtue. He allowed John to make his general confession
to him and then gave him good advice. Evidently the
good advice did not include the prohibition to do the
peculiar public penance, for soon after that John was
again running through the streets as a madman doing the
ridiculous things which had attracted the attention of the
public to him. Now he was deemed truly mad, and the
authorities had him arrested and confined for observation
in a madhouse where he was treated with the utmost
severity in order to curb his insane propensities. But
severe as was the treatment John did not resent it. It
was truly very little suffering for one who had so deeply
offended God.

John's one earthly friend at that time was Father John
of Avila, who alone understood him. He came to the madhouse to visit John and found the poor penitent near unto
death from his sufferings, covered with wounds and sores,
yet longing for still greater penance. He knew that the
madness of the man was the searching for sanctity. He
told John that he had done penance enough of this kind
and that now it was his duty to give himself to a course
of life that would be of more benefit to his own soul and
to the good of his neighbor. John listened to him as to
the voice of God, and immediately became calm, much to
the astonishment of his keepers, who very likely thought
that a miracle had been done by the great preacher. He
put off his madness, ready as always in his humility to follow the advice of the holy priest. He remained for some
time longer in the hospital, devoting himself after his
own recovery of strength to the other patients.

That short period of caring for the sick was the beginning of the work which has made the name of St. John
of God a blessing among the afflicted. On leaving the

hospital he was advised by Father John of Avila to make a pilgrimage to the shrine of Our Lady in Guadalupe in order to ask her advice as to the work that God wished him to do. It was during that pilgrimage that Our Lady manifested to him that the rest of his life he should devote to the sick and the poor. As he returned to Granada he knew not how that work was to be done, but, as if he must be doing something for the poor while waiting for God's will to be made manifest to him, he began to collect wood in the forest and carry it to the marketplace, where he sold it to get money to supply his own little wants and to help the needy.

In this condition of destitution there came to him the inspiration to found a hospital. One would think that John was not yet over his madness. He had nobody to vouch for him, he had not a cent in the world, yet he felt that his life work was to care for the sick and that in order to do so he must have a hospital. One day as he was walking through one of the streets of Granada he chanced to see a house to let with the sign, "House to let, to lodge the poor". It was like a divine invitation to him. He sought out the owner, who, judged by the standards of the world, would seem to be as mad as John himself, for without finding out whether John had money or not he let him the house. And John knew just as much as the proprietor when the rent would be paid. It was rather an uncertain beginning of a life-work, but strange to say this unbusinesslike method of procedure was the beginning of the great hospital of Granada. John had his hospital; the next thing necessary was the patients. But to get enough patients was the easiest part of the work. The humble little hospital was soon discovered by the unfortunate and John was impatient for the place to be filled. He was the only attendant for some time, but, after working hard all day long about the hospital, he would go out into the city at night to bring in new pa-

tients, carrying them on his back if they were too weak
to walk with him.   At night also he would go begging
the necessary supplies, but after a while it was unnecessary
for him to worry about the means to carry on the hospital.

It was soon discovered that John was not mad after all;
that he who once had been followed by the rabble in the
streets of Granada could now be seen in the darkness of
the night carrying some helpless individual to his home.
Before long the good people of the city, seeking to have a
share in the pious work of the holy man, brought him
more than enough of supplies.   And in addition to that
many of the priests and physicians, seeing that the new
work must be of God, nobly seconded him in his efforts
and gave him invaluable assistance.   The archbishop of
Granada, seeing what an excellent institution this new
refuge was, gave it much material aid and, greater than
all, his protection and approval, and the king's chaplain
sent him enough money to supply the place with suitable
beds.   Everybody, in a word, wanted to have a share in
the charitable work.   As John used to say as he went
through the streets, rain or shine, begging, "Do good to
yourselves, my brethren," so they felt that in helping him
to help the sick they were conferring an everlasting benefit
upon themselves.

With John it was first of all a spiritual work.   To re-
lieve the physical distress of the patients was not his only
concern; he wanted to save their souls.   So no matter how
vile the applicant was he was received into the hospital;
the viler the better.   That course, however, brought criticism upon him, and even the archbishop spoke to him of
the danger of such a course to the good name of the hospital, telling John that he had heard how he received
tramps and fallen women.   John admitted that he had
taken in such persons but, said he, "If my illustrious pre-
late and superior will condescend to visit the hospital he
will find no abuse, and he will be convinced that there is

no one in it who deserves to be driven out but myself. Were I to receive only the just our infirmary would soon be empty, and how should I be able to convert sinners? I confess that I do not acquit myself as I ought of such a ministry and that I do not correspond to the grace of my vocation, and, therefore, I say to Your Grace that I deserve to be driven out from this holy house." Even the archbishop could find no argument against that, and John was permitted to receive whomsoever he wished, and that was anyone with ills of body or soul to be cured.

The work of the hospital was an assured success from the beginning. The patience, the charity, the simple modesty of John impressed everybody. It was an honor to help him. The hardest thing was to restrain his generosity. He actually gave the clothes off his back. If he met a beggar poorer than himself he was not content unless he exchanged cloaks with him. The bishop of Tuy, an admirer of the humble servant of God, thought out a plan to prevent that. He designed a habit for him and ordered him to wear it. This dress became later on the religious habit of the Order which was founded for the followers of John. He himself in his humility had never thought of founding an Order, and it was not until six years after his death that the rules which now bear his name were drawn up. Not only did the bishop give him his new habit but he ordered him to be known by the name which the Infant Jesus had given him—John of God.

It is related that the Marquis of Tarifa who had heard such wonderful stories of the charity of John determined to put him to the test. He came to the hospital representing himself as one in distress who needed money to carry on a necessary lawsuit. John gave him all the money he then had. This so impressed the marquis that he sent him a great sum of money and ordered that every day he remained in Granada there should be sent to the poor in the hospital one hundred and fifty loaves of bread, four sheep and eight hens.

Not from his neighbors only did John receive help. We read in his biography that help came to him in those early days of struggle even from Heaven, and that St. Raphael appeared in person to aid in the work. The worldly wise might sneer at such stories, but there is nothing incredible in them to one who reads of the ceaseless devotion of this poor penitent. Surely God Himself was there in the midst of that devotion to the sick and poor; why scruple to believe that the angels also delighted to be there?

It is related in the life given in his office that one day the hospital took fire. Fearlessly he rushed into the midst of the flames and carried out on his back every patient and, even though at one time he remained in the burning building a full half hour while the flames seethed about him, he came forth unharmed.

But the humble man was not master of the elements only. Not only did he conquer the flames; he conquered also the more destructive passions of men's hearts. Shortly after its establishment the hospital of Granada was the scene of such a victory. The story is told by Digby in his *Mores Catholici.* Antony Martin had imprisoned Don Pedro Velasco on the charge of having killed his brother, and had come to Madrid to hasten on the prosecution. Antony, though a proud knight, abandoned to a life of worldly pleasure, had nevertheless become known to St. John of God by means of a practice of visiting his hospital, and the holy man had recourse to prayer in hopes of reconciling these two enemies. Meeting Antony in a street he presented him with a crucifix which he always held in his sleeve, and urged him to pardon his enemy if he himself wished to be pardoned by Jesus Christ. "If your enemy," said he, "killed your brother, our Lord died for you and me; and if the blood of your brother cried for vengeance much more should the blood of your Saviour move you to forgiveness." These words pronounced with a pathetic tone pierced the heart of Antony Martin; falling on his knees before the servant of God he promised with tears that, from that moment, from being the mortal enemy and the proud grandee he would become the friend of Velasco and the servant of the poor. "I will now lead you to the prison," said he, "where I shall embrace Velasco in your presence and then deliver him; and do you in return lead me to your hospital where I may consecrate myself to God."

After these words they walked together to the prison where Velasco was each day expecting death. Great was his terror on seeing Antony Martin enter, but the servant of God gave him speedy encouragement. The two knights embraced and gave each other the kiss of peace; they mutually vowed an everlasting friendship; and thenceforth their hearts were wholly fixed on Heaven. They both declared their resolution to serve the poor in the hospital with St. John of God during the remainder of their lives. It was an admirable spectacle shortly afterwards, as soon as Velasco could leave the prison, to behold the holy man walking through the streets of Granada having on each side those two friends, once such implacable foes, now so closely knit together in bonds of grace; they were on their way from the prison to the hospital which they never left afterwards. A long retreat and a course of instruction developed and completed the conversion of these two noblemen, who became eminent servants of Jesus Christ.

And thus these two men, who had once been the scandal of the city on account of their dissipated lives and their enmity to each other, became models of virtue, all through the kind example of John of God. So much did Pedro Velasco humble himself that he used to call himself "Peter the Sinner," while Antony became so devout, so earnest in his charitable work, that John recommended him as his successor in the management of the affairs of the new society.

The charity of John, however, was not confined to his own hospital, much as he loved it. Wherever there was distress there was he to alleviate it. All the poor were his brethren. He sought to save them from the sins to which their poverty might lead. Thus one particular class of people that claimed his attention were poor young girls who through poverty might be induced to fall into evil courses. Others who claimed his special care were the fallen women. He took pity upon these poor outcasts, sought them out and, holding his crucifix before them, exhorted them to turn back to God as he wept for his sins and theirs. No wonder that by such wonderful kindness and compassion he was able to make many converts. No wonder that the movement of which he was the head succeeded miraculously. The beautiful sight of this man devoting himself for the love of Christ to the poor was a perpetual sermon, a sermon all the more effective in that he who silently preached it was too humble to think that he was doing anything extraordinary.

The poor soldier, who once had been a wanderer over the face of the earth, was now sought out by the kings and queens who, knowing his great virtue, wished him to be their almoner. But great as was their confidence in him, it never turned his head. He was ever in his own eyes the unworthy sinner to whom should be given no glory, only humiliation. The story is told that once a woman who had imagined that she had reason to have some grievance against him called him a hypocrite and loaded him with abuse. John quietly slipped her a piece of money and begged her to repeat in the market place all her abusive language. In another that would be a fine bit of sarcasm; in John it was merely the desire of the saint to have greater humiliations. It was an echo of the early days of his conversion when he would insist on being regarded as a madman.   Nothing is said as to the woman's subsequent action, but we may wager that she was too much ashamed of herself to do as the holy man entreated her.

Thus was John of God the helper of the poor, the friend of tramps, of poor students, of widows and orphans, of the fallen women, the friend of everybody indeed, but more than all he was the penitent, the seeker of his soul's sanctification.   "What doth it profit a man if he gain the whole world and suffer the loss of his own soul?" were the words that directed his life.   His was a life of action, but with the action went prayer and meditation.   He was forever tending the sick, yet he was forever practising the most severe austerities.   He never forgot that there were long years in his life for which he must make atonement. The years were short in which to do penance; he must make up for lost time.   His meditation was ever Christ crucified.   "Lord," he would say, "Thy thorns are my roses, Thy sufferings my Paradise."

It was a short time, indeed, as years go.   Ten years he had labored in his work of superhuman charity and at last the worn-out body succumbed.   It was fitting that his final illness should result from an act of heroic charity. A great flood had come upon that part of the country and John as usual was in the midst of the distress caused by it.   He had overworked in helping the poor by saving wood and other necessaries, and in this weakened condition had jumped into the water in order to save a drowning man.   He had failed in the attempt, but wet to the skin had kept on working, making light of his condition.

His companions in the hospital insisted on putting him to bed even though he rebelled at the enforced inactivity. He could not imagine why a man with only a slight cold should be compelled to coddle himself while there was so much to be done for others who were so much worse off than he.   He was not inactive at any rate, for he took the time of what he considered an enforced vacation to straighten out the accounts of the hospital and to settle many matters about the government of the institution.

But everybody else knew how serious the illness was even though John himself made light of it.   Quickly the news spread through the city that he was dangerously ill, perhaps near unto death.   To the hospital hastened the sick and the poor who had been the object of his benefactions.   They found him in his cell, lying in his poor habit, his only covering an old coat and his pillow the old basket in which he used to collect his alms, now taking the place of the stone which had ordinarily served him for a pillow. Among those who came to see him was a noble lady, Anne Ossorio, who had always been one of his benefactors. Seeing him in such a pitiable state, pitiable to her though it was a delight to the man who so loved penance, she secretly sent word of the conditions to the archbishop and begged him to command the sick man to do her bidding. Thus armed with the authority of the archbishop she made John consent to leave the hospital and suffer himself to be brought to her home where he might receive the proper attention.   It was far from pleasing to the dying man but in his deep humility and spirit of obedience he made no objections so long as it was the will of his superior.   Perhaps he felt that he never again would return to his beloved hospital.   If so, God's will be done.   He that had divested himself of his cloak for the poor of Christ would not object to forego the happiness of dying under the beloved roof so long as that too was the will of God.   He gave his last instructions to his brethren and appointed Antony Martin superior in his stead.   Then a last visit to the Blessed Sacrament in the chapel and he was ready to leave.   During those last days in the luxurious home of the noble lady he chafed under the kindness of his attendants.   Who was he to have such comforts when his Lord had suffered so on the Cross ?   His Saviour, he said, had been given gall to drink and they gave him—broths.

The room of the dying man was the resort of all. The nobility came, so too the magistrates of the city begging the saint to give his dying blessing to their city. It was the supreme humiliation to John. Who was he, poor miserable sinner who had been such a scandal to all, to presume to give them his blessing? If they wanted a real blessing let them seek the prayers of the poor and of his brethren. And it was only when the archbishop commanded him that he finally assented, giving his blessing to all while at the same time he exhorted them to do penance for their sins. John never preached better than in those last hours as he stood at the threshold of death. It was a sermon to draw the tears of all who heard him.

To give John all the honor in his power the archbishop himself came and said Mass in the room and prepared him for death. He could die happy now for the archbishop promised him that he would pay all his debts and continue to look after the poor. As the end approached the dying man insisted upon getting from his bed and laying himself in the form of a cross on the floor. Then he arose on his knees and in this position, before the altar, rendered his soul to God on the eighth day of March, his birthday, in the year 1550, the very year in which was born another great servant of the sick, St. John Camillus, a penitent, too, in many ways like to John of God.

And now the man who was once pursued through the streets of Granada as a madman had come into his own. There was no honor too great to give him. His funeral was one of great pomp conducted by the archbishop and attended by all the clergy and nobility; and more than all by the sick and the poor who realized that they had lost their best friend.

St. John of God was not soon forgotten. His few possessions became holy relics. The staff which he had used as he went about collecting for the poor and seeking out cases for his charity became a relic celebrated throughout Spain.   It was deposited in the hospital founded by a noble Spanish lady who had given her own house and her fortune for the purpose.   It was finally encased in silver by certain persons in gratitude for miraculous cures through the intercession of the holy man.

A beautiful touch in the story of the mourning for John's passing is that he was quite as much lamented by the Moors as by the Christians.   It was a proof that he had been a friend to all.

The work established by John of God still endures.   It is needless to go into the history of the order of the "Brothers Hospitallers of St. John of God," the name given to the Order of which he was the real founder, although the rules were drawn up only after his death. Speedily it spread all over Europe.   Today it numbers more than a hundred hospitals in Europe with some thirteen thousand beds, and over fifteen hundred religious who to the three solemn vows of poverty, chastity and obedience take a fourth one to serve the sick in the hospitals.   Still do these followers of the humble penitent meditate upon his words of advice to his first followers: "Labor without intermission to do all the good works in your power whilst time is allowed you."

Many miracles were wrought through the intercession of the saint, who was beatified in 1638 and canonized in 1690.   Leo XIII made him the patron of hospitals and of the dying in 1898.

THE JESUATES

I REMEMBER hearing the late Abbé Hogan of Brighton Seminary, who did so much for the formation of clerical opinion here and abroad, warmly defend the Salvation Army when a thoughtless person made fun of its bass drum and popular song methods of religion. With his broad mind he saw what moral good was effected here, and especially in London, by the irrepressible army. He saw it in its philanthropic work—and if philanthropy is not the sublimest motive power to the human soul, it is better than laziness, better than a quietistic mode of existence that suffers the submerged tenth to sink so far beneath the waves as to make rescue impossible.

To praise the Salvation Army is not, as some would seem to imply, a rejection of the infallibility of the Church, nor an assertion that their propaganda is not amenable to criticism. The ulterior motives may be at times those of the anti-Roman proselyte. Be it so or not, it is for us Catholics to utilize the present results of their work, to perfect what they have begun, to lead into the true Fold those who are brought by other hands out of recesses into which we might not be able to go. Cardinal Manning, in his great apostolate for the poor and the children, recognized this. His "sympathy with the philanthropic work of General Booth was never disguised," says Hutton in his life of the great churchman, "and he was too much of an organizer himself not to look with admiration on the order and discipline of the Salvation Army." And he goes on to say that with their simple faith, belief in God, sin, a Redeemer, the Bible, Heaven and Hell, far

19

from Catholicism as they still are, it ought to be easier to guide them aright than many others who have higher theological and ritualistic pretensions and a less real, less ardent faith. Some have quarreled with the methods of the Army. Men who choose to fancy a religious message in a Wagnerian music drama, or feel compelled to cut into a Pomegranate of Browning for a substitute for the Sermon on the Mount cannot view the Brigade on the street corner but as a travesty on religion, of the same genus to their thinking as vulgar Catholicism—something for the poor, ignorant crowd. There are many Catholics who share in this antipathy to the advertising of God to the public. By them religion is confined to the church, or the innermost recesses of the private chamber, and of a necessity it must be tabooed in polite society. In fact, any extraordinary means to gain a hearing, and to win souls to God, is frowned down as non-traditional and therefore to be scorned.

The Catholic Church, it is true, does not take kindly to the ink of the advertising agent. She is always at the same old stand where she has been for centuries, preaching the same gospel. Knowing that her faithful children will come to her, she leaves the three columns of the Saturday night paper to the passing strange titles of sermons and musical fixings, which vie with one another in the effort to attract the sinner to a dissertation on the Jewish massacre accompanied by Gounod music, or to a denunciation of the wily Jesuit, made patriotic by the sentiment of "My Country, 'Tis of Thee." They tell us that advertising is life in this twentieth century, and while we know that the Church of Christ needs no splashing of ink to live, are we not allowed to think that more of the scattered sheep would be brought into the right fold if we went after them and compelled them to come in? Too much conservatism is not a good thing. Street corner religion, combining exhortations with brass band accompaniment, has to many a horrifying sense of innovation, and is assumed to be an emanation of fanaticism, or religious dementia, yet it is not so necessarily, unless one wishes to call fanatics many of the holy souls whom Mother Church has raised to her altars.

The Salvation Army idea is not a special acquisition of the nineteenth century and General Booth. In the Middle Ages the idea of the army for attracting listeners and winning souls to Christ was utilized by the Church in the Order of the Jesuates. It is a far cry from the slums of the English or American city of to-day to the poetical Tuscany of the fourteenth century. To read the history of the Jesuates and the life of their founder, the Blessed John Colombini, is like a romance of chivalrous days; a *romance* it is of those old poetic days, for this army of the past is quite forgotten save for its memory in ponderous tomes. Yet it should not be forgotten, for the life of Colombini and his companions is an inspiration, an incentive to us to accomplish what they did in Siena.

Old Siena, how poetically has a gifted writer described it!

"Walls and towers that flush rose red at dawn and sunset above a sea of vivid green, flecked with silver gray—a craggy island in a billowy ocean; brown roofs that climb in broken tiers, a sheer hillside crowned with a high plumed aigrette of white and black and gold, narrow sinuous streets flanked with palaces which Dante may have seen."

Such is Siena the old. Such it was in the glorious fourteenth century. This was the outer appearance that would catch the eye of the poet, but within how like the modern city, with its varied life, its passions, its aim at the beautiful in art and poetry, and the unsated hunger for wealth and luxury and pleasure. It was here, in 1304, that Giovanni Colombini was born of virtuous parents, of the famous Strozza Vacchae family, which for the past century had been known by the more familiar name of Colombini. It is not surprising to find him in his early youth engaging in a mercantile career. That was the passion of the Sienese. In the preceding century they were known as the nation of shopkeepers, oftentimes engaged in the then disputed traffic in money. Even the heads of the noblest and proudest houses did not consider it unseemly to be in business, which explains the readiness with which young Colombini became a merchant. Siena occupied the foremost position in the financial world, due principally to the fact that its bankers had the patronage and business of the Holy See, and on the strength of that they had banking houses in the great cities of France and England. A business career then was the high road to honors.

Colombini entered the wool business, a lucrative one, for the Sienese had a heavy trade in Flemish cloth. Strictly attentive to business, he was able soon to open counting houses in other cities. We can picture to ourselves the young merchant of the day, proud of his good family, polished to a fault, loving money and having it in abundance, acquainted with all Christendom, patronizing the arts with a chivalry which was a certain inheritance. It was Siena's period of glory and prosperity, and on this account the arts, being encouraged, were in a flourishing condition. Yet in the midst of it all there was a prodigality of luxury which became a folly, so much so that (1262) the State was invoked to check the extravagance of the women. Thereupon was decreed by law the length of a woman's train, the amount of gold and silver ornaments, and such like. But if the women had the proverbial failing of vanity the men were addicted to the greater fault of avarice. The accumulation of wealth and its wanton use in luxury, the continual pursuit of pleasure, and the consequent oppression of the poor, were the characteristics of those years.

Undoubtedly, Colombini was not a whit different from

the nobles of his acquaintance. He was of the earth earthy—egotistical, proud, avaricious, considering it no dishonor to grind the poor unmercifully. His pride of life was intensified by the fact that he had belonged to the celebrated Nine, shortly before the Black Death and the consequent overthrow of the existing government, and that his rule was one of the most brilliant eras of the Republic in its great rivalry with Florence. That he had a powerful will and astounding activity is evident in his later life as well as in the events which led up to his conversion.

He had little thought of marriage till he was more than forty, believing no doubt that he had little time to concern himself about domestic affairs. Years before, however, a wife had been selected for him in the person of the beautiful Biagia, daughter of the noble Cerretani family. The interests of the two families were common. The union was most desirable to the parents, and so in 1343, Giovanni became a benedict. It was a happy union of which were born a son and daughter who died in early life, the daughter as a young novice. So they lived happily for twelve years till the eventful midsummer day in 1355. On that day Colombini was in bad spirits. Business cares occupied his mind and he scarcely spared the time to come home to dine. To increase his ill humor the dinner was late. He fretted and fumed, and loaded everybody with reproaches—especially his wife for presuming to keep him waiting. To make matters worse Biagia told him to have patience, and, as the crowning bit of impertinence, she took from the table a volume of the Lives of the Saints and gave it to him with the suggestion that he should read it till the dinner was served. That was more than he could bear, and in disgust he threw it into the middle of the room, while Biagia fled in fear of her husband's anger.

Left alone, Colombini had the grace to be ashamed of himself. Regretting the manner in which he had abused the holy book, he picked it up. Chancing to open it at the

life of St. Mary of Egypt, something in it held his attention, and he sat down to read it. It was the old story of
crime and atonement.

Colombini forgot that he was hungry. Nobody dared
disturb him and he read till morning. The narrative
plucked at his heart strings. It opened his eyes to the
condition of his own soul, taught him that there are things
more important than laying up treasures on earth. The
work was done. It was the "tolle, lege," repeated once
again. Another soul had turned into the narrow lane that
leads to saintship. Here was one more sign of the favor
which Heaven showered down upon Tuscany, a province
beyond all others in the founders of Orders, which produced such saints as St. Francis of Assisi, St. Bernar-
dine of Siena, and the great St. Catherine.

Colombini's conversion was not the pietistic sentiment
that prevails a moment and is gone. He had put his hand
to the plow, and his nature was too noble to think of looking back. To atone for past forgetfulness he assumed a
practical penance. He took account of stock and declared
himself ready to return whatever he might have acquired
unjustly. He gave great alms, spent much time in visiting churches, the poor, the sick, took the vow of chastity
together with his wife, and from the day of his conversion
used for his short sleep a simple plank. The beautiful
garments of the wealthy merchant were cast off, and, the
butt of jokes from his friends, for his apparently insane
conduct, he walked the streets of Siena as a poor man.
He was not long a solitary figure. The grace of God
worked through his example. Francesco Vincenti, of an
aristocratic and wealthy Sienese family, was the first convert to the peculiar ways of his friend Colombini. It was
a hard struggle, however, before the tall and handsome
Vincenti capitulated to the exhortations of his short and
delicate adviser.

The reproaches of friends increased. Such an unheard-of thing for two wealthy men with all the pleasures of the world at their command to waste their fortune, dishonor their families by their strange behavior, and think and talk only of the poor, the Holy Name, and the salvation of souls!

There is a beautiful story about the neophyte days of the holy man, which shows better than all else what great love for the poor consumed the heart of one who erstwhile had despised and ground them. One day the two friends met with a leper at the door of the church. The unfortunate was a repulsive sight to the world, but to these men he was an image of the Master, "despised and the most abject of men." Home to Colombini's house they brought him immediately, washed and bound his sores and put him to bed, and, as a final penance to strengthen his soul still more, Colombini drank of the water wherein the leper had been washed. They then returned to the church, leaving behind them an indignant woman. Biagia had not advanced in sanctity as rapidly as her husband, and it is no surprise to find her incapable of looking on with equanimity while her beautiful home was used as a hospital for the poor, and her best bed and daintiest linens taken for the comfort of despised lepers. But the indignation soon passed away. "How be a Christian," she asked herself, "if one did not love the poor?" And so she went to comfort her guest. As she approached the room there came a perfume thence sweeter than the richest flowers. Soon Colombini returned to continue his kind offices to the beggar, and lo, the bed was empty, the leper had fled! The astonished man fell on his knees. His heart told him who the visitant was, and as he prayed in humility and thanksgiving there appeared to him in a radiant brightness the Divine Leper, "struck by God and afflicted."

This miracle was followed by a greater abandonment of self on the part of the two men. After having provided for those who depended on them they gave away all their fortune in order to be more like the Master, and with bare head and feet they begged their bread like the lowliest of mortals. "Lady Poverty" had captured other devoted suitors, like to her greatest knight, St. Francis of Assisi. Many have remarked the great similarity between him and Colombini—both poets and musicians, both preachers of the love of God, and both martyrs to poverty.

The Salvation Army methods, as any attempts destined to obtain religious notoriety are now called, had already begun. The man who had been so proud, the nobleman, the ruler of Siena, determined to humiliate himself. It is easier to be poor than to sacrifice one's pride, but Colombini was equal to the task. He acted as servant to the nobles who had been his equals in the old days, and to humiliate himself the more he rode an ass through the streets where once he had held his head as high as a king. Eccentric as such actions seemed to his compatriots, there was in the conduct of the man a deeper purpose than self-abasement. The sight of a man who had voluntarily renounced wealth and station was well calculated to arrest the attention of passers-by, and he, thirsting for souls as once he had thirsted for money, profited by the furore his presence occasioned, in striving to lead others to the things of God. Simple layman though he was, the love of God made him an eloquent evangelist. Standing on posts, or on the steps of some Sienese palace, he held his hearers entranced as he spoke so earnestly of sin, of eternal punishment and especially of love of God. Street corner preaching was not such a rarity in those ages of faith, peculiar as it seemed when the modern Salvation Army revived it. It was common enough in those days to hear the word of God preached out under the blue sky in the public square, in the fields, in the narrow streets, in the highways and by-ways, wherever a soul was to be saved. So in Protestant England in the eighteenth century had Wesley and Whitefield gone out among the people, preaching Christ in the fields, in the factories, in the mining districts, and with such effect that hardened men sobbed like children.

Colombini's preaching, united to his good example, was most persuasive. In a few months he had the happiness of beholding a thousand converted to a better life, many of them abandoning the world entirely in order to surrender themselves wholly to God. It was from these that this spiritual general got the first recruits for his army which was called then "The Poor of Christ." Soon the army numbered seventy, comprising many of the foremost citizens of Siena, an astounding thing to the populace of that gay place. It is still more astounding when we read of the manner in which prospective vocations were tried. Oftentimes the new disciple was compelled to ride through the streets seated on an ass, with his face towards the tail, and again bound as a criminal while his companions exhorted the passers-by to pray for the miserable sinner.

To men who had been full of the pride of life, who lived in luxury and knew no opposition to their will, such proceedings were far from being the tomfoolery which men of to-day consider them, but evidenced in a striking manner the fact that the love of God can induce men to be "fools" for Christ's sake. "Have you the courage to let yourself be spit upon in the face and not say a word?" asked Lacordaire of the young pianist Hermann, who had consulted him about his vocation. "Yes," he replied without a tremor. "Then go," said the great Dominican, "and be a monk."

The brass band and tambourine element was not despised by the army. Colombini's powerful voice, we are told, was like a clarion of gold. Loving music passionately, as one of the celestial pleasures, and comforting his heart with it, he saw therein a means to stir up the souls of his followers as the martial air strengthened the battling soldier. In mighty chorus they sang the hymns which he himself composed. It was the battle hymn of an army making war upon the powers of darkness. Occasionally there was one of the disciples like Boccio who sang the hymn to the accompaniment of the viol. Attract the crowd was Colombini's motto, and then keep them by the word of God.

Apparently the army had attracted too many recruits. The people of Siena saw fathers, sons and friends seduced from the world by this new enchanter. Therefore they murmured long and bitterly against him, and as a result of their enmity Colombini and Vincenti were banished from the city and condemned to perpetual exile. But they did not go alone. Twenty-five companions, tried and true, voluntarily suffered the punishment with them. Heaven, however, did not permit its valiant soldiers to be treated thus with impunity. A storm and pestilence swept over the city, striking terror everywhere, and the afflicted populace, ascribing such a visitation to their unjust treatment of the army, immediately despatched messengers to entreat Colombini to come back. But he would not. In this enforced exile he saw the finger of God pointing to other cities where he could spread the good work of converting souls, and thither he led his willing army. Triumphant band it was, singing hymns as it marched along, converting sinners and gaining new recruits for the ranks!

It is not a fancy that leads us to refer to Colombini and his disciples as an army, for the army idea was one of his own. "Chevaliers of Christ," he calls them, and above all "The Brigade." "Do you recall," he writes to the abbess of Santa Bonda, "that the way of combats and battles has been followed by our Captain, Christ?" That is the figure he uses so often in his letters, the true Salvation Army of Christ. It was likewise a favorite one with St. Ignatius, who considered Christ as the King, the Leader of an army, the "Captain-General." Whether the founder of the Jesuits was indebted to the founder of the Jesuates for this idea, or borrowed it from his former knightly career in the world, it is hard to say; perhaps it was due to both. At any rate we are told that one of Ignatius' favorite books was the life of Colombini.

It is interesting to follow the army in its campaign over the fair land of Italy, its only weapons the love of God, and the Holy Name of Jesus. It was on this tour that they received their distinctive name of Jesuates. Pope Urban V had left Avignon to return to Rome, in 1367. None was more pleased at this than the Poor Soldiers, and, in order to show their joy and their loyalty to their Holy Father, sixty-six of them repaired to Corneto, where the Papal party was to land. As they marched along, singing as usual, the children on the street cried out, "Look! look! here are the Jesuates!" It was the most fitting name for men whose entire will was to bring honor to the sweet name of the Saviour. It was a fruitful journey in many ways. The Pope was struck by the simple faith of the men, interested himself deeply in their work, approved the Order, even selecting the garb they should wear, and, in spite of the opposition manifested towards them on many sides, defended them and allowed them to be called "The Pope's Poor."

Colombini's cup of joy was full. Back to Siena he started, but the old body, now sixty-three, was worn out by its labors. Alive he did not return, but there, almost at the gate of his beloved city, surrounded by his sorrowing companions, he breathed his last. As the body was brought into the mourning city, who more fitting to be the first to touch it than the faithful wife Biagia, to whose sacrifices and devotion much of his success was due?

But if Colombini died, his army endured for three centuries. It extended over Tuscany and the neighboring country, founded many convents, as did the similar Order of women which he may claim the honor of establishing, since it was through his prayers and exhortations that his rich cousin Catherine left the world and founded the Jesuate sisterhood.

One would have an incomplete idea of the Jesuates if he imagined them only as a Salvation Army, singing hymns and exhorting to holiness of life. Beautiful as this work is, it was supplemented by another. The sick were cared for, the dead buried, and remedies were made and supplied to the poor who could not get them elsewhere. The Jesuates were certainly all things to all men. Hard labor, too, was their portion, with the discipline morning and evening, and the recitation of one hundred and sixty-five Paters and Aves daily, together with the Office of the Blessed Virgin, for it was not until 1606 that they were admitted to the priesthood. In some places distilleries were established, the proceeds of which went to give succor to the poor. As time went on, however, the Order ceased to remember the simplicity of its founder. It became too wealthy, and that was its undoing, for it is said the Venetian Republic demanded its suppression in order to obtain its wealth to carry on a war against the Turks. However it may be, it was Clement IX, who, in 1668, three hundred years after the death of Colombini, suppressed the Order for reasons which reflect naught upon the holy men who had done such loyal service to the cause of Christ.

So ended the Jesuate Army. It is now scarcely more than a name, its history embalmed in ponderous tomes where one seldom digs, and yet as we conjure up those long forgotten forms we see them live and breathe again, as men of to-day fighting the battles of the King, doing all, daring all; and in that vision of the olden days we learn to understand somewhat the grandeur of the great Captain Who could make of men such a noble army.

THE GAMBLER—ST. CAMILLUS DE LELLIS

PENITENCE and gloom are not necessarily synonymous. It would be a mistake to think of the great exemplars of sorrow for sin as useless mourners kneeling in the corner, beating their breasts, with ear for nothing but their own lamentations. The science of the penitential life is the determination to atone. Into that enters personal mortification, suffering, self-affliction. .The body has sinned; it must pay the penalty. It must suffer not only for the evil it has done, but it must be subjected against the possibility of the soul being again dominated by it. Penance looks not only to the past; it looks to the future as well. It wants to make up, to redeem the time.

Hence it is no surprising thing to find your penitent a man of superabundant activity; not a mere regretter of the past, but a maker-up of lost time. He has wasted his life; the days to the end are all too short for him to have something in his hands when he comes before God to give an account of his stewardship. So he works incessantly. Constant tears, constant prayers and, too, constant charity. Alms, to redeem one's sins. Alms of kindness, generosity to God and neighbor. How plain all that is in the life of St. Peter. Lovingly we recall the old tradition that his sin was forever before him; his eyes were continually flooding with their penitential tears, so that furrows were worn into the old cheeks. But who was more active in charity, in the service of the flock committed to him than the first great white shepherd of Christendom?

It is this penitential activity that charms in the life of

31

St. Camillus de Lellis. The grace of God opened his eyes one day. He saw himself as others saw him, a good for nothing, rowdyish, swaggering, lustful soldier. A foolish life surely. But the realization of that fact and the determination to make up for the squandered years, gambled away in more senses than one, reached its final fruition in the establishment of one of the most beneficial Orders to suffering humanity that the world has ever seen. The tears of Camillus for his years of sin were rivers of mercy to the afflicted.

Camillus was a contemporary of Shakespeare. He was a lad of fourteen when the great poet was born. They never knew of the existence of each other, but I like to think that when the poet was penning the immortal lines as to the quality of mercy the converted gambler and swashbuckler was giving a sublime example of the exercise of mercy in his tender care of the sick of Rome.

It was in 1550, then, that Camillus de Lellis was born at Bacchianico, in Abruzzo, in the kingdom of Naples, then under the domination of the Spaniards. His father, Giovanni de Lellis, belonged to a race of soldiers. Militarism was in the blood. But it was rather poor, thin blood by the time it had reached Giovanni. His was hardly the soldierness of patriotism. He was a soldier of fortune. He fought wherever he was hired to fight, irrespective of the cause, and had no scruples even about hiring himself out to the Turks, the avowed enemies of Christianity. As to his ability there can be no question, for we find him acting as an officer both in the Neapolitan and later in the French army.

But the life of a soldier of fortune was hardly conducive to morality, and Giovanni did not scruple at taking his pleasures where he found them. He was dissolute, with all the vices of the soldier life of his time. Indeed, those Renaissance days were nothing to be proud of from the point of view of morality. Yet no doubt there was a time when he too was something worth while, otherwise one cannot imagine that fine woman, Camilla Compellia, marrying him. But the noble Roman girl soon realized that her marriage had been a mistake. The soldierly husband had nothing noble about him but his name. Her happy days, if happy they could be called, were when he was away from home on some fighting expedition. Her first baby had died, and she had not been sorry, for there was ever the fear in her heart that a child of such a father must be worthless.

So passed the years. Camilla had lived a life of sorrow, a neglected wife. Her only hope was for the peace of the grave. Little she guessed that in her old days God was to use her for a great work in His kingdom. She was old and gray, nearly sixty years of age, and she was about to bring forth another child. The biographers of her son tell us that she was alarmed at the prospect. Another child, perhaps to inherit the father's vices and thus be a reproach instead of a blessing. Besides she was old, she must die before the child would be reared. What chance would any child have, being left to the care of Giovanni de Lellis?

A few days before the birth of Camillus there came a dream to alarm her. It seemed to her that she saw a child, her child, with a red cross stamped on his breast, and after this child came many others following him, all wearing the same sign. Such a dream would have been a consolation to her had she read it aright, but it only increased her melancholy. Might it not be the threat of disaster, the child signed with a cross of blood.

The early years of young Camillus were such as to increase her fears that God had punished her in sending this son. Many a tear he made her shed. Many an act of penance she did, many a prayer she said that the sins of the father might not be visited on the son. But all seemed hopeless. The boy Camillus was a chip of the old block. There was nothing winning about him. He was the product of the camp. It was useless for the quiet, gentle mother to seek to train him. He would have no books, no education. His soldierly father was his ideal, not his retiring mother. Even in those days he longed to be a soldier, and all that education did for him was to teach him to read and write. The poor mother did her best, but her conviction must have been, when she came to die, that she had failed. Little she guessed that one day this son who now caused her so much grief would be raised to the altar of God. She was denied that consolation. Camillus was twelve years old when the poor old mother was laid to rest. No doubt he grieved; surely he had reason. But the grief of youth is short and anyway there was one more restraint taken from the life of the lad who burned to be a man and a soldier. One can fancy him even then begging his father to take him with him on the next campaign but, worthless though he was, Giovanni had some little regard for the welfare of the boy. He sent him to school, glad no doubt to get him off his hands. But the school days accomplished little. Camillus learned nothing but vice, the propensity to which he had inherited from his father.

It was a happy day for Camillus when he left behind him the prison walls of school and strode off at last by the side of his father to be his companion and a soldier of fortune.

Like father, like son. Giovanni de Lellis hardly knew what were the duties, the obligations of a father. He had none of the parental instinct, or he would have been the last one on earth to permit the lad to become a soldier. But he did not care. Camillus was to him only a boon companion. The father had walked the way of vice; why not the son?

But Camillus needed not the example of his father. He was an apt pupil in the ways of the world. He became like his companions, a loose liver, to whom the only manliness was sin. The young soldier had little choice in sins, but if there was one passion more than any other that held him captive it was gambling. The lazy life of the soldier of fortune had induced that. It gained possession of him, body and soul. It became a second nature. He was powerless to resist it. Sometimes he even lost the clothes off his back, but that did not change him. There was always the chance to win back what he had lost, the old gambler's chance.

The destitution to which the son was so often reduced must have at times disturbed the conscience of the father who had been the teacher and abettor of the son's vices. He was now getting to be an old man, with nothing but a wasted life and a son who seemed destined to outstrip him in vice, difficult as that might be.

And then came the end. The old soldier was struck with his last illness, and at the same time Camillus was slightly attacked. I like to fancy that the son had contracted his sickness while caring for his father, a beginning of the life work which was to cover his name with glory.

The desire of the old soldier was to go home to die. Home for the end, to be laid by the side of the wife to whom he had been so faithless. But he never reached home. They recovered sufficiently to begin the journey home, but Camillus saw that his father would never reach there alive. He was dying. The son brought him to the house of a friend, and there Giovanni de Lellis fought his last fight—against death. No longer the brave soldier, no longer the swashbuckler that could laugh at death. He was vanquished in body, but happily unvanquished in soul. He who had so long forgotten God was permitted to come back to Him at the end. The good friend brought the priest to him, and the dying man made his peace with God, and surrendered to the Cross. They buried him there.

The death of his father was the beginning of the change in young Camillus. He had loved his father, had admired his soldierly qualities, had been his companion for years. And now he was no more. But it was grief that had impressed his heart the most. He had seen a great thing. He had seen this brave man, his father, this soldier who had been afraid of nothing, now vanquished. He knew how evil the old soldier's life had been; and he had seen the tears of his repentance. It was all in vain then—this service of the world. The day comes when passion is powerless. He saw the emptiness of a life of sin. It was then, very likely, he made his vow to become a Franciscan.

So it was a changed youth that left his father's grave, and still weak from illness and sorrow resumed the journey home. Not only was he weak from his recent sickness, but a wound in his leg was beginning to bother him. It was to bother him to his dying day. He had laughed at it as a mere scratch, but now it was becoming infected. Crushed in soul and body he trudged along, but thinking not so much of his physical as of his moral condition. He was sicker in soul than in body. His father had repented, why not he? If it was a desirable thing to repent at the end of life, why not in the flush of youth? And moreover might it not be that life was near its end for him even in his youth?

Camillus could go no farther. He sat down to rest, and to think, think, think, of the death of his father. God was tugging at his heart; and seeing two Franciscans passing in deep recollection, he took it as a sign that God had inspired him to make the vow to become a Franciscan. His mind was made up at once. He would do this thing, do it while in the first fervor of what he believed to be his conversion. An uncle of his, Fra Paolo Lauretana, was a Franciscan, a man of saintly life and of certain influence in his Order. Why not go to him for advice? And at once he went off to beg the good Father to use his influence in getting him into the Order. But the uncle was first of all the priest, and then the relative. He was not over impressed with his young soldier-nephew. He knew the blood of de Lellis, and his discerning eye could not see any sign that the conversion of Camillus was to be a lasting one. So without giving a decided refusal, he kept the youth for a while under observation. The trial did not win him over. He could discover no sign of a vocation, and moreover Camillus was far from being in the state of health required for one who would live the hard life of a poor Franciscan. He pleaded his case, but the old uncle was hard as a rock. At last he sent him about his business.

To say that Camillus was angry is to put it mildly. It is easy to imagine him using pretty strong language in talking about this uncle of his who did not understand a fellow. Camillus was incensed. Why try to be good, no doubt he asked, when your own won't take you seriously? Off he went in a huff, decided that there was no use in trying to reform. He wouldn't try to be a religious any more. He had offered himself, and had been refused. The sin be upon his uncle's head. And right away, very likely, Camillus went looking for a game of cards. No sense in being good; we can hear the old companions whom he rejoined now laughing at the soldier who wanted to be pious.

Camillus was in a sorry fix. He wanted to be a Franciscan, and the Franciscans would have nothing to do with him. He must keep on soldiering. But again who wanted a soldier with a crippled leg? For the supposed slight scratch had now become a serious running sore. In vain he sought remedies to heal it and fix him up to resume his old avocation, and all the time he was so mortified at his appearance, a soldier limping along from a little scratch— not a glorious scar received in battle—that he hid himself as much as he could, sneaking from one town to another.

At length fate, or rather the grace of God, brought him to Rome, and he came to the hospital of St. Giacomo to put himself under the care of the surgeons. In return for the medical treatment, he offered his services as a servant in the hospital. A fine big strapping servant, no doubt the hospital authorities were glad to get him. But the trouble was he had not come alone; he brought a pack of cards with him, and to while away the time he had initiated the other servants into the attractive art of gambling. Soon all work was neglected for the fascinating cards. Search was made for the chief culprit who had destroyed the discipline of the hospital, and lo, under the pillow of the big lanky young soldier a pack of cards was found. Needless to say he was dismissed at once, even though his sore was not entirely healed. What if it wasn't? They were not going to permit him to disrupt the entire hospital.

A pretty worthless customer, indeed, this limping soldier with his feet on the threshold of sanctity. In desperation he tried to hide his infirmity as much as possible and entered the army again, this time as a soldier of fortune in the Venetian army.

It was the old, old story. The good resolutions were forgotten; the young soldier-that-would-be-a-monk was discouraged and he threw himself into the thick of every fight, not caring if he were killed. He became as he was before, a roustabout, a sinner. Life held nothing for him. Yet often as he lay ill, seemingly unto death, he would shudder at his sins and promise to begin a new life. But outside dealing the cards the easiest thing Camillus did was to make vows.

He was a veritable tramp in those days, and with him there went a soldier chum, Tiberio, whom he greatly loved, both of them half clothed, half fed. One day when they were begging at the door of a church they were accosted by a rich noble of the place. He was at that time paying for the erecting of a building for the Capuchins. There may have been something in the attitude of Camillus that impressed him, or again it may merely be that the nobleman was a shrewd business man who did not believe in giving charity to vagabonds. His alms was to ask the beggars if they wanted a job. Camillus replied at once that he did, but before giving a definite decision went to ask the advice of his chum who had very likely gone on as soon as he heard work mentioned. Camillus would decide nothing without the advice of Tiberio. And Tiberio scorned the idea of menial labor for noble soldiers like them. What! give up the free life of the road for such lowly work? Why, Camillus must be a fool to think of it, and he the son of a nobleman. The easily led Camillus thought the same himself as long as Tiberio thought so, and off he went with his companion to let the building go up of itself for all of him.

As Camillus went on, however, his conscience began to trouble him. He had vainly striven to quiet it since that day when at the death of his father he had seen the wisdom and the beauty of repentance. Impulsive as usual, he turned about and set off for the man—it was back twelve miles—who had offered him a job, while Tiberio, ridiculing him, went on his own tramping way never knowing that this tramp chum of his had just turned into the road of sanctity. But he soon missed the company of Camillus. Back he turned, too, to the Capuchin monastery and asked for a job. He got it. And thus they met again, Tiberio covered with whitewash and Camillus driving the ass that carried the building supplies. It was too much for Tiberio, and after a few days of this menial employment and after vainly trying to win over Camillus to his way of regarding work, he left for green fields again, thinking that his old chum was a poor kind of fool.

The soldier spirit of Camillus never appeared to better advantage than in these days when he was winning the battle over himself. It is true, he had little notion of spiritual betterment, for he did not stick to his work from a spiritual motive. The old soldier instinct was still strong in him. He still wanted to be the active soldier. He wanted to redeem his good name, he wanted to show the world that there was something in him, and he regarded the present work, humble as it was, as the means to make enough money to rehabilitate himself, get himself new clothes, new equipment. He was truly a sorry sight, raggedy, with no care of his personal appearance, so that even the children used to congregate about the place where he worked in order to have some fun with him. He did not see the joke of it all; he was silent, almost morose, and made no friends among his fellow laborers.

It may be that the friars saw the real man in this queer looking youth driving the ass. Anyway, they became interested in him and trusted him, sending him occasionally on an errand which showed their confidence in him. One day they sent him to a neighboring monastery. It was rather a long journey and Camillus was not able to get home that night, so they put him up at the monastery. The Father Guardian felt himself attracted to the youth and engaged in conversation with him, calling attention to an old scar on the wrist of the young soldier and asking him about it. Something in the kind soul of the friar won Camillus. He saw in him a friend, and—perhaps the first one in whom he felt he could confide—he told the whole story of his short yet checkered life, short in years but long in sin and misery. It was not an easy task for him to bare his soul, and he blushed with shame at the recital of his evil deeds, even while he scarcely knew why he was recounting them to this stranger. But he had found a sympathetic listener. There was no reproach from the good friar—in this he was very different from Uncle Paolo who had seen nothing good in his nephew—he gave him sympathy, kindness.

All the night long Camillus stayed awake. He paced

the floor or stood looking out the window, the friar's words of advice, of warning, ringing in his ears. Again he heard the call to repentance. He could hardly wait for the morning to return home, determined to seek the will of God in earnest and to do it.

As Camillus rode along, meditating on the words of the friar, suddenly he seemed to hear a voice speaking to him. It halted him; he knew it was from God. He threw himself from his horse and knelt in the dust of the road like another Paul, begging God to make known to him His will. For a long time he remained there thinking of his past. He saw the wickedness of his misspent life. His sins frightened him. He beat his breast with sorrow, and moaned over and over again his fervent, tearful act of contrition, calling on God to show him mercy; and then as if calling him to the service of God he heard the sound of the church bells ringing. It was the Feast of the Purification. The grace of God had entered the young man's heart. The way of penance towards which his steps had been so many times directed was entered upon at last. He would tread it willingly to the end. He was then twenty-five years of age.

Speedily Camillus returned to the monastery where he was working and told the Father Guardian all that had happened. The friar believed him and assured him that everything would be done to enable him to become a Capuchin. It was enough for Camillus, and immediately he began a life of sincere penance, a life of austerity. The friar was as good as his word. He succeeded in making arrangements for Camillus to enter the novitiate at Triviento and thither he repaired with a great joy of spirit. There could be no turning back now. Camillus had seen the light. He must efface himself, and this he did so well in the first days of the novitiate that his fellow novices called him the "humble brother."

But the days of trial were not gone. The old sore,

that miserable, inglorious scratch, broke out again, and
the novice, zealous as he was, was dismissed, heartbroken,
yet not discouraged, for the friars had promised him that
if he were cured they would take him back. He would
be cured then! So off he started for the hospital of St.
Giacomo where the telltale pack of cards had been found
under his pillow. Again he was given a job as a servant.
But what a change in him! No longer the lazy, gambling
soldier that had set the whole hospital by the ears, he was
now a slave to duty. He devoted himself to the care of
the sick with such kindness, such unction even, that the
other attendants wondered if this could be the same man
who had been ejected a short time before.

In the Rome of that time the greatest personage was the
humble Philip Neri. The saintly man, through his untiring labors in the confessional, had changed the face of
the city, so long suffering from the evil days of the pagan
Renaissance. To him Camillus, as well as everybody else
in Rome, came to confession. But great confessor that
Philip was he had no end of trouble with this new penitent of his. Things went along very nicely until the old
sore began to heal. And then nothing would do Camillus
but that he must go back to the Capuchins, since he felt
that he was obliged in conscience to do so. Philip felt that
the youth had no vocation for the Capuchins and sought
to deter him from going back, assuring him that if he did
have his own stubborn way and go back the sore would
break out again. But the headstrong soldier persisted.
Back he went to his old friends, but inside four months
he was out again, and this time for good, with a written
document to show that he was ineligible ever to enter the
Order on account of an incurable wound. Nothing daunted,
he went to another house of Capuchins and sought admit-
tance, but the friars would not take him.

Surely Camillus was having a hard time finding his
vocation.   God was getting things ready for his own good

time. Philip Neri laughed good naturedly at the crest-fallen ex-novice when he next met him. "God bless you, Camillus," he cried out, "did I not tell you to give up the thought of being a Capuchin?" Poor enough comfort to Camillus, however.

Well, since he could not be a monk there was nothing for him to do but go back to his work at the hospital. So back he went and was given his old position of superintendent of the wards. But even then he had no idea that here was his lifework. He still had it in his head that some day he would be a monk. Meantime, he was where God wanted him to be, for Camillus was needed in the hospital.

The hospital of those days was not the institution it is today. It had many faults. The methods of caring for the sick had not reached the perfection of modern times. No one knew the faults better than Camillus, for in his early days as servant at the hospital he had committed many of the sins of negligence. He knew that the attendants often neglected their duties. And in order to catch them in this neglect and reprimand them against the further repetition of them he would hide himself between the beds. He saw that the patients often called in vain for assistance, that beds were unclean, patients uncared for, parched often with thirst with no one to give them a drink, sometimes left to die without the sacraments. So great was the carelessness that sometimes patients were buried alive!

Beholding these things now from the point of view of faith, Camillus saw the great need of reform. The sick must be cared for. They must not be left in incompetent hands. It was for him to get good men to devote themselves out of the spirit of faith to the work of caring for the poor afflicted ones. He found the beginning of his work in the hospital. Among the attendants he found five men who had something of his same spirit of love for

the sick, and who deplored as he did the lax condition of
the hospital. To them he told his plans, indefinite as
they then were, to obtain better care for the sick. These
men all heartily agreed with him. The little group of
reformers gathered in one of the rooms of the hospital
and there before a shrine of Christ crucified, which they
had made, they knelt, and prayed, and even scourged
themselves. In this the moving spirit was, of course,
Camillus. To him there was nothing new in the scourging. Long before this, even in the first fervor of his conversion from sin, he had been accustomed to spend most
of the night in prayer, whipping himself, and torturing his
flesh with a girdle of tin and hair shirt. And added to
these mortifications, he had half starved himself in his
desire to do penance.

And from that penance, that realization of his own un-
worthiness, there came to Camillus the desire to help
others. It was all planned in his mind. He and his companions at once put their charitable thoughts into execution. They watched and tended the sick, especially the
dying, exhorting them to pray, trying in every way possible to help them to their sanctification. It was the practice of the spiritual and the corporal works of mercy. But
the methods of the little association, strange to say, were
a novelty to the hospital authorities and some people never
take kindly to novelties. What was good enough in the
past is good enough for all time according to their way of
thinking. Yet one must not be too hard on the authorities.
The Christian world was suffering in those days from un-
checked novelties. At any rate the meetings in the oratory
were discontinued and Camillus was ordered to dismantle
his beloved shrine. He could not understand the opposition, so convinced was he that his mission to the sick had
been given to him by God. Even when Philip Neri sided
with the hospital authorities and advised Camillus to be
obedient and to submit, he found himself up against the

stone wall of the stubborn convert. Camillus would submit because he had to, but he kept his own opinion still. He even went so far as to change confessors believing that Philip did not understand him.

Though all the world was against him and his pet project Camillus still felt that God wished him to establish an Order for the care of the sick. It might be presumption in some one else, but in one who had felt the very presence of God it could be nothing but an inspiration. It must be done. But how? Must he be a priest in order to fulfill the will of God? Well, if that was so, he would become a priest, that was all. It seemed an impossibility, it was true, but God would show the way if he wanted him to do that work.

Camillus was then thirty-two years old. He had little or no education; he could read and write, that was all. What courage it required for him to face the long course of studies necessary before he would be admitted to sacred orders! But why let that daunt him if God was with him? So while still serving in the hospital wards he conned his new lessons, very elementary lessons at that. But so earnest was he that it was not long before he was able to enter the junior classes of one of the Jesuit colleges of Rome. It is inspiring to think of the tall, ungainly man of thirty-two or more sitting on the benches side by side with the small lads who could not resist the temptation to make him the butt of their good-natured jokes.

But what cared Camillus about discomforts, humiliation? Zeal lent speed to his feet. Determination aided him in his studies, and at last with the help of a pious gentleman named Firmo Calmo who gave him enough money for his patrimony—the same man when he came to die gave all his wealth to the hospital—he was ordained priest at Pentecost in 1584, at the age of thirty-four, and had the wonderful privilege of offering up the Holy Sacrifice of the Mass. It was an event beyond the wildest dreams of the soldier. How happy poor Camilla would have been could she have foreseen that glorious day. Her son, for whom she had feared every ill, a priest of God!

Father Camillus had intended to remain at the hospital after his ordination, still serving God in what he believed to be his life's mission, the service of the sick, a service all the greater now that he was a priest. But he soon realized that his activities here must be limited. He still felt that God wanted greater things at his hand. He was at the time chaplain of a small church. He lived in a poor small room in the rear of the church—hardly fit accommodations for one who had visions of founding an Order. But there he made his home and with him Bernardino and Curzio, two poor ignorant men who had served with him in the hospital, the only ones left of that band of five lovers of the sick who used to kneel in the little hospital oratory before the crucifix. It was in this humble room, however, that the great Order of the Camilians was begun. The three men lost little time in planning. Theirs was a practical work, to serve the sick and dying. So immediately they began the rounds of the hospitals, Camillus exercising his priestly functions while old Bernardino and Curzio instructed the sick, advised them, comforted them and helped them to die well, besides giving them all the material comfort which they knew so well how to give. Wounds and sores were cared for, the most menial and repulsive tasks were performed with holy joy. The sick man was made king; more, he was regarded even as Christ crucified.

"Praised be God," the sick exclaimed, "these are His angels. Christ himself has come to His own."

Soon the reputation of these few holy men spread throughout the city, and they were besieged with requests not only from the hospitals but also to visit and tend the sick in the private homes. It was heroic work, but crushing. Camillus and Curzio broke under the strain and

contracted an illness so serious that they had to be taken
to the hospital themselves and put to bed for treatment.
But their courage, their faith, was not lessened. No
sooner were they able to stand on their feet again than
they tottered back to the loved work of caring for the sick.

It was about this time that the kindness of a good man
enabled them to leave the poor room which, being in a
malarial district, had caused the serious illness. A more
fitting dwelling was obtained and Camillus, now with a
home of his own, began to think of the foundation of his
Congregation. He was one of the most persistent men
that ever lived. There was still a good deal of the soldier
blood left in him. The very persistence of the man won
him helpful friends. Not only did he find a good pro-
tector in the person of the charitable Cardinal Mondovi,
but even the Holy Father, Sixtus V, took a personal interest in him and his work of kindness. At once he gave
his approval to the proposed Congregation of Ministers of
the Sick, and at the request of Camillus, who had never
forgotten the story of his mother's dream of the red cross,
the Pope permitted the members to be distinguished by
this insignia. They wore a long black garment with a
red cross on their breast. They were to live together with
the vows of poverty, chastity and obedience and, added to
these, a vow to serve the sick. Gradually the Congregation attracted new members, priests and laymen, and soon
at every hospital bed in Rome there was a wearer of the
red cross tending the sick, facing death if need be in the
heroic exercise of true Christian charity.

It would take too long to review the annals of the Congregation. They are filled with beautiful stories about
the work of these men of God. In the humblest cottages,
in the fever-filled galleys, in whole districts where pestilence raged and men were dying like flies, there you would
see the red cross. Shortly after the approval of the Congregation the members were put to a severe test. A plague

had broken out in one quarter of the city where the velvet weavers lived. Camillus and his companions were immediately in the thick of it. One gets a beautiful picture of the big lanky Camillus now worn to skin and bone from his austerities, taking care of the infants, washing them, dressing them, feeding them. "Suffer the little children to come unto me." It was a time of heavy trial, with many hundreds dying, and as the result of their labors five of the Congregation died, martyrs to charity. But the danger of death deterred no one, least of all Camillus. He was still at his post, even going about from door to door begging for food and clothing for the poor unfortunates. He knew no rest. Life was a time of penance. "The true apostolic life," he used to say to his followers, "consists in giving one's self no repose or rest."

It was this spirit that ensured the success of his undertaking, and only three years after the establishment of the Congregation it was made an Order with solemn vows. Much against his will Camillus was made the Father General. Gradually the Order spread from city to city. Institutions were established everywhere, for wherever there was suffering there was an appeal to Camillus, and it was not in his big heart to be deaf to any appeal from the afflicted.

It was all the work of Camillus, but in his deep humility he took to himself no glory. He wanted to keep himself in the background; hence it is not surprising to learn that as soon as the work was well established he begged to be released from the generalship. He was suffered to resign, and he was glad; glad not at being relieved of care, but because now he would have more time to give to the sick. The most desirable holiday to him was the time he spent in the Hospital of the Holy Spirit in Rome. He hated to take time to sleep. Four or five hours sufficed him; the rest of the time he spent in visiting the patients of whom there were four hundred in the hospital, and so exhausted did he become that he had to drag himself from bed to bed, falling sometimes from sheer weakness.

But the joy of it! "There is no music," said he, "sweeter to me than the voices of the sick, all clamoring at once to be assisted, no perfume more delicious than the odor of drugs and ointments that bring such relief to the sick; and if it were a thousand times more offensive I would gladly endure it if thereby I could gain anything for the souls of the sufferers."

It was work enough to kill a strong man, and Camillus was only the wreck of a man. In watching him tend the sick no one could guess how much he himself was suffering. For forty-six years the sore in his leg troubled him, getting worse as the years went on; for thirty-eight years he suffered from a severe rupture which he got in caring for the sick; one of his feet had two great sores which caused him perpetual agony; and added to this was a painful kidney trouble. He ate so little that he was but a shadow. He was without a doubt the sickest man in the hospital but the most uncomplaining. The more he suffered the more he felt impelled to come to the aid of others. "So great is the happiness I hope for, that all pain and suffering is a pleasure." His strength was from God. The Blessed Sacrament, the Crucifix, the Precious Blood which were the great objects of his devotion—there he found that superhuman strength. He knew himself as a great sinner; how little were all these pains if they could atone for his evil youth. Always he felt that sense of sin. "O Lord," he would pray, "I confess that I am the most wretched of sinners, most undeserving of Thy favor; but save me by Thy infinite goodness. My hope is placed in Thy divine mercy through Thy Precious Blood." Every day of his life he went to confession with sentiments of the greatest sorrow.

At last the old body worn out by vigils and pains could stand it no longer. Camillus was not afraid to die. He could look back on a wonderful work. No less than six-teen houses of the Order had been established in Italy and hundreds of members were serving the sick while hundreds more had died the death of saints. So, calmly on July 14, 1614, he passed away in his sixty-fifth year, universally mourned as universally loved. Eleven years after his death the body was exhumed and lo! what had been full of sores in life was now fresh, incorrupt. Many miracles were wrought through his intercession, and it was very easy for all to believe that this was a saint. St. John Camillus was canonized by Benedict XIV in 1746. Leo XIII chose him as the patron of the sick and of those who at-tended them. The soldier of fortune had won life's great-est battle.

ABBOT DE RANCE

STRANGE as it may seem, the history of the Bourbon kings of France makes excellent spiritual reading. It is a story in great part of chicanery, of utter worldliness, of crime; yet underneath the gay laugh of the de Montespans, the Pompadours, the DuBarrys, one always hears "the burden of the desert of the sea"—that the world and its glory are but vanity and affliction of spirit. Guizot says somewhere that everybody in those days, no matter how evil his life may have been, sought to die well. One could make a very edifying collection of testimonies, from Voltaire down, of men and women who after a life of sin, of forgetfulness of God, were compelled to admit that life had turned to ashes on their lips. As young Cinq-Mars, once the favorite of Louis XIII and afterwards a traitor to his benefactor, wrote to his mother just before he paid the penalty for his crime: "Now that I make not a single step which does not lead me to death, I am more capable than anybody else of estimating the value of the things of the world."

But amid much that was corrupt, and much also that was worthy of France and its noblest, there is nothing more edifying than the conversion of the young courtier, Armand de Rancé, whose subsequent holiness and austerity gave so much glory to the abbey of La Trappe, with which his name will be forever associated.

When Don Pierre Le Nain, prior of La Trappe, wrote the life of de Rancé,—the most complete biography we have of that wonderful penitent—he spoke of him as, "the illustrious and pious abbé of the monastery of Notre Dame de la Trappe, one of the most beautiful monuments of the Cistercian Order, the perfect mirror of penance, the complete model of all the Christian and religious virtues, the worthy son and faithful imitator of the great St. Bernard."

A glowing panegyric, indeed, yet an accurate description of de Rancé. But these words do not tell all. They do not tell from what depths this great penitent ascended to the spiritual heights. De Rancé is a great example of what the grace of God can do in a man's heart. It was only the grace of God that could take that worldly, sensual, flippant courtier, that pleasure-loving abbé of the salon, and mould him over into a model of rigorous asceticism. Much of it is an unpleasant story, as the story of sin must ever be, but to understand the real man and the glory of his accomplishment one must know the poor material he had at hand when he began the work of forming the spiritual man. To know de Rancé the sinner and de Rancé the penitent is to realize that with the grace of God every man may aspire to sanctity. One is not scandalized at the early life of the man so much as he is edified by the manner in which he broke away from that life and wept bitter tears over it. One forgets the denying Peter when one sees the tear-furrowed cheeks of the penitent apostle.

Armand Jean le Bouthillier de Rancé was born at Paris, January 9, 1626. The family of le Bouthillier was one of the oldest and most illustrious families in the kingdom. A le Bouthillier had been archbishop of Tours, another had been bishop of Airé, and another had been secretary of state and grand treasurer. Originally the family had belonged to Brittany and was related to the dukes of that province. Armand's father, Dennis, a seigneur, had held several offices, and at the time of Armand's birth was secretary to Queen Maria de Medici, the "fat bankeress of Florence," as one of the court had dubbed her when she came to marry the king of France. Dennis de Rancé had married Charlotte Joly and by her had eight children, five daughters and three sons. Most of the daughters became religious; of the sons, the eldest was a canon at Notre Dame in Paris, the youngest, the Chevalier de Rancé, entered the naval service.

Armand was the second son. When he was born Richelieu was powerful with Maria de Medici, the queen-mother; he was the great power in France. It was before the break between the great cardinal and the queen-regent. Dennis de Rancé's position as secretary to the queen brought him into contact with Richelieu, who must have thought favorably of him for we find him acting as godfather to the new baby de Rancé and even giving him his own name, Armand Jean. It was surely a great honor, for the name of Richelieu was a mighty one that year of 1626, when the Cardinal had succeeded in a master stroke for the unification of France by causing the destruction of most of the feudal castles. It may be noted that there is a similarity in the cases of Richelieu and de Rancé. Richelieu had prepared for a military career, with no notion of the ecclesiastical state, and it was only when his elder brother, disgusted with the world, had refused the bishopric of Luçon and had become a monk of the Grande Chartreuse that the younger brother, in order to keep the revenues in the family, was persuaded that he had a vocation. It was an evil of the times, and the Church and religion suffered deep wounds because too often unworthy bishops were foisted upon her for the sake of material gain. It was one of the evil results of Gallicanism, for the Concordat of Francis I had put the Church in France and the episcopate in the hands of the king.

It is not that Richelieu was unworthy. Whatever we may think of his politics, he was at heart religious, and devoted himself to his poor diocese before he came to his great position of power. He was a zealous reformer and did lasting service to religion in writing his "Instruction du Chrétien," to be read every Sunday at Mass in all the churches of his diocese, at a time when the great evil was ignorance of religion. The Church benefited by the strong hand of the Cardinal. When he was convoking the Assembly of Notables, he declared, "We do protest before the living God that we have no other aim and intention but His honor and the welfare of our subjects." When he was dying in 1642, he stretched out his hands towards the Holy Eucharist which was being brought to him, and said, "There is my Judge before Whom I shall soon appear; I pray Him with all my heart to condemn me if I have ever had any other aim than the welfare of religion and of the State." But great statesman though Richelieu was, and one of the greatest servants France ever had, no one would presume to call him, save perhaps in his early days as a bishop, a great shepherd of souls.

Just as Richelieu had not been destined for the Church, so was it with his godson. The younger Dennis de Rancé had been from his very cradle the abbot of La Trappe. It was another of the evils resulting from the interference of the State in the affairs of the Church when a family could presume to claim the right over Church property. Dennis died and Armand thereby becoming the heir inherited the abbey. This meant, of course, that whether or not he had a vocation to the religious life he would enter the ecclesiastical state.

However fine a mind the young Armand had, events proved that he had little vocation for the Church. That, however, did not appear in the beginning. It never seemed to enter the minds of his elders that any special preparation for a religious life was necessary. Enough that the lad knew his Latin and Greek, and had the fine manners of a gentleman. The future abbé had his three teachers, one for Latin, one for Greek and a third for his manners. He was remarkably precocious, and his biographers say that he was scarcely out of swaddling clothes when he could explain the Greek and Latin poets. It was this very precociousness that served him in good stead when there was question about his appointment to a certain benefice. When the benefice became vacant his name was put on the list of those recommended. Naturally the clergy objected to such an appointment. They did not want this "abbé in jacket." The friends of the le Bouthillier family, however, urged the competency of the boy, and finally Caussin, confessor to the king, Louis XIII, decided to test the fitness of the boy whom the king desired to honor. And as the test for the appointment—queer test for an ecclesiastical benefice—Caussin gave the boy Homer to translate! Armand did it and did it well; and Caussin was so pleased at this exhibition of precocious learning that he withdrew his opposition to the appointment. The whole affair would be ridiculous, if it were not so sad. No wonder the real churchmen sorrowed at such appointments of babies to ecclesiastical offices, or rather to ecclesiastical revenues.

Armand was so precocious that we find him at the age of twelve publishing a translation of *Anacreon* under the protection of Richelieu. The young translator even dedicated the book to his godfather in a Greek letter! It was not a great contribution to classical learning, but it was a marvelous thing for a boy of twelve to accomplish. Time came when de Rancé threw into the fire all that remained of the edition. Afterwards, when he was at La Trappe, a penitent after a stormy youth, he spoke of this literary *début* of his, and said that he had kept in his library only one copy of the *Anacreon* and had finally given that away, not, however, as a good book, but "as one very strong and very well bound." He then went on to say that in the first years of his retreat before becoming a religious he had wanted to read the poets, but that since it only recalled old ideas, and since there was in such reading a subtle poison hidden under its flowers he at last gave it all up.

But that was only long afterwards. De Rancé penitent
must have smiled sadly as he thought of those early days
in the sunshine of the court.

No youth ever had better worldly prospects. The
protégé and godchild of Richelieu, he was on that account,
as also because of his father, a favorite with Maria de
Medici. She loved the bright lad, and would carry him
in her arms, hold him on her knees, kiss him and call him
her son. Richelieu, too, was very fond of him, chiefly
no doubt on account of his wonderful talent, just as he
had promised great things for young Pascal and his sister,
and he showed his favor in a practical way by giving the
lad many benefices. Fortune surely smiled on him. He
was canon of Notre Dame, abbot of La Trappe, guaranteed
a life of opulence, and all at the age of twelve.

When the break came between Richelieu and the queen-
mother, the de Rancé family was in a perilous position,
but Dennis de Rancé was well drilled in politics; he had
studied in a clever school. He remained faithful to the
queen, who tried to make him keep away from Richelieu,
but de Rancé was also faithful to his benefactor, and continued to see the Cardinal, though only in secret, till
Richelieu's death in 1642. Richelieu, the mighty, had
gone the way of all flesh. "Treat me as the commonest of
Christians," he said to the priest who came to prepare him
for death. He saw the littleness of worldly glory as he
lay helpless on his death bed. "Let those who cannot re-
frain from showing the excess of their weeping and lamen-
tation," he said as his friends bemoaned his passing, "leave
the room; let us pray for this soul." The great Richelieu
was at last but *this* soul seeking mercy from God. So
passed, too, Louis XIII, who in the light that comes from
beyond the grave saw what a puerile thing is all pretended
royal magnificence. One of his historians tells us that in
his last illness, "he was seen nearly always with his eyes
open towards Heaven, as if he talked with God heart to

heart." Toward the end he cried out, "My God, receive me to mercy." And to the Bishop of Meaux, who came to attend his last moments, he said simply, "You will of course see when the time comes for reading the agony-prayers. I have marked them all." The King of France was but a sinner that needed mercy.

During the regency of Anne of Austria and Mazarin, who had succeeded Richelieu, young de Rancé continued his ecclesiastical studies. He attained great success in philosophy and theology, and—a sign of his favor with the ruling powers—dedicated his thesis to Anne. He was, moreover, a successful preacher and, had he applied himself to that work, might have reached an eminence as great as that reached by Bossuet, who was his fellow pupil. But successful as de Rancé was in his studies owing to his abundance of natural talent, he did not accomplish so much as he might. The reason was that his heart was divided. He was not primarily an aspirant to the priesthood because he felt that he had a vocation. That was but secondary. The priesthood was simply a career, a necessary state for the benefices conferred upon him. No man can serve two masters. But he would be an ecclesiastic and a man of society at the same time. He did not see the incongruity of that; he had all too many examples before him of men who had thrust themselves upon the priesthood that shrunk away from their worldly touch.

So we find young de Rancé, because of his social position, his family name, his royal connections, a frequenter of the salons. The most illustrious salon of the time was that of Madame Rambouillet, which became the centre of the world of nobility as well as the rendezvous of the literati. It was a brilliant, clever, worldly society. It was a time when a new desire for things intellectual was being felt. It was the reaction from the licentiousness of the court of Henry IV. Refinement, grace, intellect were the valued things at Madame's, and here was laid the

foundation of the French Academy with which the name
of Richelieu will ever be associated. Here, too, reigned
the blue-stocking, of which Molière made so much fun;
and that artificiality is the worst that can be said of the
Hotel Rambouillet. To all the salons—for others succeeded Madame's—de Rancé had the entrée. Needless to
say, the influence of these worldlings, however intellectual
and refined, was far from happy upon the impressionable
youth who was destined for the sanctuary. Mingling with
worldlings he became a worldling, too. After the Fronde,
that war of the people and Parliament against Mazarin and
his taxation, he resided sometimes at Paris, sometimes at
Veretz, his patrimony. But wherever he was he was the
man of the world. With an abundance of money he could
indulge his luxurious tastes to the full. He could always
go his friends one better. No feasts were more sumptuous
than those given by him, no fêtes more brilliant than his.
He was always planning new pleasures, which assured
him his position as a leader in society. In a word, he
was in those days a worldling, nothing more.

One of the pastimes to which de Rancé was devoted was
that of hunting. One day while out hunting a chance
shot from a hunter on the opposite bank of the river hit
him, but by good luck, or, as he knew later on, by the
Providence of God, the bullet hit the steel chain of his
pouch and thus saved him from death. "What would
have become of me," he meditates in his penitential days,
"if God had called me in that moment?"

At another time when he was staying at Veretz certain
hunters came poaching upon his grounds. De Rancé,
angered, attacked the leader of them, who wondered afterwards what had prevented him from killing de Rancé.
But these narrow escapes from the judgment of God did
not trouble the soul of the young courtier at the time. The
grace of God had not yet touched him.

With such worldly preparations he advanced to the

priesthood. He had been tonsured as a boy of nine in
1635. In 1647 he had received his degree of Bachelor
of Theology when he was twenty-one, and his Licentiate
in 1649. In 1651 he received Minor Orders, and in that
same year was ordained to the priesthood. How unworthy
he was of the sacred office he himself must have had some
suspicion, for though magnificent vestments had been made
ready for him to say his first Mass at Paris he withdrew
to Chartreuse and there privately offered up his first Holy
Sacrifice. But the humility, if such it was, was but temporary. De Rancé wanted to advance. His sole idea in
entering the priesthood was preferment; the spiritual
counted for nothing. He had Richelieu's ambition without
Richelieu's stable character. But times were hardly favorable for his advancement. He had been a protégé of
Richelieu, and that was enough to discredit him with the
reigning powers. Moreover he had taken part in the
Fronde against Mazarin, and Mazarin would not put himself out much to assist those who had opposed him. Rather
did the Cardinal take delight in opposing the protégé of
his predecessor. But de Rancé was not much disturbed by
that. If advancement came he would welcome it, but he
would not think too much about it if it interfered with his
convenience and pleasure. For that reason he refused the
bishopric of Leon, because the revenue was not big enough,
and also because it was too far away from the brilliancy of
the court. He had no notion of sacrificing himself for the
ministry. The Church was to him just what a military
career might be, a means of livelihood and a certain power.
It seems almost incredible that any such notion could be
entertained by him, but there is no sense in minimizing
things. All tends to the greater glory of the penitent de
Rancé once he had opened his eyes to the enormity of the
crime he had committed in forcing himself into the sanctuary without a divine call.

So the priest passed the time as any worldly baron

might. Passionately fond of hunting, he would follow the
chase three or four hours in the morning and then come
to the Sorbonne to sustain a thesis or preach at Paris with
all tranquillity, without any qualms of conscience. One
day his friend Champrallon asked him, "Where are you
going, abbé? What are you doing today?" "This morning," replied the abbé, "to preach as an angel, and this
evening to hunt as a devil."

One is not surprised when told that de Rancé had a
strong inclination towards the military life. At any rate
he had little inclination towards the sanctuary he had sworn
to serve. He was the typical court abbé, more interested
in the vanities of the world than in the care of souls. Even
his dress betrayed him. He wore a violet robe of precious
stuff and also wore a wig. There was a diamond on his
finger and an emerald on each glove. When hunting there
was about him absolutely no sign of the priest. He carried
a sword and pistols and dressed accordingly. At home in
quieter company he dressed in black with gold buttons. He
was a man of courage and spirit, and a fearless horseman,
though many accidents happened from which he narrowly
escaped with his life. He had all the accomplishments of
the soldier, none, or few, of the priest. He rarely said
Mass.

It would be a mistake to consider de Rancé as a priest;
he was merely a man of the world who for financial reasons
had taken orders. So also would it be a mistake to consider
him as the typical French priest of his age. His bad example was as shocking to the good people and the clergy of
his time as it would be to us today. It was the result of
secular interference in affairs of the Church, and the
Church never ceased to protest against it.

The Church in France in the seventeenth century needs
no apology. History, it is true, loves to talk about
Richelieu and Mazarin and De Retz and the court abbés,
and from their lives to make platitudes about the weakness

of religion in the France of the Bourbons. It has little or nothing to say about Bossuet and Bourdaloue and Fenelon and Flechier. For the seventeenth century in France, in spite of the noise that is made by Voltaire and Rousseau and the other Encyclopedists, was a great Catholic era. St. Francis de Sales, St. Jane Frances de Chantal, St. Vincent de Paul, Father Olier of the Sulpicians, Cardinal de Bérulle, founder of the Oratory; the founding of the Sisters of Charity, of the Ursulines, of the Christian Brothers and the bringing of the Carmelites from Spain, under the protection of Cardinal de Bérulle; the wonderful work of the Grand Seminaries, and perhaps more than anything else the great missionary activity, with the establishment of the Seminary for Foreign Missions; the mission labors of the Jesuits in China and Canada, with such heroes as Lallemant and de Breboeuf—these are but a few names picked at random from Catholic France of the seventeenth century.

It was the prevalence of this spirit of faith that eventually worked for the conversion of de Rancé. The event which led to that conversion was his association, unhappy as that association was, with the Duchess de Montbazon. The Duke de Montbazon was a relative of de Rancé's father. His life had been a wicked one. He was a roué up to the time of his death in 1644 at the age of eighty-six. He had married the young Duchess when she was but sixteen, a wonderfully beautiful girl. She had even decided to become a religious, when, flattered by the offer of the Duke so many years older than herself, she sacrificed all for the social position he could give her. The young Duchess soon forgot all religious sentiment. She determined to enjoy the world to the full, and enjoy it while she was young. It was a *bon mot* of hers that one was good for nothing after thirty and that she wanted to be thrown into the river at that age. De Rancé, owing to his relationship with the Duke, was a welcome visitor. In this way

he came to the notice of the young Duchess, and was soon
a great favorite of hers. When the old Duke finally died
she was thirty-two and did not look more than twenty.
She had changed her mind about wanting to be thrown into
the river. No wonder people talked about the attention
paid by the young abbé to the frivolous Duchess. Even
had the association been innocent it was scandalous, showing what little conception he had of his dignity. Her
name was a byword. At one time she came near being
drowned; in fact the rumor had spread that she had per-
ished. No such luck. The accident but added to her fame,
or rather notoriety. The Duke of Beaufort with all his
wealth became her slave, and de Rancé seemed to have
passed out of her life. The Duchess cared not so long as
she had money. She cared not where it came from. She
loved the easy way of the world; there was nothing she
would not sacrifice for social position and power—a far
cry from the days when she yearned to become a nun!

De Rancé was twenty-six when his father died. He
became thereby the head of the house of de Rancé, and
was in a position to live in great style. He had been
worldly enough before; he was more so now. He became
noted for his luxurious living, his fine table, his beautiful
equipage. He rode in state drawn by eight horses, with
elegant livery and followed by a great train of dependents.
Even the King did not enjoy a greater magnificence or
show greater éclat. No wonder that the Duchess strove
again for his notice.

Speaking of this period in de Rancé's life, his biographer
Le Nain, writes: "A youth passed in amusements of the
court, in the vain search for success, even damnable, after
being engaged in the ecclesiastical state without any other
vocation than his ambition which carried him with a kind
of fury and blindness to the first dignity of the Church—
this man, plunged wholly in the love of the world, is ordained priest, and he who had forgotten the way to Heaven

is received as doctor of the Sorbonne. Behold what was the life of Monsieur le Bouthillier up to the age of thirty years, always at feasts, always in company, in play, in the diversions of the promenade or the chase."

De Rancé's uncle, the Archbishop of Tours, was unable to get him appointed as his coadjutor, but he succeeded in making him his deputy to the Assembly of the Clergy in 1645, and then had him appointed as first Almoner to the Duke of Orleans. The natural ability of de Rancé came to the fore. He did excellent work in his new position, and when it was finished returned to his estates at Veretz, perhaps with new designs to feed his ambition. But the day of God's grace was nearing.

The Duchess de Montbazon died, so suddenly that even de Rancé had not heard the news. One day he came to call on her. He entered her apartment, and instead of beholding the sprightly, beautiful woman, he came face to face with her corpse lying upon the bier. The shock to him was a terrible one. Even long afterwards he would say nothing about that day or about the woman who had made him almost lose his soul. Once he wrote: "Those who die, well or ill, often die more for those they leave in the world than for themselves." Stunned, grief-stricken, he returned to Veretz to bury himself in solitude. The blackest melancholy fell upon him. He passed the days riding, trying to forget, but then came the long, torturing nights, so unbearable. He even consulted the dead, seeking to summon the Duchess back to speak to him. But the answer came in a way he did not expect. One day he seemed to have a vision in which he beheld the woman suffering in the midst of flames. It was very likely in reference to this event that he afterwards wrote: "While I followed the disorder of my heart, I not only swallowed iniquity as water, but all that I read and heard about sin only served to make me more guilty. Finally the blessed time came when it pleased the Father of mercies to turn Himself to me; I saw at the dawn of day the infernal monster with whom I had lived; the fright with which I was seized at the terrible sight was so great that I cannot believe I will recover from it as long as I live."

The hand of God touched the sinner. He was converted in that instant, and determined to devote the rest of his life to penance to seek to expiate the scandal he had given. In this first fervor he went at once to consult an old friend, Mother Louise of the Visitation, at Tours. She directed him to Père Seguenat, and from him he went to Père de Mouchy, a learned priest who belonged to one of the first families in France. But after these spiritual consultations he returned to Veretz without having reached any decision as to his future course. But Veretz, where he had lived like a king, had lost all its charm. The fine home with its furnishings of gold and silver, its luxurious beds, its priceless paintings, its lovely gardens, its whole atmosphere of softness disgusted the young penitent who had come to realize what a poor thing is life. He began his reform at once by practising frugality, by discharging most of his servants, by giving up hunting and even by renouncing the more innocent amusement of drawing of which he was very fond. His whole time now was taken up with works of penance, in the company of a few friends who joined with him in his practices of piety.

Shortly after his conversion de Rancé came to Paris on business. While there he avoided his former friends, kept away from the salons where he had been so popular, and instead went to lodge at the Oratory. It was not an easy task for him to give up his world. Old thoughts haunted him, temptations to the old life afflicted him. It was hard for his social set to regard his conversion as other than a joke. It was no joke, however, to de Rancé; it was a struggle to the death. To end it all and to enable him to get away from the temptations of the old life he was advised to go to the foreign missions, even to India.

He did not go; not that he shrank from the hardship, but God had other work for him to do.

Still undecided, de Rancé repaired to Blois as it was his quarter to serve as Almoner to the Duke of Orleans. Gaston, Duke of Orleans, had revolted against his brother, Louis XIII, but had escaped. He had reappeared at court when Louis was dying, but had then retired to Blois, a discredited, deserted man. When de Rancé arrived at Blois the Duke, who was coming to the end of his useless life, was thinking of doing penance. Surely he needed it. He withdrew to the Chateau of Chambro, and de Rancé was one of the party who accompanied him. De Rancé owned a priory near Chambro, served at that time by seven or eight religious, and for a time he went to live with the monks in the midst of those solitary woods. He returned to Paris, but was hardly there when a messenger came from Blois to tell him of the serious illness of the Duke. He repaired thither at once, and had the satisfaction of seeing the Duke die in sentiments of great contrition. De Rancé's prayers and example had no doubt contributed much to this happy ending. He was left almost alone with the corpse, and was deeply affected by the sight of death, another warning of the emptiness of life. When the funeral was over he went to Mans and there hid himself for two months, even changing his name so that he might pursue his life of penance without interruption. He was fighting against himself and the evil inclinations that he had so long indulged.

For a long time de Rancé had been considering submitting his future conduct to the bishops of Aleth and of Comminges, and January 27 he arrived at Comminges. He accompanied the bishop on his diocesan visitation. He thought of building a hermitage in the mountains, but the bishops wisely opposed this extreme idea. "You," said they, "think only of living for yourself."

The bishop of Aleth approved of de Rancé's determination to get rid of his fortune, but he counseled him against a life of solitude. The abbé agreed to give up his benefices, recognizing the fact that appointment merely for the sake of material revenues, was not according to the spirit of the Church. It was, however, a problem for him to know what to do, for he did not like going to live in a regular monastery.

De Rancé returned again to Veretz, decided to put his plans into execution. Needless to say, there was much opposition on the part of his friends, and of his servants who did not fancy being sacrificed to the penitential desires of the master of the house, no matter how highly they regarded him. It was hard for them, but it was harder for him to part with all his worldly grandeur. He had no intention, however, of turning back. There was sorrow in his heart; never again could he enjoy life. So he sold his silver and gave the proceeds to the poor. He owned two houses in Paris. One of them he gave to the Hotel Dieu, the other to the General Hospital. Finally he sold his ancestral estates of Veretz and gave the proceeds to the hospitals. Of all his benefices he reserved only La Trappe, which was to be the scene of his later life. He had effectually broken with the past.

The abbey of La Trappe was situated in Normandy at a distance of eighty-four miles from Paris, in a solitary valley surrounded by forests and lakes. It had been founded in 1122, having been built by Rotron II, Count of Perché, who while returning from England had made a vow that if he escaped shipwreck he would build a chapel in honor of Our Lady. The chapel which he built was changed into a monastery in 1140, and in 1147 was united to the Cistercians. At the time it was founded St. Bernard was abbot of Clairvaux. St. Louis had taken the abbey under his protection. Subsequently, when the English ravaged France, it was pillaged many times. In the sixteenth century it was one of the abbeys given "in commendam," and in this way it finally came into the de Rancé family. It was not much of a prize, for the glory of La Trappe had long ago departed. Before de Rancé came to live there and reform the abbey its doors were open day and night, and men and women were permitted freely to enter the cloister. It was a sorry place, fallen into decay. It was far from attractive to the man who had been a dainty courtier, but, as he wrote to Madame de Guise, "It pleased God to send me here. What matter where one lives since one must die?"

Not only was the building in ruins; the spirit of the monastery was also in need of reform. The few monks who kept the place were content to let well enough alone, and when de Rancé in his new zeal spoke of reformation they opposed him. Finally they gave their consent unwillingly, but de Rancé, seeing what little help they would be to him, let them go or stay as they pleased, giving a pension to those who wished to leave.

It was a problem for de Rancé when he determined to settle at La Trappe. One day he was nearly crushed by the falling of a ceiling. He took refuge in the chapel, and while praying there heard the monks chanting the psalm— *Qui confidunt in Domino—Who trust in the Lord*. It came to him as the voice of God, and he had no more fear. He went to Paris to seek the King's permission to establish himself in the abbey. Some of his friends, holy men, sought to deter him on account of the difficulty of restoring the abbey to the rule. "I see no other door than that of the cloister," he replied, "at which I could knock to return to God. I have no other resource after so much disorder than to clothe me with a sack and haircloth and pass my days in the bitterness of my heart."

A friend of de Rancé's, an abbé, said to him: "I do not know, sir, if you understand well what you ask. You are a priest, a doctor of the Sorbonne, and otherwise a man of position; nourished in delicacy and luxury, you are used to having a great train and the making of good cheer; you are on the road to be a bishop at the first opportunity; your temperament is extremely feeble, and you ask to be a monk, which is the most abject state in the Church, the most penitent, the most hidden and even the most despised. It will be necessary for you henceforth to live in tears, in work, in retreat, and to study only Jesus Christ crucified. Think seriously of it."

De Rancé replied: "It is true, I am a priest, but I have lived up to now in a manner unworthy of my character. I am a doctor, but I do not know the alphabet of Christianity; I make some figure in the world, but I am like those posts which show the way to travelers yet never move themselves."

The new life was not easy for the converted courtier. Many a time memories of the past sought to lure him from his good intentions, many a time did he have to battle with temptations. He wrote to the Bishop of Aleth: "I cannot understand how I have the hardihood to undertake a profession which wants only detached souls, and how, my passions being as vivid as they are, I dare enter into a state of veritable death. I conjure you, sir, to ask of God my conversion in a circumstance which ought to be the decision of my eternity, and that after having violated so many times the vows of my baptism He will give me the grace to keep those I am now going to make, which are as a renewal of it, with so much fidelity that I may repair in some manner the errors of my past life."

In April, 1663, de Rancé wrote to some friends: "I am sure you will be surprised when you know the resolution I have taken to give the rest of my life to penance. If I were not held down by the weight of my sins, many ages of the life I am going to embrace could not satisfy for a moment for that life I have lived in the world." He finally got the King's permission to have La Trappe restored to the rule, but on condition that at his death it should become a commendatory abbey again.

To prepare himself for the work he was about to undertake de Rancé went to Perseigne and spent five months in the novitiate, learning his new profession. While there he became very ill, and the doctors assured him that his health would be worth nothing if he did not give up his idea of following the monastic life. But the warning did not deter him. When he went to La Trappe he was cured. The great Physician of souls was watching over him.

Before pronouncing his vows at Perseigne, de Rancé made a visit to La Trappe and there read his will by which he gave to his monastery whatever property still remained in his possession. He had made his adieus to the world.

On June 26, 1664, de Rancé made his profession at La Trappe. His real life work was begun. His first care was to repair the buildings and make them habitable, and during those days he worked as laboriously as the humblest brother. "Are we less sinners," he asked, "than the first religious of Citeaux? Have we less need of penance?" The reply made to him was that they were weaker and could not practise the same austerities. "Rather say," he replied, "that we have less zeal."

The abbot's good example soon prevailed and the monks gave up the use of wine, fish, meat and eggs. Labor became sweet, and de Rancé, to set the example, devoted himself to the cultivation of a piece of wild land.

During those days the cause of the reform of the abbeys, which meant their restoration to the austerities of the primitive rule, was in the air. Many abbeys had instituted the reform. Those of the strict observance tried to form an independent order under the government of the abbot of Prières. De Rancé was appointed by the regular community to go to Rome to plead the cause of reform. He arrived there November 16, 1664, and had an audience with the Holy Father, Alexander VII. It was a hard task. Reformers were regarded as singular men, very close to schism, even when they were well intentioned, and seeing his cause lost, de Rancé returned home. When he arrived at La Trappe with the unwelcome news the abbot of Prières ordered him to go back to Rome and again plead the cause of the reformed rule. De Rancé obeyed. He redoubled his penance, living on bread and water only, and thinking only of God. Back in Rome, he frequented the churches, caring for no other sights, and went as often as possible to pray at the tombs of the apostles and martyrs. But he had to return home again without having accomplished his purpose. On the way back he visited different monasteries, gaining information to help him in the work of governing his own monastery, and getting new zeal for the task.

When de Rancé arrived at La Trappe word came from Rome that the Pope had not sanctioned the strict observance proposed. In the Bull *"In Suprema"* he settled all disputes by making certain concessions and by laying down certain rules to govern the abbeys. De Rancé of course submitted with true obedience, confident in the wisdom of the Holy Father, and certain that if God wished it the strict observance would in due time prevail. The new regulations were accepted by the General Chapter at Citeaux in 1667, though even then de Rancé expressed his opposition before the vote was taken.

De Rancé's whole heart now was taken up with the desire to do penance. He was a changed man. There was a majesty even in his exterior, due to the deep spirituality that had come into his life. He aimed to sanctify himself and to make his monastery a holy place. During his brief absence from the monastery in May, 1666, there came a relaxation in the discipline of the abbey, but as soon as he returned he made peace at once and set about needed repairs, built cells, and two chapels. His penance was not a mere idle moaning over the past, but hard work for God's glory. Gradually the discipline became more strict. The monks slept on pallets of straw, with a block of wood for a pillow. In Lent they kept the strict fast, and spent their time in prayer, silence and work. Guests were welcomed with kindness and no questions asked. Already the good influence of the monastery was being felt. The poor were fed, schools and workshops were established. De Rancé preached to his brethren in the abbey, heard their confessions, and in every way fortified them in their spiritual combat.

Thus passed five or six years. The abbey grew as its good fame spread. Up to the time of his death in 1700 de Rancé had received ninety-seven religious and forty-nine brothers. He kept account of them all and wrote their history. One such edifying story is that of Pierre or François Fore, who had been sub-lieutenant in a corps of grenadiers. He was a brave man, and had been often wounded in battle. He had been the victim of all kinds of vice and was convicted of a dozen different crimes. Obliged to flee the country, he knew not where to turn, whether to England, or Germany or Hungary. He even thought of going to the Turks. Somehow he heard of La Trappe, and he decided to go there. He made the journey of two hundred miles, and after a frightful struggle arrived at the abbey at the end of winter. He knocked at the abbey door, and was admitted. He was a pitiable sight, his face was hardened, his eyes haggard, he looked more like a ferocious beast than a man. De Rancé kindly received the poor penitent, who was plainly near death from tuberculosis. Scarcely was he inside the haven of penance when he poured forth his life blood and died. It was such cases that brought consolation to the heart of de Rancé and repaid him for all his sorrows.

But as the renown of the abbey increased, so also did the slanders against de Rancé spread. He was sneered at, the errors of his youth were retailed, and his conversion was regarded as mere vanity, as a matter of self-advertisement. But the penitent did not mind what was said. He felt he deserved it all and more.

In 1672 de Rancé again asked the King to allow the reformed rule to be established. The request was the signal for abuse, heaped upon de Rancé by those who did not approve. He was denounced for his doctrines, accused of hypocrisy in seeking to introduce new ideas. The King submitted the matter to his advisers. De Rancé's adversaries opposed him at Rome and again the request was refused. But he was not disheartened. He went about his personal sanctification, no matter how great the obstacles. And the obstacles, indeed, were many. In 1676 he contracted the disease of which he eventually died. The pain did not stop him from working. He was compelled to spend three months in the infirmary, but as soon as possible he rejoined the community. In 1689 he was the victim of a great fever, but when that was passed he was back at work, though a relapse soon laid him low again. Sickness did not worry him. He was not afraid to die. "The life of a sinner like me," he said, "always lasts too long."

Bossuet, who had been his fellow student, came to visit him several times. He loved the place and would assist at the offices day and night. De Rancé had thought of giving up the abbey but Bossuet, knowing the great good his friend was doing, advised him to wait. One loves to think of the Eagle of Meaux, the great orator who would not mince words even when he was talking to the King and thundering at him the warnings of eternal damnation if he did not break with the infamous de Montespan, resting his soul in prayer in the solitude of La Trappe. Bossuet knew as well as de Rancé, though in a different way, the foolishness of the life of sin. When the Grand Monarch, Louis XIV, lay upon his death bed he must have remembered the many warnings of the preacher. At any rate he made a good end. "Prayers are offered in all the churches for Your Majesty's life," said the parish priest of Versailles. "That is not the question," said Louis; "It is my salvation that much needs praying for."

Always patient under abuse and calumny, de Rancé knew how to sympathize with others. It was no doubt due to his prayers and his good example that others left the sinful world to do penance. Like Louise de la Vallière, discarded mistress of the king, they could say as she: "I quit the world without regret, but not without pain. I believe, I hope, I love." La Vallière led a hard, penitential life for thirty-five years. How many moralists since have sneered at her wickedness, and how few have had the courage to imitate her penitence. When the sermons of de Rancé—"Of the Sanctity and Duties of the Monastic Life"—were gathered together, Bossuet, no mean judge, wanted to have them printed. De Rancé in his humility threw them into the fire, but happily the manuscript was rescued and published. The book aroused a storm. It was attacked by Protestants, and even Mabillon entered into a controversy with de Rancé over some of his ideas put forth as to whether or not monks in an abbey like that of La Trappe should devote themselves to study. But the controversy ended, and Mabillon came to visit La Trappe.

De Rancé was dead to the past. He never referred to his life in the world. That was a closed chapter to him; he wanted it to be closed to everybody else. But he had no softness because of his own past sins. He had no pity on evils. "You are made for the cross," he would say. And again: "One dies only once; one cannot repair in a second life the mistakes of the first. What one is at the moment of death, that he is always." There was but one idea in his mind it was penance, penance, penance. No other cry escaped him.

De Rancé was a prodigious letter-writer. He wrote to everybody, and always with the one thought, to bring his correspondents to the service of the Cross. His work is amazing when one considers that his illness was continuous. One hand had become useless from rheumatism; he suffered from a cough, from insomnia, from toothache, and long days and nights were passed in a chair in the infirmary. But he never would relax his penances. Before his chair he had placed the words, "Lord, forget my ignorances and the sins of my youth." He always considered himself the most wicked of sinners. Hence he had no mercy on himself. The monks complained to the Pope of his self-afflictions, and the Pope thereupon ordered him to relax his austerities.

Severe as he was with himself, de Rancé was ever kind to others. He was full of sympathy for the sick, ready at all times to listen to the troubles of others, always all things to all men for the sake of winning them to Christ. In spite of his continued sickness he ruled his monastery. It was a marvel how one in his condition could accomplish so much. And all the while with patience, no matter what happened. His enemies wrote against him, preached against him. He was called a heretic, a fanatic. But, in his trust in God, he remained calm through it all. When he was very ill his brethren begged him to have the doctors. "I am in the hands of God," he replied. "It is He Who gives life, He Who takes it. He knows well how to cure me if it is His will that I should live. But why cure me? For what good am I? What could I do in this world but offend God?"

What good, indeed! For an answer to that one must ask the many souls in Heaven who were led thither by the penitential example of this true convert. Whenever the name of Trappist is heard, one thinks at once of this great abbot of La Trappe who made the name a benediction. Many a soul had found new strength in the presence of de Rancé. Thither in the lifetime of de Rancé had come the ill-fated James II. Whatever one may think of the ability of James, one thing certain is that he had remained loyal to his faith at all costs. When he was dying in 1701, the year after de Rancé's death, he said to his son: "I am about to leave this world, which has been to me nothing but a sea of tempests and storms. The Almighty has thought right to visit me with great afflictions; serve Him with all your heart, and never place the crown of England in the balance with your eternal salvation."

De Rancé's continued illness at last made him helpless. Thinking it for the good of the abbey he resigned to the King in 1695, and much to his relief another superior was appointed. In his sincere humility he became a simple religious, and was given the work of caring for the infirmary. He still kept up his penances. Penance was his life. He made his general confession. As the end approached he was serene, his countenance shining. They laid him upon a bed of ashes, and while answering the prayers for the departing he died, October 31, 1700, at the age of seventy-five, after thirty-five years spent in penitential solitude.

His life reads like a page from the Fathers of the Desert.

The name "Trappist," from this abbey of La Trappe, was long given to those Cistercians who followed the reform instituted by de Rancé. Today the Order is known as the "Order of the Reformed Cistercians," but the popular name of "Trappist" will continue long.

La Trappe, sanctified by de Rancé, suffered many changes after his death. In the years between 1713 and 1790 there were three hundred professions there. In the Revolution the Commissioners took from the monastery everything they could carry away and dispersed the religious who sought asylum in foreign lands, some even coming to America. In 1815 the Cistercians repurchased the place. It was nothing but ruins then, but they rebuilt it and improved it till now it is a glorious abbey where the spirit of de Rancé is still vigorous.

SILVIO PELLICO

ONE of the treasures of the library of the University of Notre Dame is a copy of the tragedy of "Thomas Morus" inscribed by the author, Silvio Pellico, to that other great lover of liberty, Daniel O'Connell. Looking at the two illustrious names side by side one inevitably thinks of the other greater bond between them, the Catholic faith which both so prized.

To Pellico, indeed, religion was everything. In the silence of his prison cell he had come to see the value of that faith which in the pride of his youth he had cast aside. Through tears of pain he had got again his vision of God. The little cell was a new Mount of the Transfiguration.

A bulky book could be made out of the spiritual experiences of famous prisoners. Many there have been to whom the enforced retreat has been a grace from God. It was the only place where God chose to visit them. "I was in prison, and you came to me."

Benvenuto Cellini, egotistic and boastful though he is, can stop long enough from his tirades and his self-laudation to write a long poem about the blessings of his experience in jail. Part of it runs thus:

Whoe'er would know the measure of God's strength
And how far man can borrow from that source,
He must in prison lie, I firmly hold,
Harrow'd by thinking of his kindred dear,
Wearied and sick with his own body's pain;
And far must be his exile from his home.
Now if you fain would prove yourself of worth,

Be dragged to prison guiltless; and then lie
Month after month, while no man lends you aid.
And let them rob you of your little all,
While you face death and outrage every day,
Hopeless of any bettering of your fate.

In prison Paul Verlaine, "pauvre Verlaine," found
his Heaven, only, perhaps, to lose it again. And Silvio
Pellico found in his ten years of imprisonment not only
the material for one of the classic books of the world, but
more than all that, a sense of sin, a renewed faith in God,
and a spirituality that was to deepen till the day of his
death. "Silvio Pellico," says one of his biographers, "owes
a great celebrity to a great misfortune. Spielberg has been
for him a pedestal which has raised him up and placed
him in the light; his contemporaries spoke of him with
emotion, many with enthusiasm; his name is European."
This was said because of his literary talents. But to
us his fame is greater, not for what he wrote—the day
came when literary renown meant nothing to him—but
for the whole-heartedness with which he served God once
he had set his feet on the penitential road of the Cross.

Silvio Pellico was born at Saluzzo in Piedmont, June 24,
1788. His parents were good simple people of the middle
class, and at that time were in very good circumstances.
There were six children, Luigi, Gioseffina, Silvio and his
twin-sister, Rosina, Francesco and Marietta. Onorato,
the father, was then employed in the post-office. According
to all accounts he was a most excellent man, and his wife
was one worthy of him. Her name was Tournier, and she
came from Chambéry in Savoy. She was a woman of
distinguished character, with all the Savoyard virtues, first
and last the devoted wife, the devoted mother whose jewels
were her children, ever filled with tenderness and solicitude
for them.

Silvio Pellico was always proud of his humble birth,

proud of those parents who never lost their wonder to him. "No child," he writes in "My Prisons," "was ever more loaded with benefits by his father and mother than myself." A good description of that Christian home is given by one of his biographers: "Perfect purity of manners, hospitality never refused but always proffered, an uninterrupted exercise of Christian charity which recognized as a neighbor not only the Christian and the royalist, but everyone, and especially everyone who was unhappy, made the home in which Silvio was born and lived, a temple sacred to every social virtue."

The queen who reigned over that home was especially dear to Silvio. Religious, as was also her husband, she had moreover a simplicity, a courtesy, a modesty that help much to explain the later character of her famous son as suffering formed him. "When he speaks of his mother," says his friend Maroncelli, "his soul is an incarnate, living hymn of adoration to God as manifested in His creatures." This tender love of Pellico for his mother was developed in a great measure by his years of absolute independence upon her. He was a weakling at birth, so much so that it was not considered possible that he would live long. His early years were one continued suffering where one sickness followed another. The doctors shook their heads dubiously; he would never live to be seven. When he did reach his seventh year they prophesied that he would die before fourteen, and again when he passed that crisis that he was doomed to die at twenty-one. Evidently seven was not considered his lucky series.

But the lad continued to live in spite of the doctors, even though life was to him a miserable thing, filled with melancholy thoughts and an overabundance of self-concentration. "Long sufferings," he writes, "long sadnesses oppressed my early years. The children of my age ran and leaped around me, happy and proud of their beauty, but I was plunged in a mournful languor and afflicted with spasms the cause of which was a mystery. My short joys vanished before the pity which my frail and miserable nature inspired. I ran away tó hide my tears in solitude." It was in those early years, indeed, that the first germs of doubt were lodged in his soul. One evening when he was very sick one of his young companions said to him: "Silvio, there is no God! God would be good and He would not let you suffer so." The day came when his whole soul was to be poisoned with these sins against faith. But, it was no wonder that in the childhood days he regarded death with indifference. It was a feeling he never lost. In later years he would say, "The most delightful day of my life will be that on which I die." Many a heavier cross he had to bear, however, before he found the peacefulness of death.

When it came time for the boy to be put at his books, he and his elder brother studied together in their own home under the tutelage of a priest, Don Manavella, who prepared them for examination for admission to the public schools. Even in those early days the future dramatist displayed a passion for the theatre. His father would compose little plays and verses, and Silvio and his brother Luigi would get up on the family bureau and declaim them. The child is father to the man. Silvio attained great fame as a dramatist, and Luigi enjoyed a certain popularity as a writer of good comedies. In those days when the whole family loved play-acting it is not hard to credit the story that Silvio, chancing to read an Italian translation of the poems of Ossian, delivered himself of a Scottish tragedy at the age of ten!

It was about this time that the Pellico family came to live at Turin. The father had tried his luck at the manufacturing of silk at Pinerolo, but the venture had not prospered, and he got another position with the government. Life for Silvio was not changed much by the change of dwelling. He and Luigi continued their studies under Don

Manavella, and continued also their play-acting. More-over, these early days at Turin had more than a literary influence. Turin was then a republic. Onorato Pellico was at heart a monarchist, deeply attached to the royalist ideals then so violently attacked by the spirit of revolu-tion in France and Italy. He had suffered, indeed, for holding those ideals, since being known as of the king's party he had been obliged some time before to be a fugi-tive in the Alps accompanied by his wife, soon to become a mother, and by his little children. Thus early in life Silvio had learned the lesson of misfortune. In Turin he and his brother Luigi accompanied their father to the popular assemblies. There they received strong impres-sions about popular government and got that strong love of liberty which later was to be the cause of Silvio's im-prisonment. At Turin, too, he had his first and only love affair. One of his companions in acting was a girl, Car-lotinna, who died at the age of fourteen. It is too much, perhaps, to seek to find any influence from this childhood love affair in the life of the grown man, yet it is said that Silvio never forgot the love of his boyhood days.

The day came all too soon when the boy, now grown to young manhood, put aside the simple Catholic life in which he had been trained and entered upon the course which finally led to the ruin of his soul. The change came about through the marriage of his twin-sister Rosina, who is said to have been as beautiful as an angel. A cousin of his mother's living at Lyons had obtained her hand in mar-riage. Silvio and his mother accompanied the young bride to France, and when the mother returned home Silvio decided to remain at Lyons. It was an evil decision for the youth, who was thus deprived of all the safeguards of home at the most impressionable time of life. Lyons worked the ruin of his innocence and his faith—he was to regret his life there with bitter tears. Filled with pride, and with no other god but his desires, his soul was an easy prey for the powers of irreligion. He was unfortunate enough to meet an apostate priest who was inclined to scepticism and went about preaching it. The impressionable Silvio was attracted to him, and through the association lost his respect for the religion in which he had been so carefully educated. He was never, however, a blatant unbeliever. There is question if he ever did really lose his faith, for as one of his biographers tells us, "sometimes the churches had for him a mysterious attraction. He fled from the impious gatherings, and solitary and discouraged went to the churches and there prayed and meditated. He wept over his darkness, his doubts, his passions and the God he had lost."

Silvio Pellico was to find that God again only on the way to Calvary. Just now he had no need of God. He was young, happy, surrounded by the many friends whom the gentleness of his manners won to him. He loved the world, especially this new French world which offered youth so many attractions. He loved France, French customs, French literature. He divided his time between the study of this literature and the pursuit of pleasure. Later on he deplored the irreligious doctrines he heard preached, the bad books he read, the hardening of his heart, the pride of his thoughts. Yet he also consoled himself with the thought that in Lyons he had seen the rebirth of Catholicism, which somehow was always a light shining for him in the midst of the darkness of his intellect. It would have been quite impossible for Pellico to get to the low level of the unbelieving Encyclopedist.

So the youth spent four years in Lyons, thoroughly content with himself, enjoying life to the full. And then one day in 1806 he chanced to read Foscolo's poem, "I Sepolcri." It was a voice from home. It made him Italian again, homesick, and under its spell he became sad, a dreamer. The French life he had thought so wonderful palled on him, and at once he determined to go back

home. The Pellico family was then living at Milan, where
the father was employed in the war department and where
Luigi was secretary to the Grand Equerry of the Kingdom
of Italy.

The home influence soon resumed its power over Silvio.
Shortly after his return he was made professor of French
in the college of military orphans, an easy position which
required only an hour or two daily. The rest of his time
he devoted without restraint to the cultivation of his poetic
talent. His position in the college he soon lost, being
removed by the Austrian government, but the removal did
not distress him much since it gave him more leisure for his
beloved literary work. This desire for literary fame was
furthered by his friendship with the writer Foscolo, who
was then one of the literary leaders of Italy, the others
being Monti and Manzoni. Luigi Pellico had been a friend
of Foscolo and thus Silvio was introduced to the great
writer. The friendship between the two was a lasting one.
Foscolo, who alienated his friends by his roughness, was
always full of tenderness for Silvio, and on the other hand
Silvio had for him a tender veneration. The two writers
planned to form a literary partnership, Foscolo to do
tragedies and Silvio rhymed stories.

The literary association, however, was not lasting, owing
to what would seem to us now a bit of professional jealousy
on the part of Foscolo. Silvio had written a tragedy on
the subject of Laodicea. Shortly after that he was so impressed with the acting of a young girl of twelve—afterwards the celebrated Carlotta Marchionni—that he composed for her his famous "Francesca Da Rimini." He
submitted the tragedy to Foscolo, who after reading it told
him to throw it into the fire and let Dante's dead rest in
peace. Silvio then submitted to him his tragedy "Laodicea." Foscolo pronounced it beautiful, even lauded it
to the skies. It may have been an error of taste, but we
rather think it was the master's jealousy of his disciple.

Anyway Pellico threw into the fire the "Laodicea" and not the "Francesca." It was the wisdom of the poet who knew the value of his own work, for it was "Francesca Da Rimini" that made Silvio's reputation when two or three years later, in 1819, it was played at Milan by Carlotta, then an unrivaled actress. Silvio, however, entertained no enmity toward Foscolo on account of the biased criticism. Rather does he always speak of him with tenderness, even while he sadly remarks that Foscolo "does not understand the consolations of the faith and has opened his strong intelligence to miserable doubts."

A more worthy friend of Pellico's was the famous physicist, Volta. He was quite the opposite of Foscolo, being a fervent Catholic, and took every occasion to preach to his young friend Christian humility and the benefits of grace. Silvio in those years had his days of anger and revolt, and was very much inclined to satire. Volta fought against this disposition. "Poetry of anger benefits no one," said he. "If it happens that you feel angry and inclined to pour out your bile in verse, have the fear of becoming wicked. I would wish on the contrary that you would seek then to soften your heart by working on some noble example of charity and indulgence." Pellico followed the advice. He wrote a rhymed story, "Aroldo E Clara" in which a sister pardons her brother's murderer and persuades her father to do the same in the name of Jesus Christ. Silvio later on was to give in his own life a lasting lesson of forgiveness of injuries. Volta died in 1826 when Silvio was yet in prison. Who knows how much the remembered advice of the great scientist contributed to the softening of the heart of the man who must have felt that the hand of the world was against him.

Silvio had need of the lesson in those days, for he was soon to be tried by fire. Italy then was ground down under the heel of the oppressor. To the Napoleonic era had succeeded the Austrian domination, and Vienna treated Lom-

bardy as a conquered country. Though the Pellico family
had returned to Turin, Silvio remained at Milan, where he
had charge of the education, first of the children of Count
Briche and afterwards of the children of Count Porro
Lambertenghi. Count Porro loved Silvio as a son and did
all he could to advance him in the world. The association
meant much to the young poet, for the Count's home was
the meeting place not only of all the eminent men of Lom-
bardy but even of all the illustrious strangers, from every
nation, who came to visit Milan. Here Silvio met Madame
de Stael, Schlegel, and especially Byron, then at the height
of his fame, to whom Pellico refers as, "this surprising
genius, who unhappily accustomed himself to deify now
vice, now virtue, now error, now truth, but who was tormented, however, with a burning thirst for truth and virtue." The friendship of the two poets was very close.
Pellico translated "Manfred" into Italian and Byron translated "Francesca Da Rimini" into English.

They were happy days but Silvio's association in the
house of Count Porro finally led to his imprisonment. It
came about in this way:

The Count was a thorough Italian patriot, one of the
leading opponents of the Austrian domination. It was
thus that the journal "Il Conciliatore" was established.
The idea very likely originated with Pellico. The reunion
of so many of the intellectually elect inspired him with
the idea of a paper which would serve as a forum for these
men. The project appealed to Porro inasmuch as the
journal which was to defend the romantic school as against
the classicist would serve as a means to combat all foreign
domination.

So the association was formed. It met three times a
week. Silvio was elected secretary. The paper was
avowedly a purely literary one. No politics were allowed
in it, for the eyes of Austria were very vigilant, so vigilant
that even in the literary articles many passages were sup-

pressed which were regarded as showing a tendency to think too much about liberty. Scarcely a number of the "Conciliatore" that was not mutilated by the censor. It was a busy time for Silvio, yet in addition to his work on the paper he had the intention of publishing by subscription a great history of Italy, and a society was formed with this object in view. But nothing came of it. His pen was busy otherwise, too. He wrote his second tragedy, "Eufemio Di Messina" on the subject of "Judith." It was considered by the censors, however, as having an inner political meaning, and they allowed it to be published only on condition that it never would be played. The tragedy never reached the stage.

"Il Conciliatore" did good work inasmuch as it brought about a renaissance in Italian art and letters; but it was necessarily doomed to failure. Owing to the many mutilations from the censor, it was soon little more than titles and signatures, and after existing a year it was given up. But Pellico's association with it was fraught with evil consequences. It made him suspect to the Austrian government and thus finally led to his downfall. The Revolution in Naples and in Piedmont had produced a great fermentation in the Lombard and Venetian states. As a result the Italian army was disbanded, all political debate was suppressed, the press was silenced, and national industry paralyzed. Out of the tyranny arose the secret societies, especially the Carbonari, all of which aimed at the constitutional independence of upper Italy. This was the unsettled state of affairs when the revolution of Piedmont and the Two Sicilies occurred. Austria was alarmed, and fulminated a decree against the Carbonari. By the decree of August 25, 1829, Article 53 declared for the death penalty for all who joined the society, and Articles 54 and 55 declared for severe and most severe imprisonment for those who neglected to stop its progress or to denounce its members. Hence the editors of the "Conciliatore" were treated as Carbonari. Count Porro and others escaped the death penalty by fleeing the country.

Silvio had gone to Turin to attend his dying friend, Breme. On his return to Milan he was told that the officers of the law were looking for him. "They know where I live," said he; "I shall go and wait for them." He found them waiting for him. They took all his papers, poems, etc., and conducted him to the prison of Santa Margherita. It was October 13, 1820.

Silvio Pellico did not belong to the Carbonari. He was not even in the secrets of the conspirators. He had written a letter making inquiries about the organization, giving his correspondent to understand that if his conscience permitted he would join. The letter had been intercepted. All the others had fled, and Silvio, unsuspecting in his innocence, remained. But he must be found guilty at any cost. He must be the scapegoat; and so he was condemned without even a trial.

The prison of Santa Margherita, in the center of Milan, had once been a nunnery. When the nunnery was suppressed the building was used for the general office of the police. It had a long range of cells connected with it, some for criminals, some for unlicensed prostitutes, some for political prisoners. The cells were damp, so much so that the prisoners soon lost their hair; they were dark, gloomy, fetid, comfortless, with all kinds of loathsome insects. They were fittingly called "Dante's Dens." It was there that Silvio for several days underwent an examination. He tells the story of it in the book he wrote afterwards, the book which keeps his name in everlasting remembrance, "My Prisons," one of the classics of the world, "this book, of a simplicity so sweet and a tenderness so religious," the simple baring of a man's heart, the story of Christian resignation under ten years of suffering.

"A century ago," he writes, "this was a monastery; the holy and penitential virgins who dwelt here never imagined that at this day their cells would resound no more with the sighs of women and with pious hymns, but with blasphemies and indecent songs, and would contain men of all kinds, the greater part destined to hard labor or to the gallows."

He thought of home, and wept like a child, grieving as he regretted that he had not been more tender with his parents on his last visit to them. When he awoke in his prison cell he thought of them again. "Who will give them strength to bear the blow," he asked himself; and a voice within seemed to say, "He Whom all the afflicted invoke and love and feel within them! He Who gave strength to a mother to follow her Son to Golgotha, and to stand under His cross! The Friend of the unhappy, the Friend of mortals."

For years Silvio had been forgetful of God. He had put Him out of his life in the Lyons days when pride ruled his will. Now God was knocking at the door of his heart. "This was the first moment," he writes, "that religion triumphed in my heart; and I owed this blessing to filial love." He continues his confession: "Hitherto, without being hostile to religion, I had felt its influence but little and imperfectly. The common objections which are brought against it had not appeared to me of much weight, and yet a thousand sophistical doubts had weakened my faith. These doubts had not for a long time related to the existence of God; and I had continually repeated to myself, 'If God exists, it necessarily follows from His justice that there is another life for man who suffers in a world so unjust, hence follows the great reasonableness of aspiring to the blessings of that second life; hence follows a worship consisting of love to God and our neighbor, a perpetual striving to ennoble ourselves by generous sacrifices.' I had for a long time gone on repeating all this, and I had added, 'And what is Christianity but this perpetual aspiration after perfection?' And Christianity in its essential character being so pure, so philosophical, so unimpeachable, I marveled that an age should have arrived when philosophy should dare to say, 'Henceforth I will fill its place.'

" 'And in what manner wouldst thou fill its place? By teaching vice?'

" 'No, surely.'

" 'By teaching virtue? That will be the love of God and our neighbor. It will be precisely what Christianity teaches.'

"Although I had thus felt for several years," he continues, "I had avoided the conclusion, 'Be then consistent! Be a Christian! Be no longer offended by abuses, no longer dwell perversely on some difficult doctrine of the Church, since the principal point is this, and it is most plain: Love God and your neighbor.'

"In prison I determined at last to embrace this conclusion, and I did embrace it. I hesitated somewhat from the fear that if anyone should happen to learn that I was more religious than formerly he might think he had a right to consider me a fanatic, made abject by misfortune. But knowing that I was neither fanatical nor abject, I felt complacency in disregarding the possible blame I did not deserve; and I resolved from that time forward to be and to avow myself a Christian."

It was some time before this became his settled resolution; but once taken, he felt peace come into his heart. It was a time of trial; he was abandoned, deprived even of the materials with which to write. He tells us that in order to write a letter to his friend and fellow prisoner, Maroncelli, he pricked his finger and used the blood as ink. The old man who carried the letter was beaten mercilessly. Soon after he was permitted to have a Bible and a Dante, and to use the jailer's library. He began to love the Bible more and more. Meditation on the word of God gave him to understand what prayer was and he learned to put himself in the presence of God.

"This purpose of always considering myself in the presence of God," he writes, "instead of being a fatiguing effort of mind and exciting my fears, was delightful to me. By remembering that God is always near us, that He is in us, or rather that we are in Him, solitude became daily less terrible to me. 'Have I not the most excellent society?' I used to say. And I became cheerful; I sang and whistled with pleasure and tender emotion."

There came into his soul a strong faith that God would sustain him. Written on the wall of his cell by a previous occupant were these words: "I bless the prison, since it has made me know the ingratitude of men, my own misery, and the goodness of God."

The soul of Silvio Pellico was a tender one. There is nothing in all literature more touching than his description of his friendship with the little deaf and dumb boy, the child of a criminal. Of like beauty is his tribute to the poor Magdalen whose voice he heard but whose face he never saw. In the room next to his were women prisoners. One of them, Maddalena, never gave utterance as the others to vulgar thoughts. When her companions related their troubles she pitied them and said: "Take courage, my dear; the Lord never forsakes anyone." "Innocence," writes Silvio, "is to be honored; but how much is repentance to be honored also! Did the best of men, the God-Man, disdain to cast His compassionate looks upon sinful women, to regard their confusion, and to associate them with the souls whom He most honored? Why, then, should we so much despise a woman who has fallen into ignominy?" The voice of this penitent woman often cheered him. Often when he was tempted to hate the world her voice brought him back to compassion and indulgence. And he concludes beautifully: "Mayst thou, O unknown sinner, not have been condemned to a heavy punishment! Or, to whatever punishment thou hast been condemned, mayst thou profit by it to recover thy worth, and to live and die dear to the Lord. Mayst thou be com-

passionated and respected by all who know thee, as thou
hast been by me who know thee not! Mayst thou inspire
in everyone who sees thee patience, gentleness, the desire
of virtue and trust in God, as thou hast in him who loves
thee without having seen thee! My fancy may err, when
it paints thee beautiful in person, but I cannot doubt the
beauty of thy soul. Thy companions spoke with coarse-
ness, thou with modesty and courtesy; they blasphemed,
and thou didst bless God; they quarreled, and thou wert
the composer of their strife. If anyone has taken thee by
the hand, to withdraw thee from the career of dishonor;
if he has conferred benefits on thee with delicacy; if he
has dried thy tears, may all blessings be showered upon
him, upon his children, and upon his children's children."

All the while Silvio was learning to pray again, to re-
new again his faith in God, by walking the way of the
cross.

On February 20, 1821, he was brought to Venice and
confined in the state prison, The Leads, so called
because the upper part of this former palace of the Doge
was entirely covered with lead. He was subjected to a
harrowing examination for hours, and then restored to
his cell, so enraged by the injustice of it all that he would
have committed suicide if the voice of religion and the
recollection of his beloved ones at home had not restrained
him. Again his faith weakened. He ceased to pray, began to question the justice of God, and for six or seven
days cursed the world and all mankind. "My Bible,"
said he, "was covered with dust. One of the jailer's boys
said while caressing me: 'Since you have ceased to read
that ugly book, you are much less melancholy, I think.'"

He took up the Bible, wiped away the dust, and opened
the book at random. He read the words (St. Luke XVII,
1, 2): "And he said to his disciples: It is impossible that
scandals should not come: but woe to him through whom
they come. It were better for him that a millstone were

hanged about his neck, and he cast into the sea, than that he should scandalize one of these little ones."

When the boy left the cell the man exclaimed: "And had I abandoned Thee, my God? And had I become perverted? And could I believe that the infamous sneer of cynicism was suited to my desperate situation?" He knelt to read the Bible. He burst into tears, and repented the evil he had done. He vowed he would never again lose his God. How little now seemed his affliction. Even the scaffold was small in comparison with God. Again and again he was assailed by temptations to unbelief, but by the grace of God he conquered them all. His sufferings in the prison cell were intense, the heat was terrific, the onslaughts of the innumerable insects maddening, but he resigned himself to all the afflictions. "And examining myself with just rigor," he writes, "I found in the years I had lived only a few specious traits of character; all the rest was made up of foolish, idolatrous passions, proud and false virtues. . . . 'It is well,' I concluded; suffer, unworthy man, suffer. If through passions and without any right men and gnats should torment thee to death, acknowledge them as the instruments of divine justice, and be silent! Does it need an effort for man to be sincerely humble? to be sensible that he is a sinner? without self-abasement, without the scruples of a fanatic, contemplating myself with all possible tranquility of mind, I perceived that I deserved the chastisements of God."

The struggle to conquer himself was not over yet, however. He busied himself with writing several tragedies and other poems. On May 29, 1821, he finished two tragedies, also four rhymed stories. Later, when he was leaving Italy, being removed to the prison of Spielberg, he asked permission to pass to his family the two tragedies as his literary testament. Permission was granted but nothing was done. The government was afraid the plays would be published and thus bring honor to a man who was a criminal. They decided that even his name must perish. And all the while they were preparing, unwittingly, to make his name immortal.

During those days Silvio meditated much, writing the meditations on his table and then scraping off the writing. He made verses, and prayed. Yet would the old tortures return to his mind. The temptation came to him to consider himself abandoned by God, and he yielded to the temptation. He denied the excellence of religion, even denied God. To this there succeeded a serious illness. His heart softened under it. He recovered, and his soul was filled with gratitude to God. He was now getting ready to die. "If the end of my life has arrived," he wrote, "am I not fortunate that it is in such a manner as to give me time to recollect myself, and to purify my conscience by holy desires and acts of penitence worthy of a man?" From that time on he meditated on death and the sacraments.

From The Leads Silvio was removed to the prison of San Michele. There he was tried again, and condemned to the death penalty. At once the punishment was commuted to fifteen years severe imprisonment in the fortress of Spielberg. To the reading of the sentence the prisoner simply answered, "The will of God be done," but back in his cell again the awfulness of his fate struck terror into his soul and again he put God out of his life. Spielberg, in Moravia, was the hardest prison of the Austrian government. It was a terrible place to Silvio, never of robust health, now weak and suffering, his lungs affected by what he had endured in the Italian prisons. He burned with fever, his stomach revolted against the coarse fare; his feet were chained together, his bed but hard planks. Yet in the midst of the afflictions he composed a tragedy. He had no paper, no ink, but memorized the lines as he composed them.

Count Antonio Oroboni, a young man twenty-nine years

of age, one of Silvio's fellow prisoners, exercised a good influence upon him. The two prisoners became confidants. "Let us take advantage of the short time that has been granted us anew," said Oroboni one day, "to console each other by religion. Let us speak of God; let us excite each other to love Him; let us remember that He is justice, wisdom, goodness, beauty; that He is everything excellent which has been the object of our love. I tell you that my death is not far distant. I shall be eternally grateful to you if you will contribute to make me as religious in these my last days as I ought to have been through life." So the two prisoners talked of religion, and prayed together. Silvio was taken very ill. He sent for the chaplain and made his confession, and prepared himself for death. But he did not die. Oroboni, however, died June 13, 1823. His was a holy death, a blessing which might not have been his had he been permitted to pursue his life in the world. He deserves to be reckoned among the great penitents. Silvio had loved him devotedly and prayed earnestly for his soul. In his dreams he seemed to see the man redeemed to glory through the door of his prison cell.

An Augustinian priest, Father Battista, was appointed confessor to the prison. Silvio lovingly calls him, "an angel of charity." The priest brought books to the prisoners, visited them every month and heard their confessions. "Oh," says Silvio, "how unhappy is he who knows not the elevating influences of confession! how unhappy is he who thinks himself bound to regard it with scorn, that he may not appear one of the vulgar!" The ministry of this good priest continued for a year, and then the authorities forbade him to come any more. During the years from 1824 to 1827 a severer discipline was instituted. The prison was made a tomb, and the prisoners were deprived even of books. In 1825, however, a new confessor was allowed them in the person of Father Stephen Paulowich, who obtained for them the privilege of hearing Mass.

To know the great reputation which Silvio Pellico en-

joyed in the world it is sufficient to know that when in
1828 the news of his supposed death was given out there
was profound sorrow everywhere. The world had the
most sincere sympathy for the man it regarded as a martyr.
But he was not destined to die in prison. In the September of 1830 he was liberated. He piously attributed his
release to the prayers of his baby sister, Marietta, who had
become a nun and had died soon after her profession. He
concludes "My Prisons" with these moving words: "And
now, for my past misfortunes, and for my present happiness, as well as for all the good and ill which may be reserved for me, blessed be that Providence, in whose hands
men and things, whether they will or will it not, are the
wonderful instruments for accomplishing purposes worthy
of their divine Author."

What must have been the emotions of the man on returning to the home to which he had been as one dead for
ten long years! But he wasted no time in useless lamentations; there was nothing of the posing martyr about Silvio
Pellico. On his return to Turin he took up again the
thread of his literary work. His tragedy, "Ester D'En-
gaddi," was played with success in 1831, but the production was soon stopped by the censors. A new tragedy
met the same fate. He was still considered politically
dangerous. His tragedy on the great Catholic, Thomas
More, was to him a labor of love. He wrote eight tragedies, but he was never a great success as a dramatist. Besides his dramas he wrote a dozen novels in verse, the
subjects of which were taken from the Middle Ages.
His unedited poems contain a paraphrase of the "Imitation," elegies on his youth, souvenirs of his past loves.
Nearly all his poems have a religious ending. The most
severe Italian critics consider his canzone on the sun, composed at Spielberg, perfect, "a jewel to be set in gold."
"Shine on the face of the father," it runs, "shine on the
face of the mother of this poor captive, and may thy joyous

ray enchant their sorrow. But what matters where goes lamenting this abandoned spoil, if God has given me a soul which nothing here below can enchain?"

But Silvio Pellico came not back to the world to seek literary fame. He wanted more than all else to serve God with his pen. So he wrote his "My Prisons" as well as "The Duties of Young Men" with the object of showing by precept and example the necessity of sufferings and expiation for the moral perfection of man. So he writes in his "Duties of Young Men," an excellent treatise which might have been written by a master in the spiritual life: "Let us not be daunted by the weight of the obligations which are insupportable alone to the slothful, let us be of good will, and we shall discern in each duty a mysterious being inviting us to love it, we shall feel an admirable power augmenting our force in proportion as we ascend in the arduous way of virtue; we shall find that man is vastly more than that which he seems to be, provided that he will, firmly will, to compass the noble end of his destiny, which is to purify himself from all base tendencies, to cultivate in the highest degree those of a superior order, to elevate himself by these means to the immortal possession of God." What a pity that the English translation of this excellent book is now out of print. It deserves a better fate.

The other great prose work of Silvio Pellico is the book which has made his name famous—"My Prisons." Some time after his return to Turin he had selected as his spiritual director an old priest of eighty years, Dom Giordano. After listening to Silvio's account of his experiences in prison he urged him to write them and give them to the world. Silvio hesitated. Even then there was too much political rancor in Italy and he did not wish to increase it by the account of what he had endured for a supposed political crime. However, he spoke to his mother about it. She replied simply, "Let us pray over it." A few days after that she asked him if he had prayed. He replied that he had, and that he felt the book of his experiences would do good.

The book was soon written. Needless to say it met with great success. It stirred up some criticism, too. Some accused the writer of too much bitterness, others of too much leniency because he was so forgiving. Some would have had him make political capital of his sufferings. But such a plan was furthest from his mind. Indeed—and that is the tragedy of his punishment—Silvio Pellico was never a politician. He suffered because of his friends rather than for what he himself had done. Hence he was very indifferent to politics after his release from jail. He was reproached bitterly for the indifference, but the reproaches could not disturb the serenity of his soul. He had found the pearl of great price. The book was criticised on other scores. The Protestants charged the author with having attacked the divine nature and truth. Many Catholics also found fault with it because of the "additions" made to the book by Maroncelli who was a very different man from Silvio. But no one regretted the additions and the "Life" by Maroncelli more than Silvio himself. He protested that Maroncelli had put forth many propositions of which he could not approve. It is a pity that Maroncelli is still allowed to glorify himself by associating himself so intimately with the man who was so immeasurably superior to him. For "My Prisons" is a great book, simple, true. It is that which makes it immortal. Silvio Pellico, after all, was not a great writer, but he was a human writer. In all his works the ruling sentiments are family love, love of country, love of man, love of children especially, and love of God. It is said that "My Prisons" did more harm to Austria than any military defeat.

One effect of the book was to gain for Silvio the friendship of the Marchesa di Barolo, the reformer of the Turin prisons. In 1834 he accepted from her generosity a yearly pension of three hundred dollars. It was a lasting friendship. On the death of his parents in 1838 he went to live at the Casa Barolo, and there he remained till his death, assisting the Marchesa in her charities and writing on religious subjects. The library of the Casa Barolo was to him a happy retreat. He had come from the prison broken in health. It was a wonder that one always so weak had borne the burdens of prison life so well. Those who looked at him, small of stature, continually ill, marveled that such a one was regarded as a conspirator; they wondered that the very sight of him had not disarmed suspicion.

But Silvio Pellico did no whining about what he had endured. He had no bitterness against the prison, simply because it was there he had found his God. All else was insignificant beside that fact. He renounced the world, letters, fame. He gave up writing for the theatre, gave up writing romances. All was spiritual now. The illusions of his youth about fame were gone. He had no desire but to come to peace in serving God. His first occupation was prayer, then the reading of books of piety, especially the most ascetic. He loved to converse about such books; he became more and more mystic. He was religious first, and literary only secondly. "I often have need," said he, "to make verses in order to pray; thus now is produced an ode, now an elegy, where I spread my soul before God, and it is enough for me to restore serenity." "Pray God for me," he asked of everybody he met. He had but to think of death. "There is for him," wrote the Marchesa, "only the thought of God and eternity."

Silvio's life toward the end was serene. He taught French and Italian in a convent school, composed little plays and canticles for the students. He went to the church a great deal, never into the social world. All of his family died before him with the exception of a brother

who had become a Jesuit, and a sister, both noted for their
piety.   The world held little for him now.   February 14,
1839, he wrote to his friend Arrivabene: "I write little;
my health is always very bad, and I would say to you that
I am tired of life were it not that I know that one should
never say he is tired of carrying a gift we hold from God,
and that one should rather arm himself unceasingly with
sweet patience and courage and bless life as death.   Let
us suffer then with the smile and the strength of soul He
demands: the years flee with such rapidity that to find
their sufferings long would be truly foolish."

Again in 1844 Silvio wrote to the same friend: "Let us
bless God in our consolations and in our sufferings, and
let us go forward with love."   It pained him to be useless,
he wrote, but he found consolation in the thought that the
number of useless beings is infinite.   He admitted that he
was always suffering, but, he concluded, "Patience and
courage to the end!   Let us adore the will of God and
trust in His goodness."

So passed these years of prayer, of atonement for sin,
of deep repentance in sweetness and gentleness.   On January 31, 1854, Silvio felt that he was going to die.   He sent
for his confessor and received him with a smile.   "Father,"
said he, "I feel that I am going.   In two or three hours I
shall be in Paradise.   If I have sinned, I have expiated.
When I wrote 'My Prisons' I sometimes had the vanity to
believe myself a great man, which was untrue, and I have
repented of that all my life."   Then with a loud voice,
with a face peaceful and even gay, he read the prayers of
the agonizing.   When the priest had finished reading he
looked at Silvio.   He was dead.   All his prison days were
over.

PAUL FEVAL

SOME time ago I chanced to pick up in a second-hand bookstore an historical romance—*Les Deux Femmes du Roi*—by Paul Féval. It was only necessary to read a few pages to discover that the romancer was far from being a clerical. "The Popes," he wrote, "fomented revolt. The Popes are the fathers of the Revolution. . . . In crying out to the people—to obey is a crime—the Popes, imprudent, dug the abyss at the edge of which totters their own throne. They committed the greatest of all the social crimes." This romance bore the date of 1865. But what a familiarly modern ring it has! How like to the violent talk of the anti-clericals of our own times, whom the great war happily has silenced, for a while at least.

But the day came when Paul Féval blotted out these words and many like them with his penitent tears. In all his long literary career he never wrote such a thrilling romance as his own life was in reality, a poor boy who attained great wealth and fame, wandered far from God, lost all faith, and at last by the loss of all his worldly wealth got the grace to see the true value of things and returned a humble penitent to the foot of the Cross. Paul Féval in his day was a "best-seller." Much of his glory is departed, as realism has taken the place of romance. Most of the books which he turned out with such incredible speed are now forgotten. But the true glory of the man remains in the ardor with which he defended the recovered faith of his childhood and in the untiring zeal with which he labored to correct his books and undo the harm his pen had done in the many years of his religious indifference. Féval is a shining example of true repentance.

Paul Henri Corentin Féval was born September 29, 1817, at Rennes in Brittany. He was always a thorough Breton, and a great deal of his best work deals with the history, the legends of his native province. "They sometimes ask me, my dear good mother," he writes in his wonderfully beautiful dedication of Le Comté Barbebleu, "why I am always speaking of Brittany, and why the name of Rennes so often escapes my pen. It is because you are at Rennes, and with you all that I love. I speak of Brittany and Rennes, because I am thinking always of thee, because my heart is with thee, and because in talking of Rennes and Brittany I seem talking of thee or to thee. I send thee this book, and if it gives you some pleasant hours, it will be my great success." The Févals were an old family of lawyers. Paul's father was a lawyer, a learned man, a counsellor at the royal court. He was, however, very humble and very pious. When Paul, after his conversion, wrote his most beautiful book—"Les Etapes d'une Conversion"—he painted the portrait of his father who had died in 1827 when Paul was a lad of ten. It is the picture of a wonderfully holy man, and it was a sad day for the boy when he was deprived of the guiding hand of the saintly parent. He made his First Communion; it was his last for many years, until the time of his conversion back to God.

Paul Féval was not a very promising youngster. He was weak and sickly, something of the coddled and spoiled child, with an inclination to make fun of others. That habit made him very unpopular with his teachers and his fellows in school, and many a good beating he got for his mean disposition. In those early days at school all he cared for was play, giving very little evidence of a taste for books, and absolutely no indication of the talent which later was to bring him fame and fortune. He was stub-

born. An example of that was given when he was thirteen
years of age, at the time of the Revolution of July. His
teachers and fellow students wore the tricolor, but Paul,
no doubt from sheer perversity, wore the white cockade.
He was whipped again and again for his obstinacy, but
he still stuck to the white. His school days thus were not
a great success and finally his mother took him out of class
and brought him to live with her in an old manor belonging
to a member of the family. The neighborhood was the
rendezvous of conspirators, and the mysteries, the dangers
that surrounded them went a great way towards the development of the spirit that was to make of the lad one
of the great romancers of his age. He was filled with
warlike desires, of which the struggle to hold fast to the
white cockade was perhaps a manifestation. Anyway,
these youthful experiences, while they did not make a soldier of him, laid the foundation of his literary success, for
when he came to write he found his materials ready in the
old traditions, the old legends to which he had listened
at the big fireplace and later pondered over as he lay in
bed, his hair standing on end.

Féval entered the college of Rennes in 1831 and remained there two years. He did not accomplish much as
a student. He was the same weak, sickly boy, with a
mean disposition, always teasing his companions and getting many a good beating that did not, however, reform
him. And all the while there was the growing indifference
in religion. The good mother thought it time to choose
a career for him. She insisted on making a lawyer of him
since that was the family tradition. Paul was not keen
about it, in fact he did not know what he wanted; he had
no ambition. It was a problem for the mother how to
manage the finances. She was poor through the death of
her husband, but a relative of the Févals sent her three
thousand francs to pay for the legal education of the boy,
and at once he was sent to the University of Rennes to

prepare for admission to the bar. It was the same story, lack of interest in his studies, but at any rate he succeeded in obtaining his degree and was admitted to the bar at the age of nineteen.

He was not cut out for a lawyer; he had no oratorical talent. His first case was to defend a peasant who had been accused of stealing a dozen chickens. It was the young lawyer's great opportunity and he was determined to make a lasting impression on the judges. He prepared very carefully according to his college exemplars of the great orations of Demosthenes. When he arose to speak he launched out into a solemn oration in defence of the chicken-stealer, and with such pomposity that even the judges burst into laughter. To make matters worse, the presiding judge asked the culprit what he had to say in his own defence and the poor thief gave a dissertation on the art of stealing chickens while preventing them from making any outcry. Needless to say he was condemned, and Féval lost his first case. The young lawyer was disgusted, ashamed of the manner in which he had humiliated himself, and he left the court determined never to enter it again. He wanted no part of the law. He left home at once and went to Paris with the intention of making his living by writing, though up to that time he had discovered no special talent in that line.

Meanwhile, to keep himself from starving while he was getting ready for his literary career, he got a position in a bank as a clerk. He did not last there very long. He neglected his work and devoted most of his time to the reading of novels. The climax came one day when his employer came upon him while he was deeply interested in a novel. It was one of Balzac's, one in which bankers were satirized. Féval was ignobly dismissed, and had to face the world again with only a few louis in his pocket.

He would have to be an author now, he decided, and he

bought a ream of paper and a bottle of ink and began—
nothing less than a tragedy. The only thing he accomplished was to lessen the number of louis. One of his
good friends came along then and borrowed all that remained of his fortune. Paul waited for a while and then
demanded that the loan be paid. Arguments followed; the
two friends fought it out and Paul wounded his adversary
without, however, getting his money back. He was in a
bad way, without a cent in his pocket and pretty close to
starvation. Some of his former fellow students at the university came to his aid and gave him a lodging with them.
It was a charming life he led for nine or ten months, supported by others while he continued the tragedy which
he hoped would give him entrée to the literary world of
Paris.

When it came time for his friends to go home for vacation the five acts were finished and in addition to the
tragedy he found himself possessed of reams of poetry and
other literary baggage. It was one thing to write, it was
another thing to buy bread with verses. He could not
sell his wares. No one would even read the tragedy from
an unknown author. In desperation he decided that he
most do something for a living. What seemed a fine opportunity came with the offer from an absolute stranger to
start a journal provided, of course, that Paul would fur-
nish the funds. The gullible youth succeeded in borrow-
ing four hundred francs from his sister as his contribution
to the capital. The eager partner took it all and Paul
once more was penniless and jobless. Shortly after this
business failure we find him working with an advertising
concern of bill posters, but not a cent did he receive from
his work.

He tried job after job, but he was a miserable failure at
everything. He had to sell his watch, his clothes, his books
to get enough to eat. He would not go back home. He

was too proud to admit that he was a failure. He lived in a mean attic, hungry, his only possessions the cherished manuscripts which later were to bring him fame and fortune but which now were worse than waste paper. He was actually dying of hunger in his attic room when some of the neighbors, noting his long absence, broke into the room and found him lying unconscious on the bed. By his side, strange to say, was the only one of his books he could not bear to sell—an "Imitation of Christ!"

The good neighbors, full of pity for him, helped him, and he soon succeeded in getting employment as a proof reader in the office of *Le Nouvelliste*. Gradually the opportunity came for him to slip in his own articles. His talent was recognized and he received small orders for articles, for material for the vaudeville stage, while he continued at the work he liked best, that of writing romances. The real beginning of his literary career was with the publication of a short story, *Le Club des Phoques,* which, appearing in no less a paper than the *Revue de Paris,* attracted considerable attention, gave him a name and thus opened to him the columns of the most important papers.

Meanwhile Féval had married the girl whose devotion had saved him when he had been discovered dying of starvation, the pious, devoted wife who in God's good time by her incessant prayers was to win him back to his Breton faith. But he was still far away from that day. Success in life was to increase his indifference to religion. As he wrote later in his preface to his wonderful book— "Jesuits!"—"When I came up from my province, I fell into the midst of sparkling scepticism where the eyes were dazzled by incessant flashes of wit. My charming companions were engaged in publishing newspapers or in managing theatres. I was still young in literature. I ran wildly about after popular success, and I won it to a degree. I had my day like another, in the society of my associates and friends, Alexandre Dumas, Balzac, Frederick Soulié, Eugene Sue."

Féval came into great literary prominence with the publication of his "Mystères de Londres" in 1844. Sue had won great success with the "Mystères de Paris" and a rival house of publishers decided that the mysteries of London should prove as popular as those of Paris. The talent of young Féval was very promising. Why not get him to do the work. But Féval protested that he had never been in London, knew nothing about England. But, protested the publishers, that was not necessary to make a popular novel. Let him take one of his romances, change the locale, give the characters English names and behold the thing was done. He could go to London afterwards. Thus the "Mystères de Londres" was written. It was the story of an Irishman who tried to avenge his country's wrongs by seeking the annihilation of England. It was a book after the school of Dumas and Sue. To give the book *vraisemblance* the author was put down as one "Sir Francis Trolopp." Modern methods of booming literary wares were in vogue then. The new novel was advertised unsparingly and met with a wonderfully popular success, so popular that it was translated into many languages.

Paul Féval had arrived. The wise publishers took advantage of his success. The famous author was sent to London in royal style, accompanied by secretaries and servants, in order to study conditions there and get material for more mysteries. The distinguished visitor met with a very flattering reception. He was received everywhere and treated as the lion of the hour. A whole police force was placed at his command to protect him in his investigations in the underworld of London. The public was gullible even in those days. Paul Féval must have grinned to himself as he contrasted his present state of magnificence with the sordid garret of a few years back. And how superior he felt to the poor unintellectual things of religion! Religion was an excellent thing for his mother, his wife, but not even worthy of consideration on the part of the maker of best-sellers.

The "Mystères de Londres" was followed by "Amours de Paris." The walls of Paris were placarded with advertisements of the book, and soon the name of Paul Féval became a household word. He had really struck a gold mine with his popular, somewhat lurid, romances. It may have been a wasting of talent, as Eugène de Mirecourt in 1856 called it, but Féval did not worry about that. He had come into his own, and by his own he meant money and notoriety. He was able now by his royalties to live like a lord, gave splendid entertainments, had his salon and drove the best of horses. And with every year the wealth and fame increased.

It would be impossible to follow out in detail the literary history of Féval. He was well called by de Mirecourt a "literary locomotive." He had a facile pen—too facile, indeed—and sometimes published four novels at once. De Mirecourt wrote: "If the house Alexandre Dumas & Co. had interrupted the course of its commercial operations, the writer, still young (1856) whose life this notice is going to retrace would have been able by himself alone and with no help from the pens of others, to supply a good part of the clientèle of this immense factory of romances." And de Mirecourt ended his notice by saying—"We do not fear to speak of him with entire freedom, and with the certainty that sooner or later he will take a shining revenge." The revenge which Féval was to take on himself for his sensational fiction was a long way off, and it was to be very different from that expected by de Mirecourt. It seems almost incredible, but it is a fact that in a period of thirty-five years, up to the time of his conversion in 1876, Féval had published one hundred and three novels and dramas. From that time to his death in 1887 he wrote some twenty more books, making a total of one hundred

and twenty-three, besides innumerable articles not republished. He had tried his hand at the drama but only one
of his plays met with success—Le Bossu—dramatized from
one of his novels in 1863. Sardou collaborated with him
in making the play, which may explain its tremendous
success. This then was the life of Paul Féval for many
years. It was not a life of crime, though he wrote much
about crime and thus exercised an evil influence on the
minds of his readers, an evil which he happily came to
realize. His works never were indecent, he never could
have written the immoralities of the realistic school. Yet
for all that he was far from being an uplifting writer. He
was the flippant, sure-of-himself novelist, conscious of his
superiority, quite above the things of religion and hence
sure to say in his books many things that were not in conformity with the teachings of the Church. So we find
him on the eve of his conversion a wealthy, popular author,
a pagan romancer who long ago had put God out of his life.
He was a sinner, and what made his lot all the worse was
that in the pride of his heart he was unable to realize
his miserable condition. It needed a blow from God to
make him open his eyes.

The blow came in this way: Paul Féval had made a great
deal of money by his pen. He was really wealthy, and to
insure the future of his wife and eight children had
thought to increase his fortune by investment. He had put
all that he owned into Ottoman Bonds, which had promised
an especially high rate of interest. But the foreign se-
curity failed and Féval saw the earnings of a lifetime
swept away and at a time—he was then sixty years old—
when it was impossible to build up another fortune. He
was ruined. The news was overwhelming. For years
he had had an income of fifteen thousand dollars a year,
which had enabled him to live in the greatest luxury, and
to send his children to the most exclusive and most ex-
pensive schools. The day the bad news came he was sitting

in his study, while his wife and children, six of them, just home from school for the mid-day meal, waited for him to join them. The wife finally went to call him and found him in deep despair. She was a sweet, gentle woman, with steadfast faith in God. He blurted out the story of his bankruptcy and she turned pale at the news, her first thought being for the future of the children and the effect which this ruin of fortune must have on them. "Nothing remains," said he sadly.

"My dear," said the woman, "God remains to us. If He chastises us it is because He loves us."

"What!" he exclaimed. "God loves me?" He thought it a poor way in which God had shown His love.

"Will you pray with me?" she asked simply.

He assented and mechanically he said with her the Our Father, the Hail Mary and the Hail Holy Queen. She kissed him and together they went down to lunch.

"O father!" said one of the little girls, "you make a face just like I make when I am going to cry." Féval surely had reason to cry.

When the children had gone to school the wife said to Féval, "There is a God who sees the wound of your heart." But Paul was unmoved. His heart was not open to consolation. As he said afterwards: "I was living according to the law of God, yet without preoccupying myself about God, at the door of the sanctuary but outside. This position is of all others the most perilous, because it is not open to remorse. I was quite at ease there outside God, nothing tempted me to enter in, and this peccable indifference is like an untroubled sleep—the last hour may awaken it, indeed, but who can answer for his last hour? Indifference in itself may be, and often is, the most certain of condemnations."

In despair he turned to his wife. "What would you do in my place?" he asked.

"In your place," said she, "I should go to confession."

That had been her life-long prayer, for his conversion, and he knew it. He knew how far he had fallen from God.

He remembered his saintly parents and how his mother had prayed for him to make his peace with God. He used to tell how once when he was in trouble he did not dare go home, knowing that there he should hear only of God. And he who was the rival of Dumas, Hugo, Flaubert, with his books translated into twenty different languages was not to be bothered with inanities about religion. He remembered his saintly elder brother of whom he writes so beautifully in "The Steps of a Conversion," but religion was all right in its place, it had no place in the life of a popular author. Féval knew that there was no chance in literature for a practical Catholic. Novels must be unclean—happily he had not pandered to the underworld—or at least they must be in harmony with the times, that is with nothing to disturb the religious indifference of the readers. Hence the very mention of confession was objectionable to Féval, who knew that to earn his daily bread he must still retain his appeal to the popular ear. In his despair as he planned for the future it seemed to him that there was but one thing for him to do. His future novels must take the modern note, must be realistic, must make an appeal to pruriency. The temptation was alluring but, perhaps with a thought to his wife and children, he rejected the temptation to write immoral books. No doubt that was the decisive moment in his conversion. At any rate he decided to consult a priest even though he had no notion of going to confession. He went to see a Jesuit, the professor to one of his sons, and confessor of his wife, and told him about the financial ruin that had come to him.

Toward the end of the conversation the priest said to him—"Tell me the story of your First Communion; you have often promised to do so."

"Oh, not now, Father," said Féval, "it is too late; see,

it is nearly our dinner hour and I have eaten nothing today."

"Nevertheless, stay with me," insisted the priest, "you shall have something to eat here."

"Nonsense," said Féval. But the priest insisted.

"I am a prisoner, am I?" asked Féval, smiling, as he moved toward the door.

And the priest, his hand on the door, suddenly exclaimed, "The hour is past and gone! Let me clasp your hand, at least, for if you go now, you will never return. I have prayed to your dead and they have not heard me." And he continued after a while, "I was wrong to ask for the story of your past life. I knew it already." Féval declared that impossible, and he turned back, memories of the past coming back to him, to ask how the priest knew. The priest told him where he had got his information. "Her name is Mother St. Charles, but in the world she was called Clemena Loirier."

Clemena Loirier had been engaged to Féval's brother Charles, but Charles, on account of the family cares which had come to him on the death of his father, had never married. Clemena entered the convent. At the sound of the beloved names and the memories they recalled Féval burst into tears. The priest held a crucifix before him. "Behold your God of love!" he said, "the God of sacrifice. Behold the God of Charles, whom Charles sought to imitate. My son, go down on your knees!"

"I did not kneel," said Féval, "I fell down, with a great sigh of relief as if a burden was being lifted from me." And the priest simply pointed to the prie-dieu.

Féval repeated the Confiteor after the priest; it was so long since he had said it, he had forgotten it entirely. "My son," said the priest, "you cannot yet make your confession, but tell me now that you give yourself to God with all your heart." And simply, as a child, as the prodigal son he was, Féval answered, "With all my heart I de-

sire to belong to God, Father." A wonderful joy surged
into his soul. He left the house, his heart singing, while
he heard the priest, whom he had just left, chanting the
Te Deum in gratitude to God for the return of the lost
sheep. "I love God," Féval kept repeating to himself,
"I will love Him." He hurried home as if on wings, and
fell into his wife's arms. "It is done," said he, "I love
God. I belong to Him."

"What a contrast," he wrote, "between this night and
the preceding one! I had Jesus reconciled at my bedside and I confided to Him, with serene faith, the future
of our children. I cannot call myself resigned, for resignation presupposes a struggle, and I had no struggle,
nothing but a supernatural calm."

Féval made his confession, a confession of a life that
had done without God for fifty years. Peace came to
his soul and his heart overflowed with joy as he received
the Bread of Life, his second Holy Communion. The old
life was dead. After his reconciliation with God he took
up the manuscript of an unfinished novel and wrote as
follows: "This unfinished page is written by my other
self, it seems to me a hundred years ago. I cannot finish
it." Féval in those moments of conversion lived a greater
romance than any of those he had written.

The "penitent-romancer" as he has been called had but
one thought—to repair the evil which he believed his
writings had done. He felt that his future life must be
one of reparation. It was a practical penance he did by
working at the revision of his published works, which, as
we have said, numbered at that time more than a hundred.
"It is necessary," said he, "that all those pages disappear
—all! God will permit me to live to convert them as I
am converted myself." So he worked untiringly in the
preparation of new editions of his books, eliminating objectionable passages. His friends remonstrated with him
at undertaking a work of such magnitude. But he re-

plied: "What is the work, the pain? All is nothing when one searches into his life, when he reviews his life and retraces his steps. There is no longer question of believing, or even of practising, but of repairing. Faith does not suffice, one must have works."

Féval surely knew the meaning of true repentance. He had more than the pain of reparation to endure. Once his conversion became known he was slighted and sneered at by many of his former friends and admirers. But far from letting that disconcert him he bore it all cheerfully. One of his former friends said to him one day, "Well, I am hardly surprised, for you are a Breton, and that explains it. You have an archaeological heart, attracted by the things of the past, and you cling to your Ancient God as you do to your ancient King, but at all events you will never fall so low as to believe in La Salette and Lourdes, and what they call the Sacred Heart."

Féval in those days had never even heard of La Salette or Lourdes, which shows how far removed from Catholic thinking he was. He asked his wife about them, and she told him simply the story of them, giving him a picture of the Mater Dolorosa, weeping over France. "There," said she, "it is *that!*" From that time on the convert became devoted to both La Salette and Lourdes. Also, he developed a great devotion to the Sacred Heart. To manifest it he went on a parish pilgrimage to the provisional Chapel built in honor of the Sacred Heart at Montmartre preparatory to the erection of the great basilica toward which he was to contribute so much by his pen and his alms. His eyes were wet with tears. The chaplain to whom he was introduced asked him to write an account of the pilgrimage for a Catholic paper. Féval gladly performed the task, and signing his name to the article thus announced to the world that he was a practical Catholic.

That was the beginning of his constructive work of writing in defense of the faith. He became for the next ten years the Knight of Catholicism. He wished to write only for God. "If you knew," said he, "how sweet it is to pray and to think of nothing but the love of God, when one has spent his life celebrating the profane love of men." One thing that especially appealed to him was the erection of the basilica on Montmartre. Toward this project he was generous, on one occasion giving the proceeds of one of his most successful pamphlets, which amounted to some seventy thousand francs. In fact one form his penance took was that of giving alms. The first fruits of every payment he received were devoted to charity. He even refused to benefit by the sale of any of his re-edited works lest his repentance might bring him any material gain, but gave all the profits to the poor.

After the death of his devoted wife Féval went to live in a small house near his beloved church of the Sacred Heart on Montmartre, for which he had written such eloquent appeals. This church was his joy and his life and he wanted to be near it. So he took this little house at the foot of the hill, near the church, but not too near since he humbly believed that he was not holy enough to approach the holy place too closely. In this humble dwelling he worked at his writing, at new books and at the revision of the old. It was there he received such friends as Louis Veuillot. Once he said to a friend who expressed astonishment at this hermit's life: "Oh, I know well that everybody cannot make a hermit of himself like this. Only—listen! You also ought to convert yourself. I assure you that God loves you. Adieu! But adieu in two words—*A Dieu.*"

All his remaining years were for Féval a life of penitential prayer. His joy was to climb the hill to the church. It was not an easy task. He was old and unwell and it took him fifteen minutes to reach the church where his soul found such inspiration. "Yes," said he, "the road is rough, but less rough than the approach to Calvary.

It is the too weak expiation due to my God by the author of such deplorable writings."

"But God does not require one to kill himself," said a commiserating friend.

"God," replied the old penitent, "demands that I do my duty, and not that I should live."

But live Féval did to atone for his past indifference by writing noble defences of things Catholic, of the Jesuits, the priesthood, of his beloved Sacred Heart. One of his greatest works of apologetics was the sketch book, as it may be called, which he entitled, "Jesuits!" The book created somewhat of a sensation. Féval defending the Jesuits! Father Galivly translating the book prefaced his offering by saying: "Féval, until lately, was not what would be called a clerical—far from it. As he himself says, he was an intimate friend of Eugene Sue, and his first connection with the Jesuit controversy was as an antagonist of the Society." The American reviewer of this book in the *Catholic World* of February, 1879, wrote in this wise—which shows how strange Féval appeared as an apologist of the Church:

"Paul Féval is scarcely the man we should look to for a defence of the Jesuits or for a defence of anything that is especially worth defending. M. Féval is best known as a fairly successful writer of the customary French novel, and the customary French novel is worth very little, indeed. The same sprightliness of style and fancy, the same play of wit and conceit that once he used on the side of evil, or of very doubtful morality, he now, in his old age employs in defence of a worthy cause. . . . There is force; historical research, eloquence; there are all the gifts of an accomplished writer bent upon accomplishing a serious purpose."

The review is interesting as showing how Catholics regarded Féval in his unregenerate days, and as indicative of the courage required of the penitent to come out in defence of what he had once derided or ignored. In the preface to "Jesuits!" he writes the apologia of his return to God. He tells of his first interest in the Jesuits when he was a young writer to whom popularity had come. "Eugene Sue," he writes, "was one of the most pronounced aristocrats I have ever met; a real Sybarite who was tortured by the fold of a rose-leaf. When the enormous success of the 'Mysteries of Paris' had given him over to the democracy, Doctor Veron (a publisher) said to him, 'There is a fortune to be made in attacking the Jesuits.' And he laid a hundred thousand franc notes on the table. That is the history of the 'Wandering Jew' as related by Veron, who afterwards freely confessed that the dearly bought scythe had mown nothing at all, unless it might be the subscribers."

A rival publisher came to Féval, then only twenty-five, and, as he says, "vainer than any peacock you could find" and urged him to write a book also against the Jesuits, telling him that he had a room full of documents to help him out. Féval accepted the task, but after working hard for a month studying the question he abandoned the work in disgust and wrote as follows to the publisher: "I am going to Brittany, and I have thrown the sheets of our book into the fire. Pardon me for returning your 'documents' and your money, but I find that I undertook in a trifling way and ignorantly, a task that does not become an honorable writer, and though I am utterly indifferent as far as religion goes, I am as careful of my literary honesty as I am of the apple of my eye. Understand, I am not attacking others' honor or honesty; opinions are free; I speak for myself alone. . . . I have found out by reading your own documents that I had undertaken to calumniate for so much a line men who are not only innocent of all crime, but are useful citizens, benefactors of mankind, soldiers of science, peaceful conquerors, apostles, heroes, saints whose only fault is having excelled all other bodies of men in bringing out by the strength of their arms, their sweat, their blood itself, what is perhaps the most astonishing work of civilization in modern times." These honest words written thirty years before Féval's conversion were, indeed, heroic, at a time when "not to spit on the Jesuit was indecent!"

The publisher, nothing daunted, then urged him to write a book in favor of the Jesuits, and so create a literary sensation! But Féval was afraid. "I was afraid," said he, "of falling into bad odor with the people who disperse success. I was afraid of my enemies, but, above all, I feared my friends. To make known all the testimony unwillingly favorable to the Jesuits that I had found while bent on their condemnation amid the heap of papers livid with their adversaries hatred, would have been to compromise me forever. . . . I was afraid of the journals I contributed to, I was afraid of my readers whom I liked and who liked me. It made my flesh creep to think of the amount of popular prejudice." So the book was not written until long after, in spite of the fact that the irreligious Féval had his sons educated in Jesuit colleges. It required a grace from God to give him courage to defend the truth. "I was dozing in my worldly prosperity," he said, "I needed misfortune to awaken me, and a sorrow that should scald my eyes with tears. The misfortune came; an unaccustomed sorrow fell upon me without warning, threw me to the earth and in that solemn moment when the soul hesitates and shivers, called on one side by repentance and life, on the other by revolt and death, I was assisted by a Jesuit who touched the crucifix to my pains and lifted me out of despair. . . . I have said that before; here, there, everywhere; do not blame me for saying it over again, it would be of no use. I will say it and say it again in the thankful joy of my heart until the last hour of my life." And he continues: "My conversion constituted my nobility, my glory and my triumph in this world and it will be my salvation in the one to come. And I gather with a pious care whatever relates to my conversion. I have already made one book about it, and I shall make others, repeating: *Quia fecit mihi magna qui potens est.* Is it not my right and my duty to chant the *Magnificat* of my conversion?"

And thus he concludes: "I have spent thirty years not in making this book but in summoning up courage enough to write the first line of it. Would to God I had spent this better half of my life in getting light on the subject to the extent of my poor ability! But I have sown my long road with light pages that have been the sport of the wind. In them the name of God is dubiously honored, religion receives an empty respect, and there is scarcely one of those pages that I can read with unmixed pleasure. I have lost too much time. Thirty years! . . . I do not know if I shall be read, but I hope so. For some my bad books will serve as a passport to this book, and that at least will be good."

As an apologist Féval was untiring. The most beautiful of all his books is his "Les Etapes d'une Conversion" —"The Steps of a Conversion"—in which he gives us a charming picture of his own family in the far distant Breton days. It was a work of four volumes published at intervals and is full of faith and love. He is forever insisting on the glory of his conversion back to God and thanking Him for the mercy of it. "Every conversion," he writes, "implies at the same time criminal error and His merciful chastisement. Happy the wounded hearts! Happy the suffering that warns and converts! Happy the captives enchained by the benediction of sorrow!" Well could he write: "I was saved, having received the gift of first tears. Since then I believe, I hope, and I love. I am happy: I know how to pray!"

Féval's pen was forever going. He contributed innumerable articles to the papers, especially the Catholic journals, and at one time directed three different publications. He had in view the writing of many other books in defence of the Church. It was a hard task he had set himself and no wonder that the strenuous, ceaseless labor gradually undermined his health. A sudden stroke of apoplexy incapacitated him. He became a helpless invalid. In this condition he remained for five years. The *Societé des Gens de Lettres,* of which he was president— he was also an officer of the Legion of Honor—had him placed in the Home conducted by the Brothers of St. John of God. There he was tenderly nursed through the long years and there, attended by one of his daughters, who was a Sister of Charity, he died March 8, 1887.

He was buried from the Church of St. Francis Xavier, the funeral being attended by all the celebrities of art and literature. At the interment in Montparnasse Cemetery eulogies were pronounced by Jules Claretie in the name of the *Societé des Gens de Lettres* and by Ludovic Halévy in the name of the *Societé des Auteurs et Compositeurs Dramatiques.*

The Vicomte de Spoelbergh de Lovenjoul in his *Les Lundis d'un Chercheur* pays a glowing tribute to Féval's literary worth. "Paul Féval," he writes, "though placed in literature at a respectful distance from the great Alexander Dumas, remains, however, one of the masters of this age in stories of adventure. By his fertile imagination the power of conceptions and the astonishing variety of his inspirations, he is certainly of the race of the inexhaustible author of *Monte Cristo* and of the *Musketeers,* if he is not his equal. Both of them will remain for a long time the best amusers of the sad and morose generations which have succeeded them. . . . All these works assure him a literary rank of the most distinguished among the writers of these times."

But whatever may be said of Féval's literary glory, he deserves a place among heroic souls, who when the grace of

God came corresponded with it, considering the world and its glory as nothing, and the labor for eternal life as everything. It is not of Féval, the rich, the famous, we love to think, but of Féval, the "penitent romancer," Féval, the great penitent.

FATHER HERMANN: MUSICIAN AND MONK

IN VAIN would one search the musical dictionaries of today for mention of the boy-genius who once engaged the attention of the musical world, not alone as a virtuoso, but also, and perhaps more so, as the darling pupil of Liszt, the pet prodigy of George Sand.

Hermann Cohen was born November 10, 1821, in Hamburg, Germany. He was the son of David Cohen, a strict Jew, who traced his ancestry back to the tribe of Aaron. The father was a well-to-do tradesman, or as some would have it a banker, and occupied a high position among his compatriots, who constituted a colony numbering twenty-five thousand. This colony, as was to be expected, had suffered some modification owing to association with the outside world, and so David Cohen, in spite of his strict orthodoxy, was, like many of his countrymen of all ages, fondly in love with the goods of this world. Hence it is not surprising that greed for business reigned supreme in the household and that money and stocks were the topics of conversation from morning until night.

In this atmosphere of broad Judaism young Hermann spent his childhood. He and his elder brother were sent to the principal college of the city, where, in spite of delicate health, his progress was rapid. He was noted for his amiable disposition, though there was a seriousness about him which inclined to moodiness. This gloom was due, perhaps, to the growing ill health of the lad, which made it advisable in his ninth year to take him out of school work and allow him to continue his studies at home, a misfortune not so great as might be supposed, for he was quick to learn, and had an earnest desire to improve. But it was in music that his advance was most phenomenal. At the age of six he played well the popular airs of the day, improvised on the piano, and had even attempted composition. Such precociousness pleased the father so much that when the boy found fault with the old harpsichord it required no persuasion to induce him to purchase a grand piano. Yet, notwithstanding this zeal for the boy's advancement, there was little vigilance exercised in regard to his associates, at the most impressionable period of his life.

On leaving school he was placed under the care of a professor, whose morals were no clearer than his mental faculties. He rewarded *"le petit prodige"* for his talent by taking him to the theater and the race course, and initiating him into the mysteries of hunting and gambling.

One can easily foresee the effect of such an association upon the brilliant lad. It was well that it was soon brought to an end, though by reverses in the fortunes of the head of the family. Hermann was twelve years of age when Mrs. Cohen, seeing how she had fallen from her high estate, and chafing under the thought that she must live a life of comparative poverty where once she had been used to every luxury, determined to leave the scene of her affliction and settle where none of her old friends could taunt her with her present need; for she was a woman of lofty manners. Accordingly, leaving her husband and eldest son to try to repair the family fortunes in Hamburg, she set out for Paris, taking with her Hermann and his younger brother and sister. Possibly she thought that the earning power of the boy whose talent had been the talk of amateur circles in the days of prosperity might be of service at a time when all help would be acceptable to David Cohen. When they stopped at Mecklenbourg, on the way to Paris, the Grand Duke was so impressed on hearing the boy play, that he besought the mother to

let her son give all his time to music. Mrs. Cohen needed
no great persuasion. The lad had already made his
début successfully in Altona, and any lingering doubt
was dispelled by his success in Frankfurt and other great
German cities. And so, with the intention of devoting her son to music, she came to the city of Paris July
5, 1834.

It was not difficult for the mother to get a hearing for
the boy. His name was already known as that of a remarkable amateur, and his letters of recommendation assured him admission to the smartest salons. Here he soon
became the center of brilliant assemblies, the recipient of
the applause and even of the caresses of the beautiful
and cultured ladies of the Faubourg St. Germain. They
vied with one another in trying to spoil him, giving dinner
parties and soirées at which the twelve-year-old genius,
who looked even younger with his long girlish curls and
kilted costume, rewarded his admirers with exhibitions of
his precocious talents.

Even when the modern press-agent was only in embryo
the daily papers recorded the triumphs of the little Jew,
and he was besieged for his portrait. Alas for youth that
never knew the joys of youth! What is that poem of
Stevenson's?

> Sing me a song of a lad that is gone,
>   Say, if that lad be I;
> Merry of soul he sailed on a day
>   Over the sea to Skye.

It was so with the lad who had been saturated with the
world almost from babyhood, a man without having passed
through boyhood, "an abortion of celebrity," as he calls
himself, whom the flattery of worldly men and women
kept from his home till the small hours of the morning,

gradually destroying in his soul the remnants of virtue in the maelstrom of Parisian luxury.

It was deemed advisable to put the boy under the instruction of one of the great teachers of the day. Chopin was first selected because after a long period of neglect he was now the mode. He took one lesson from this master, and went from him to Zimmerman, from whom also he took one lesson. From this we suspect that the purpose of the boy was to make a trial of all the famous teachers of the city before submitting himself to any one of them. At length he came to Liszt, then twenty-three years of age, who, on his arrival in Paris, had undergone the course Hermann was now enduring, having been called the eighth wonder of the world. Liszt, whose name was one to conjure with in Paris, both as a pianist and as a teacher, at first refused to take the boy as his pupil, and it was only after great persuasion that he was induced to give him a hearing at all. Half unwillingly he listened to the playing of the lad, but it was so charming, so full of genius, so replete with hopes of a great career, that the famous virtuoso immediately assumed charge of his musical education, predicting wonderful things for him. From that time Hermann was the spoiled pet of Liszt, his companion from morning until night, his "show pupil," who must accompany him to the innermost circles of wealth and culture, where the master was always a welcome guest.

However advantageous this friendship was to the boy in the development of his musical talent, it could not but be harmful in the formation of his character. It familiarized him with ideas which sooner or later must bear evil fruit. The whirlpool of Paris had swallowed Liszt. The "second Mozart," whom Beethoven had kissed amid the frantic cheers of the Viennese public at the close of a recital there, had come to Paris the devout son of fervent Catholics. Even after a tour of France and a second trip to London his faith was so strong that he would have entered Holy Orders were it not for the opposition of his father. A period of convalescence, when he was about eighteen, was employed in reading Voltaire and Rousseau. Religious doubts assailed him. De Lammenais had been his resort for the solution of them, and he had followed him—alas! In 1835 he wrote of the Church: "She seems doomed to perish in oblivion." Jules Sandeau, Victor Hugo, Alfred de Musset, Planché, George Sand—these were his associates and his new evangelists. He was twenty-three when he met George Sand, who had just returned from Venice, where she had broken with De Musset. But in 1834, the year in which Hermann had come to Paris, Liszt had met and been conquered by the Countess d'Agoult, known as "Daniel Stern." This woman was so infatuated with the virtuoso that she left her husband and her three children to follow him, and that infatuation lasted for ten years.

Such was the youth who had once moaned because he had not been allowed to take Holy Orders! Such was the preceptor of Hermann! And by his side, exercising perhaps a greater influence upon the boy, was the strange woman who had the name of a man and few of the instincts of a woman—George Sand, who has immortalized the young pianist in her "Lettres d'un Voyageur." It is not pleasant to recall the low moral condition of the men and women who constituted themselves the protectors, the educators, of the little boy in a strange city, but if one would understand the full glory of his conversion one must follow him, even through the sewers of iniquity, where his feet slipped along ere they struck the solid rock of the way of the cross.

Amantine Lucille Aurore Dupin-Dudevant had been so religious during her convent school days as to have yearned to become a nun herself, but under the subsequent tutelage of her grandmother, a free-thinker who deliberately planned a course of reading destined to destroy the girl's vocation, she gradually lost her faith. Married to the vulgar Colonel Dudevant at the age of eighteen, she left him in 1831 at the age of twenty-seven, and came to Paris to make a living by her pen. She had already displayed remarkable talent, but it was some time before the new writer found her audience. When she did she became famous immediately. There was an air of mystery about her which made everybody wonder.

Young Hermann was brought to the notice of George Sand by Liszt. Fascinated by his musical genius, she made a pet of him at once, for she loved music and often declared that she would have been a musician had she received the proper training. "Music is prayer," she said, "it is faith, it is friendship, it is association *par excellence.*" For days she kept the boy at her side while she wrote, letting him soothe her with his playing or roll the cigarettes which she smoked inveterately during her writing hours. She always called him "Puzzi," a tender name that Liszt had given him from *puzzia,* meaning darling.

How beneficial was this influence to a boy of twelve, may be judged by the picture we have of the youth seated at the piano running scales mechanically while he devoured *Indiana* or *Lelia.* It was in these days, too, that he came under the influence of De Lammenais, who soon became the lad's master and hero. In the "Histoire" of Sand she tells us of Liszt coming to see her accompanied by De Lammenais and *"l'enfant Israelite, Puzzi."* Yet all the while the boy was studying hard at his music. After much searching in dust-covered folios for accounts of his playing, I have found in the *Gazette Musicale* of Paris for April 19, 1835, the following notice: "We take pleasure in announcing the concert of the young Hermann of Hamburg, pupil of Mr. Liszt, which will take place next Thursday, April 23, at eight o'clock in the evening, in the Chantereine hall. A duo for four hands, the composition of M. Pixis, executed by M. Liszt and the beneficiary, the grand potpourri of Czerny for four grand pianos, by Messieurs Liszt, Lourosky, Alkan and Hermann," etc.

In the letters of Liszt, as well as in the works of George Sand, we get an occasional glimpse of the affection which was showered upon the boy by his two older companions. In 1834 began the fascination of the Countess d'Agoult for the great virtuoso, and in the following year they determined to travel through Switzerland and Italy, taking Puzzi with them. The boy had prevailed upon his mother to allow him to go in order to continue his lessons with Liszt. Evidently there had been a little dispute between Sand and the Hermanns, for in the November of that year we have Liszt writing to her, "Come to us, then, and that as soon as possible. Puzzi has already bought a pipe of peace in your honor." Many letters passed between the friends, and Hermann came in for his share of mention, always in a playful and loving manner. "The illustrious doctor," she calls him, *"ratissimo,"* the "rat" and *"le gamin musical."* In one of her letters to the Countess she beseeches her not to give Puzzi a bon-bon for a whole day for not writing to her, and again to "pull the ear of the *ragazzo di-rosa."*

Liszt had called himself and his little pupil "fellows," and this title was often given to him as well as to Hermann by Sand. "Fellows primo" was Liszt and "fellows secundo" was Hermann. "I want the fellows," she wrote; "I want them as soon as possible, and as long as possible, I want them unto death."

In one of her letters to the maestro she says: "It is you especially, my dear Franz, whom I place in a picture inundated with light—magical apparition which arises in the darkness of my evening meditations . . . But if I made this picture I would not forget the charming Puzzi, your well beloved pupil. Raphael and Tebeldaeo, his young friend, never appeared with more grace before God and man than you two, my dear children, when I saw you one evening across the orchestra of a hundred voices, all silent to hear your improvisations. The child just behind you pale, affected, motionless as marble, yet as a flower ready to scatter its petals, seemed to inhale the harmony through all his pores and to open his pure lips to drink in the honey which you were pouring out for him." Again, "I received news of you through a letter from Puzzi; you have a mother of pearl piano; you play it near the window looking out upon the lake, looking up to the snows of Mt. Blanc." At length George Sand came to visit her friends at Geneva. "The first object in my path," she says, "was Puzzi, sitting astride of his traveling bag; but he was so changed, so much grown, he had such a head of long brown hair, his blouse was of such feminine cut, that I was mystified. I no longer recognized the little Hermann, but took off my hat and asked, 'My handsome page, tell me where Lara is?'" Very girlish the boy must have seemed at that time, for soon after when the company went to the Church of St. Nicholas, where Liszt played the *Dies Irae* on the great organ, the old organist was told that Puzzi was a celebrated Italian cantatrice who was following Liszt in disguise. Liszt established a conservatory at Geneva, and gave one of the classes to Hermann, who directed it with the assistance of a young German named Schad.

Evil example had already begun to bear fruit in the boy's soul. While in Paris, his head had been turned by the strange doctrines he had heard from the lips of celebrities. Long after he wrote to Father Ratisbonne, "They were early at work to make me a scapegoat of all those dreadful doctrines which, springing up from the bottom of Hell, were creeping out all over the surface of this Parisian den. Soon this head of only fourteen made room for atheism, pantheism, Fourrierism, Saint-Simonism, communism, socialism, riot, massacre of the wealthy, abolition of marriage, terrorism, agrarianism and the community of enjoyment in all pleasures.   Evil makes rapid strides; I soon became one of the most zealous of propagandists of sects that are sworn to change the face of the world and, consequently, the pet Benjamin of more than one of the apostles of a misnamed civilization."   Such was evidently his state of mind during the stay at Geneva, for we find the youth of sixteen making a pilgrimage to Fernay, where he rhapsodized before the statue of Rousseau.   It was not surprising, therefore, that for the new and more companionable friends he neglected the mother who had followed him to Geneva to watch over him.

When Liszt resumed his travels again Hermann had to return to Paris alone.   It was a strange gift which Liszt gave his pupil on parting with him; a Bible with these words written on the fly-leaf by the hand of the maestro: "Blessed are the clean of heart, for they shall see God." Were the old thoughts of his childhood's purity and religion pulling at the heart strings of the musical genius, and did he regret the impious associations into which he had led the boy?   We know, at any rate, that he had often tried to break away from the woman, who still clung to him in spite of himself.

Even in those days Hermann had a fancy to become a Christian; but he was uncertain as to whether he should embrace Catholicity or Protestantism, and so the fancy passed away, and the youth of sixteen was plunged again into the world and its allurements.   For a time he settled down in Paris, devoting himself to teaching and the giving of concerts.   He made considerable money, but it went in gambling and luxurious living.   Then the passion of travel came upon him, and he made trips to Italy, London, and his own native Hamburg.   "Reckless from success," he said, "and a prey to every kind of bad habits, I traveled through England and Switzerland, Italy and Germany, growing ever more mad after philosophical novelties, everywhere examining the working and finding out the novelties of the poisoned doctrines with which my childhood had been imbued. Priests I looked upon as the bane of society, but the monks I shunned as so many anthropophagi. Who would have told me, when I returned to Paris, that divine Providence intended to show me from how far it could lead a stray creature back!"

Hermann was then a young dandy who lived but for the day. According to one of his contemporaries he was the real beau, very gentlemanly, extremely courteous, careless, however, about his conversation and unreserved in telling about his exploits. And no matter where he went, whether it was to Italy to see Liszt, to London or to Venice for the production of his opera, he was ever the rabid redflagger, hot of speech and deeply interested in the designs of the revolutionary element in every country.

Such a course must inevitably bring ruin. The youth who had become the victim of every passion, of all the snares of youth, was obliged to flee from Paris and seek the protection of his father in Hamburg, beseeching him to extricate him from the plight into which his gaming propensities had plunged him. But the father, who had heard of his escapades, refused to give him any help. He was heartily ashamed of the son of whom he had expected great things, not in artistic lines only, but in the making of a substantial fortune. Nothing daunted by this cold reception, the youth traveled through Germany, where his undoubted talent gained him a hearing and flattering receptions from the noblest families. Still the gambling craze stuck to him, and when in Paris he found himself again ruined he was at the point of committing suicide. Again did he become the dandy of the Faubourg St. Germain, and still more the slave of the world's sin. We get a glimpse of him in the life which Paul de Musset wrote of his brother Alfred. "Alfred admired him, both as a

pianist and a composer; and, while the musician improvised, the poet would devise verses adapted to the movement of the music. They thus composed three songs—
'Bonjour, Suzon,' 'Non, Suzon, pas encore,' and 'Adieu,
Suzon.' Another melody by the same master adapted to
Italian words, was afterwards adopted by Steinberg for
the barcarolle which he sings in 'Bettine.' " But the soul
of the young musician was never at ease. Divine grace
was troubling the Bethesda pool of his corrupt and putrid
heart.

The great work was done in 1847, when Hermann was
twenty-seven years of age. At the Church of St. Valery,
Burgoyne Street, Paris, devotions for the month of May
were held with great solemnity, the music being under
the direction of the Prince of Moskowa, whose choir of
efficient amateurs attracted many listeners. One Friday
evening he invited Hermann to play the organ for him.
At the benediction of the Blessed Sacrament, though Hermann felt no disposition to kneel, there came over him a
strange sensation causing him to bow. The feeling returned to him on the following Friday. There came to
him then an inspiration to become a Catholic. A few
days later when, on passing the Church, he heard the bell
ring for Mass, he entered and remained for three Masses.
That afternoon he was drawn thither again and, the
Blessed Sacrament being exposed, he fell on his knees as
though compelled by some power greater than himself.
"I felt as it were a great weight descend upon me which
forced me to my knees, yea, even to bow to the ground in
adoration."

That day he hunted out a prayer-book on the shelves
of one of his friends and studied it earnestly to find out
about this great devotion of Catholics. All the night he
thought of the Blessed Sacrament. Thereafter he went
to Mass often, his mind wrought up to a high pitch of
excitement. Grace had not yet come and he knew not

what course to pursue. In this condition he went to Ems to give a concert, and on Sunday at Mass he felt the same strange emotion. At the elevation he burst into tears, and knew that grace had come. "I had often wept in my childhood," he says, "but never such tears as these. All at once I saw before me all the sins of my past life, hideous, vile, revolting, worthy the wrath of the Sovereign Judge. And yet I felt also a miraculous calm, God in his mercy forgiving me these sins, and accepting my firm resolution to love Him henceforth above all things."

He went immediately to the Duchess of Rauzanne and begged her to introduce him to a priest. Abbé LeGrand began to instruct him, giving him L'Homond's Exposition of Christian Doctrine. God alone knows the struggle that the awakened soul endured in those days. The devil does not release his prey without a terrible effort to retain it still unto its destruction. And so he made use of the concerts and parties and feasts and the joy of living, and the wit of men and the smile of women, the allurements of the world and the flesh to keep the heart of the youth from corresponding to the grace of God. On his return from Ems Hermann shut himself in his room, and devoted himself to the study of the doctrines of the Church. His conversion had been effected at Ems, August 8, 1847, and on the 28th day of that same month, the feast of the great St. Augustine, who ever seemed to play a part in the life of Hermann, he was baptized by the Abbé LeGrand in the memorial chapel of Our Lady of Zion, built by the famous convert from Judaism, the Abbé de Ratisbonne, in the Rue de Regard. To this church was attached a convent, all of whose inmates, nuns and orphans, were converts from Judaism.

The new convert was confirmed by Monseigneur Affre on December 3d, taking the name of Xavier. On the eighth of that same month he received his first Holy Communion with faith and love so ardent as to transform his countenance. His old friends could hardly believe him to be the same person, so great was the change. He was pale and reserved; he wore a long overcoat, a broad-brimmed felt hat, common shoes—far different from the clothes in which he had once taken so much pride. His room was poorly furnished—an iron bed, a piano, a trunk, a crucifix, a small statue of Our Lady, and small pictures of St. Theresa and St. Augustine. If he could abandon the world entirely and hide himself with God alone! But he must first pay the debts of the gambler Hermann, and to this task he set himself with all the ardor of a penitent spirit. Those were long and dreary years, the time spent in giving lessons and concerts to wipe out the debt of thirty thousand francs. In addition to the suspense, the dismal labor, there were customs and habits and memories to be combated, contempt and raillery of former companions to be endured. Hermann had recourse to the sacraments and prayer, the remedies which had sustained Augustine when the call of the past seemed imperative. In the intervals of his lessons he recited the rosary and read pious books; but above all put his trust in the Blessed Sacrament which was ever to be the object of his greatest devotion.

Two years of exile ended, and Hermann determined to become a monk. He had had doubts about the choice of a vocation, whether to become a secular or a religious, and had consulted Lacordaire. "Have you the courage to let yourself be spit upon in the face and say no word?" asked Lacordaire. "Yes," answered Hermann. "Then go and be a monk," was the answer. He went therefore to the Carmelite convent at Agen, and thence to the novitiate of Brouissey near Bordeaux, where, alas, for the aspirant to sanctity, there was a fresh obstacle to be met. A Jew could not be admitted into the Carmelites without special dispensation from Rome; and Rome, knowing his past, refused to grant the dispensation.

There was nothing for Hermann to do but to go to Rome and plead in person with the Holy Father. Happily, a general council of the Carmelites was then in session at Rome. Before it he laid his case and the dispensation was granted. He returned to Brouissey and was admitted October 6, 1849. On the sixteenth of that same month died Chopin, another to whom the "woman with the sombre eye," as de Musset called George Sand, had been an evil genius. He asked for Extreme Unction, confessed, received Holy Viaticum, and having recited the litany after the priest, passed into eternity. Who can say how much of that happy death was due to the prayers of the other musician buried in the silence of his retreat!

Novitiate days were full of true spiritual joy to Hermann, even though the crosses sent to try him were heavy. He immediately became an example of perfection, working out his salvation with the energy with which he had pursued the primrose path of pleasure,—cleaning the offices, sweeping the passages, gathering grapes, digging as a day laborer, yet always with the joy which comes from a good conscience. Nor was his beloved music cast aside. What had hitherto been the snare of his soul now became the wings to bear him aloft in the beautiful canticles which have since made his name famous in ecclesiastical music. These were helps to humble and strengthen his soul for one of the great trials of his life, now in store for him.

In the eyes of his countrymen, for a Jew to become a Christian was folly; to become a monk was outrageous. The news of the defection of Hermann had traveled to his family at Hamburg, and it needs no great powers to imagine their consternation. One day in the July of 1850 the mother, who had set out from home to reclaim, if possible, the wayward son, came from Paris and took lodgings in a house near the convent. That evening she came to the convent, called for her son, and was shown to the little chapel, where she took a seat in a nook by the window

opening into the cloister garden. Suddenly she started
back in horror. There before her very eyes was the son
of whom she had expected such great things, a renegade,
a monk! Her cup of misery was filled to overflow. It
seemed an age till he came to her, accompanied by the
master of novices, and she swooned and fell into his arms.
Touched by her misery, he sought to console her, but she
would not be consoled. He had to leave her when the bell
for the office rang, but she waited for the services too, and
on hearing him playing upon the little melodeon wept as
if her heart would break, moved by grief and offended
motherly love. He had slighted her before for Liszt and
George Sand. She had won him back, and now he had
gone from her even more hopelessly to the God of the
Christians. She begged him to go back to the world with
her, and went away from the convent, execrating those
who had taken her son from her. His father, enraged at
the defection, disinherited and cursed him, forgiving him
only after many years. Time softens hearts, and Hermann's prayers were ever ascending to God for the conversion of his family. He was granted the happiness to
see ten members of his family come into the Church,
among them two of his brothers, a sister and her son. His
mother remained a Jewess to the last, though the son had
reason to believe that in the final hour she called upon the
God of the Christians.

At his profession the young pianist became Brother
Augustine Marie of the Most Blessed Sacrament. He
was duly ordained priest, and said his first Mass on Easter
Sunday in 1851. In 1853 he was ordered to the south
of France to preach a mission, which was so successful
as to number among his many converts some of his own
countrymen. But his health gave way under the strain,
and ever after he suffered terrible pain.

The time came for a great act of reparation for the
scandal he had given during his life in Paris. He was

never a great orator, but he had the gift of conviction, a gift more potent to move hearts than all the powers of elocution; and so when it was announced that the once celebrated Hermann was to preach at St. Sulpice, April 24, 1854, the edifice was thronged with a curious and interested crowd. It was a wonderful sermon, in which he reminded his audience of his life of sin in days not so long distant, and told them of the coming of the grace of God and his strange conversion. Then he turned to a group of young men present and begged them to do as he had done, to follow him and share his happiness.

So it was always. The strange circumstances of Hermann's conversion, the remembrance of his fame as a pianist, brought him invitations from all sides to preach, and these, in spite of his continual sufferings, he accepted whenever it was possible. On one occasion he went to preach in Geneva where he had been at one time with Liszt. "How our old friends will be astonished," he wrote to his former colleague in Liszt's conservatory, Joseph Schad, the pianist. Surely they would have been astonished. I cannot help thinking that it was Hermann's prayers for his old maestro which led Liszt in his latter days to take orders in the Church of his childhood, where, as he wrote to Saint-Saens in 1869, "one must learn to subordinate himself in mind and deed." Here he devoted himself to sacred music and charity concerts. But, alas, for George Sand! She died as she lived, away from God. Yet Hermann had not abandoned her without an attempt to lead her back to the piety of her convent days. Once after his profession he was allowed to call upon her, but she would not listen to him. He was no longer the child of the world, the little "Puzzi" who had rolled her cigarettes, or soothed her with the music she loved. "So you have become a monk," she sneered. That was all. The interview was ended. Yes, he had become a monk, a real monk who did not spare himself for the glory of God.

He was ever working, now founding the desert of Taras-
tiex, now the Lyons foundation, where he was so beloved
by the people that they went on their knees to beg his
blessing as he passed. Cardinal Wiseman met him at
Rome in 1862, and was so impressed that he begged his
superiors to send him to England. The general of the
Carmelites refused, but the Cardinal, undaunted, appealed
to the Pope, who sent Hermann thither. The London
people remembered the young pianist who had amused
them in the olden days and knowing the story of his conversion, flocked to hear him at Kensington, where he was
established. But he was not to remain there permanently.
"In spite of my conversion, I am always the wandering
Jew," he said. He was everywhere,—at Lyons, Rouen,
Rome, Paris, Geneva, yes, and in Ireland, in spite of his
weak health and constant suffering. Finally he was appointed chaplain to the soldiers imprisoned in the German
fortress, and there his labors were brought to an end.
Smallpox was raging among the prisoners, and while min-
istering to them he contracted the disease.

"Can you sing the *Te Deum?*" he asked of the Sister
who was attending him.

She could not.

"The *Salve Regina?*"

"Yes," she replied.

"Then let us sing it together," he said. And with that
song on his lips he went to the land of eternal harmonies,
January 20, 1871. He was buried in the church of
St. Hedwidge, Berlin.

J. B. CARPEAUX

CARPEAUX was one of the greatest sculptors that France ever produced. With every year since his death his fame has grown. He is sure of his niche in the hall of fame, but it is not as the masterful artist that he appeals to us. Carpeaux at the height of his glory, in the fulness of his powers, does not thrill us so much as the poor suffering Carpeaux, stretched on his bed of pain through weary months waiting for the merciful touch of the hand of death. Carpeaux in his strength had drunk deep of the cup of sin. He wandered far from God on the primrose path; he traveled slowly back by the hard road of the cross. He who had made many a masterpiece bowed down at last before the *chef d'oeuvre* of the Great Artisan—the Crucified Christ. Carpeaux was a great penitent, even though like the penitent thief he saluted his Master only in the valley of the shadow of death.

Carpeaux was born at Valenciennes in French Flanders May 11, 1827. Here also had been born another great artist, Watteau, a statue of whom Carpeaux in the fulness of his powers made for his native city. He was baptized Jean Baptiste Jules. He was always called Jules until he became a celebrity, and then he simply signed himself, J. B. Carpeaux. His father, Joseph, was by trade a mason, though in order to keep the wolf from the door he did not disdain being a jack of all trades, now working as a carpenter, now as a thatcher. His mother's maiden name was Adèle Wargny. They were poor people, in fact their poverty was extreme, and they found it difficult to feed their children let alone have any ambitions to give them a place in the world. Consequently, Jean Baptiste received very little schooling. He had to leave the Brothers' school just when he was able to read and write and do a little figuring. He did not rebel against his lot, however. He was born of the people, was proud of that fact, and always had the tastes of the people. But the genius cannot be kept down by lack of opportunities; he makes his own opportunities. Carpeaux was possessed of a remarkably fine intelligence, of an elevation of character, and of a nobility of heart, and these spurred him on to supply later on the deficiencies of his boyhood's education. If there was ever a truly self-made man it was he. Even the humble employment of his father helped him in his career, for the work as a mason gave strength to his arm for the fashioning of his masterpieces of sculpture.

For Carpeaux was destined to be a sculptor. He felt it in him. Even as a child he had no other dream than to make statues. His father wanted him to be an architect and put him to study at the school of architecture at Valenciennes. When he had learned the elements there he came to Paris and took the courses of the royal school of design and mathematics. Mathematics appealed to him but little, design a great deal, and in his spare time he worked at his modeling, untaught by anyone but by his own instinct.

One day he came to Henri Lemaire, the sculptor, a relative of the Carpeaux family, and showed him a head which he had modeled. Carpeaux was then but a boy of fifteen, the smallest student in the school, and insignificant in appearance. Lemaire, without looking at the head, shrugged his shoulders at the sight of the aspirant to his art as if to dismiss his pretensions. The lad, indignant at the silent scorn, burst out in resentment: "You may be marshal in your art, monsieur, but who told you that I would not be prince of it ?" No difficulty, not even scorn, could daunt him. But it was an uphill road. Between classes he spent his time modeling, using as model anyone who was willing to pose for him. To make his touch surer he would work with his eyes bandaged. To fill in the education which he knew to be lacking he read assiduously, especially the books that would help him in his chosen profession.

The boy sculptor finally mustered up courage to bring one of his bas-reliefs to Rude, the sculptor, who was so impressed by the evident talent displayed in the work that he opened his studio to the youth. Rude may be considered the first master of Carpeaux. Carpeaux remained there eight months and learned much from this teacher, for whom he always had the greatest respect.

From his fifteenth to his twentieth year the life of Carpeaux was one continual struggle for existence. His father had come to Paris with his family to seek his fortune, but had retired with them to Versailles. The young sculptor, alone in the great city, needed all the strength of his urging genius to keep him from abandoning his quest. There were long months of complete abandonment, of misery, of sickness. To earn his daily bread he performed the most menial labor. Not only did he have to earn his own living, but the human vultures with whom he associated preyed upon him. It was an ugly period in the life of Carpeaux when he found his friends in the Paris underworld. There was little study then. He modeled bits and sold them. He worked by day and attended class by night. The character of his associates, the evil life he was leading, were not conducive to the formation of a great artist. For seven years the youth had wasted his body, his health, his heart, his brain. He saw at last that he never would advance in Paris under such conditions, and to be free of it all he went back to his native

city, where he found hospitality in a fine family of artists.
There he remained for a year and accomplished some
really good work.

The following year he obtained a pension of six hundred
francs, which permitted him to resume his studies at
Paris under much more hopeful conditions than during
his former residence there. He again studied with Rude,
but Rude, anxious to advance his pupil, sent him to Durer,
under whom he knew he would make greater progress.
Carpeaux was in earnest and he did advance. In 1851
we find him teaching anatomy at the *petit école,* where
he himself had studied. With his indomitable energy he
took part in all the contests of the *Ecole des Beaux Arts*
and succeeded in winning many prizes. Characteristic of
his work in those days were the many models he made of
children. He always had a special love for the little ones.
In fact Carpeaux, spite of his evident failings, was always
a child at heart.

In September, 1854, he obtained the *grand prix,* and
on this occasion his native city gave him a reception. The
son of the poor mason must have felt a thrill of pride as
he returned in triumph to the city where his childhood
had known so many hardships. But the rose was not
without its thorn. His eyes began to trouble him to
such an extent that he feared he was going to lose his
sight. Happily the trouble passed and the year 1858 finds
him entering upon his studies at Rome at the age of
twenty-eight. His talent, his genius for hard work, had
at last established him in the world. Up to now it had
been a hard struggle for recognition, a struggle against
poverty; fortune at last smiled upon him. The years at
Rome were years of hard work. Nor were they without
their struggles. Sometimes he was discouraged, and then
he would find his greatest help in the little mother whom
he always loved so tenderly. Thus, October 16, 1858, he
wrote in reference to a period of discouragement: "My

mother consoled me.   She restored to me by her letters the hope I had lost.   She gave me courage and I went back to work."

Shortly after Carpeaux nearly died at Naples.   As a result of the attack he was ill a long time, and came back to Valenciennes to recuperate in 1860.   But once more he returned to Rome, where he remained hard at work for seven years.   It was there he met with his first colossal success in his famous group of Ugolini.   Everybody in Rome came to see what was regarded as a masterpiece. When the work was sent to Paris for exhibition the French did not think so highly of it.   But in time the adverse criticism was overcome, and today the Ugolini is considered one of the great works of the age.

The now famous sculptor returned to France in the spring of 1862, but for some reason or other he was disgusted with his native country and thought of going back at once to Rome.   He went north instead, and after a short sojourn in Belgium came back to France again.

Carpeaux, though he had drunk deep of the cup of life, though his life was far from being an innocent one, was not the "Voltairian deist" which one of his biographers would make him out to be.   He never lost his faith, even though he was for many years a stranger to the practices of religion.   When he was working for the *prix de Rome* he entered one day the church of Saint Sulpice to pray. When he was leaving he remarked simply, "The Virgin has promised me that if I worked hard I would get the prize."   Asked about his beliefs, he replied once, "I love with naïveté, I believe with all the forces of my soul, and I adore with recollection all that elevates one to God." Many times he said, when questioned about religion, "Oh, me? I am a believer."   His friends used to say of him that he was "mad with Catholicism."   Later on in 1867 he said to one of his students, "If ever I am sick, don't forget to go and get me a priest."

Carpeaux was always noted for his charity. The story is told that one evening in 1872 the body of a drowned man was taken from the river. The attempts to revive him were vain; he was declared dead. But Carpeaux brought the body to his home and for six hours breathed into the man, mouth to mouth, and finally saved him. He was even full of tenderness for animals. One day his dog wounded one of her pups so that the entrails were falling out. The great sculptor threaded a needle and sewed up the wound. Many a struggling artist owed his success in life to Carpeaux's helping hand.

The great cloud came upon Carpeaux's life with his marriage. In 1864 he had written to a friend of his: "I lose from day to day the desire of struggle because my powers weaken and my will goes. Today I have only the desire to be able to raise pigs, charming chickens, to have a horse, a cow, and especially a wife, whom my art has always refused me, to find refuge in truth and the true life." At last his art allowed him to take a wife, and on April 28, 1869, he thought that his cup of joy was full in his marriage with Amélie de Montfort, the daughter of the Governor General of the Palace of Luxembourg. The wedding was celebrated with great pomp at the Church of the Madeleine. But the cup of joy was soon dashed from his lips. The marriage was an unhappy one.

Through hard struggle Carpeaux had reached his position in the world, and then suddenly came the crash which broke him in twain physically but which happily saved his soul. He had arrived at full maturity of his powers, a man with a soul of fire, with a noble intellect, with at least twenty years of activity ahead of him, when suddenly the blow fell that made him a hopeless invalid and robbed French art of one of its greatest glories.

During the Commune he had sought refuge in London and there continued his work. But the fatal disease was working at him. In 1874 he determined to go to Russia, but got no further than Brussels, where he became seriously ill. His friend, Alexandre Dumas, came to bring him home. He returned to Auteuil and remained there for a while. He wandered then to other places, seeking his lost health, but all the while he was very ill. "I suffer with patience," he wrote. He had sore need of patience. His sufferings were frightful, day and night. He could not even sleep to forget his afflictions. He wanted to go to Italy once more, thinking that there he might find peace from suffering. But he got no farther than Paris. It was evident that he was slowly dying. His sufferings increased daily. "What can I say of myself," he wrote, "except that I am lost? I suffer without respite. That which I endure, that which I suffer, that which I cry is impossible to describe. No one can help me." He was reduced to skin and bone, but he was still patient. "I submit to the will of Heaven," he said, "which has decided about my last hour."

There were mental as well as physical sufferings. In the midst of his pain he was informed that a judgment had been given to his wife against him. She had divorced him. He was dispossessed of all he owned. He was then staying at Nice. The greatest sorrow of all was to be deprived of his son, Charles, whom he loved devotedly. Carpeaux had three children, but he cared only for the first born, Charles. He begged to have Charles, but the wife, to whom the custody of the children was given, told him that he must take the three or none.

The faith that had been put aside during the years of success was making its appeal to the man who was facing death. During his illness at Nice he succeeded in going to Mass every Sunday. He was ready to come home as the prodigal son; he needed but a tender hand to set him on the road.

As we have said before, Carpeaux was not the shameless and cynical artist, the Voltairian deist, that some thought him.   He had come from a thoroughly Catholic home, where his youth had been a model one in the Brothers' school, and later on during his first studies at Paris. The relative with whom he lived in those days at Paris used to tell of the long prayers he said morning and night, filled with devotion.   The Parisian life, the company of young artists, brought about his fall into a career of sin, but through it all he kept the faith.   At Rome he had been received by Pius IX, who gave him a medal.   Afterwards he wanted to go back to Rome to see the Holy Father, for, said he, "I love him much and venerate him." As a tribute to him he wanted to make his bust.   It was this faith that at the first stroke of sickness made him resolve to return to God.   A help to that end was, no doubt, his great charity to the poor. He never refused an applicant for charity; he would bring the poor to eat at his table, and would even scatter handfuls of silver and gold to them.   There were two young Bretons who worked in his studio.   Their strong faith and piety pleased and impressed him.   "How happy you are," he said.   "You have only holy passions.   I venerate you."

One day a visitor said to him, "I have no belief." "Well," said Carpeaux, "I do not think as you.   I believe, and this belief is my strength."   On the eve of his marriage he received Holy Communion with his wife.

He said that the two most beautiful days of his life were those of his first Communion and his marriage.

When Carpeaux became ill most of his boon companions left him, but the two Bretons remained faithful to him. One of them was particularly dear to him.

"Do you believe," said Carpeaux to him, "that the good God could pardon such a great sinner as I have been? How could God show me mercy?   No, it is impossible!"

"You deceive yourself," said the young Breton.   "See St. Augustine.   He was a great sinner and yet God pardoned him, and he became a great saint. You should not doubt the mercy of God."

"Oh, St. Augustine!" said Carpeaux. "I love him with all my heart. I would like to read his life."

At another time he said: "I deserve all my sufferings. How I have offended God in my life! How can you wish me to confess? I am too guilty. God cannot pardon me." And again the Breton tried to convince the despairing man of the mercy of God to sinners.

Again he said: "If I return to life I promise God to do as much good as I have done evil. For with a little sketch of an hour or two I could solace the misery of my poor."

Day by day suffering was bringing the light to his soul. "I perceive every day," said he, "that I am a great sinner." "My greatest suffering on my bed of pain," he said to his Breton friend, "is to have abandoned my religious duties. If you wish to be happy always, be Christian always."

One day the Breton brought to him a Capuchin priest. Carpeaux took the priest's hand and held it during the entire interview which lasted an hour. It was with deep humility he said: "If I had always lived as a good monk I would have become the equal of Michael Angelo." Michael Angelo was his great ideal.

These were the sentiments of Carpeaux when Prince Stirbey met him at Nice. The Prince, who was destined to be the instrument to lead the great sculptor back to God, had never before met Carpeaux. He had bought the sculptor's last group—the *Amour Blessé*. Seeing him so ill he offered him the hospitality of his villa near Courbevoie, and during the stay at Nice got two Sisters of Charity to come and care for the new friend whose genius he had long admired.

As soon as the sick man came to the villa Prince Stirbey

surrounded him with every possible attention. Once more the dying man made an attempt to get better. He submitted to four painful operations in seventeen days. But it was hopeless. He was doomed to die, and even the joy that came to him with the receiving of the cross of officer of the Legion of Honor that August did not drive the fear of death from him. "How hard it is to die," he exclaimed.

The Prince was a devout Catholic himself and he saw the man's danger. He wanted him to make his peace with God, but he did not know how to suggest the matter to his guest. God showed the way. A little child shall lead them. A god-child of the Prince, a little girl, came to visit him at Courbevoie. She had just made her first Communion at Paris. Carpeaux loved children, and the Prince determined to make use of that affection in order to win him to prepare for death. The child was soon admitted into the affectionate heart of the dying man, and she said to him: "Will you give me a great joy, Monsieur Carpeaux?"

"Surely, my dear," he replied.

"I receive tomorrow," she replied simply. "Will you receive with me?"

Carpeaux was silent for a moment as he reflected on her words. "But I am not ready," he replied at last.

"Oh, if it is only that," she replied, "that will be fixed soon—my confessor is so good!"

She returned to Paris at once to seek her confessor. He was not at the Madeleine at the time, but in her childish wisdom she brought back another priest and to him Carpeaux made his confession. The next day they received side by side in the church at Courbevoie, Carpeaux being carried thither at his urgent request so as not to disappoint the child.

After that Carpeaux had many conversations with the priest. He went to confession several times. His last confession he made September 29, and there on the terrace of the Chateau de Beçon received Extreme Unction and Viaticum. He himself answered the prayers of the priest with deep piety. He kissed the crucifix many times. "Oh," said he, "how they treated him! Ah, if I regain my health I will make a crucifix better than that." Again and again then he kissed the sign of redemption.

In the first days of October the terrible agony began. His poor mother was faithful to the end. She and his father were with him as he passed into the dark valley. He thought of his son, Charles, and grieved that he could not see him before he died. His cries then were agonizing. *"La vie, la vie!"* he called. And then: "O my mother, my little mother, I love you with all my heart." They were his last words.

Carpeaux died October 12, 1875. His death was a great loss to the art which he had so nobly fostered. How great that loss was considered was shown by the wonderful outpouring at his funeral, where artists, authors, all of the intellectual world vied with the people in doing him honor. The solemn funeral services were held at the church at Courbevoie. Later on the body was removed to his native city, Valenciennes, the "Athens of the North," as it was called, and after the solemn religious services was laid to rest amid the tributes of those who knew that here was a great man.

For a great man Carpeaux was—a great, big, tender soul—a great artist whose fame shall ever endure. But more than all he was the great penitent who gave testimony that all is vanity except to love God and serve Him alone.

FRANÇOIS COPPÉE

SOME years ago a Frenchman, Jules Sageret, wrote a book on *Les Grands Convertis*—the four great French writers whose return to God had amazed the Parisian public. The converts were Bourget, Brunetière, Coppée and Huysmans. Sageret rather belittled these conversions. He explained the psychology of them according to his own preconceptions and dismissed all by declaring curtly that the religious experiences of these men were of no avail as a tribute to the truth of Catholicism, and of no influence whatever on French literature. So he dismisses Coppée's conversion as a purely personal matter, concerning no one but the poet himself. We fancy that in like manner Augustine was dismissed when he left his Manichean friends. How contemptuously they must have thrown aside the "Confessions" of their former defender! Thus speaks M. Sageret: "There are few of his verses which a Catholic author could not sign. One could not find in them any that smack of the free-thinker. The conversion of M. Coppée rests indifferent to literature. It is then in a word only an affair purely individual."

That is, indeed, how Coppée himself regarded his conversion—an individual matter. That is how Huysmans, so long doubted even by good men, regarded his; that is how all penitents regard their conversion. It is the Lord Himself who asks, "What doth it profit a man if he gain the whole world and suffer the loss of his own soul?" But just because the conversion was so individual, its story has power over the hearts of others; Coppée's *"La Bonne Souffrance,"* simple as it is, will always have its place among the greatest of all books—those written out of souls. A book that has gone into nearly one hundred and fifty editions must be about something more than an affair purely individual.

François Edouard Joachim Coppée was born at Paris January 26, 1842. From a worldly point of view it was not much of a family. His great-grandmother on his father's side belonged to a noble family of Lorraine and had two brothers who served in the army of the king. But that had been a long time ago. The blue blood of the paternal ancestry was of no more interest than the very red blood of Baudrit, the locksmith, the father of Coppée's mother, a firm patriot he, who had exercised his trade during the Revolution in making pikes. But the Coppées wasted no time in tracing ancestral lines. They were too busy trying to make a living for their family. Thus in his sketch—*Adieux à Une Maison*—after telling of the pain one must feel in leaving a house that has been part of one's very life, Coppée confesses: "I have not known this rending. My poor parents, laborious bees of the great city, occupied in turn one or other of those hives which are the houses of Paris. Often they had to change their shelter; and all that is left of them to me are—humble relics, indeed—two or three very old pieces of furniture saved from the dismantlings."

Humble home though it was, it was the place where Coppée the Catholic as well as Coppée the poet was formed. And one could no more neglect his parents in the study of his conversion than one could eliminate from the life of St. Augustine the influence of his mother, St. Monica.

Coppée's father was a man of high ideals, a man who might have been a poet himself had he had the opportunity. But hard work was his portion of life. He held a small clerkship in the War Department, a place to which by his natural talents he was far superior. But true as he was to the traditions of old France and out of sympathy with new movements he got no advancement. He was, however, passionately fond of literature, an evident influence in the career of his son. Whatever the accomplishments of the man, he was first of all the true, practical Catholic. It was religion that formed his character and made him, as his son describes him, "pure, humble, and fearing God." This is the picture which that grateful son paints of him: "This man of duty, this poor man, proud and pure, had to have patient and Christian resignation to gain our bread, a daily task, and to deprive himself of everything without ever complaining." We get a picture, too, of the good man telling the little François stories, sacred stories especially, which were to be of service later on in the religious experiences of the poet. He was a gentle being; and from him the poet who was to be known as "the poet of the humble" got his love for the little ones, the humble ones, and his horror of violence and brute force. More than that he got from him the piety which slept during the years of sin and wanderings far from God, but which came to life again in the days of sorrow to bring back the penitent to the cross. Thus the poet:

> "And I feel on my lips, surprised, once more
> The prayers he taught in the days of yore."

If Coppée owed much to his father, he owed still more to his mother. It was she, he says, who made him a poet. The mother of eight children, four of whom died in infancy, she had her share of the world's hard work. But no one ever heard her complain. She was always gay, always singing and laughing at her work, always hopeful and full of energy, and her system of meeting new troubles in the days when poverty and sickness pressed hard on the little family was to increase her good humor. No wonder Coppée loved her. There is in all literature nothing more beautiful than his tribute to her in *La Bonne Souffrance,* his *souvenir filial,* as he turns the pages of the "Life of St. Louis" which she, as a little girl, had won

as a school prize, and from which he had got his first lessons
in spelling. Far back as he could remember she had always been the old mother. "My mother," he writes, "was
nearly forty years old when she brought me into the world.
They say that in her youth she had much freshness and
brightness; but the only portrait of her that exists is one
that was made a few years before her death, and in the
lowest depths of my memory her beloved face never ap-
pears to me but as one already touched with age. Those
who have known their mother as young and beautiful, can
they find a particular sweetness in so recalling her? I
know not. But in my opinion they are privileged whose
first glances saw leaning over their cradle a face marred
by life's fatigue, and to whom their mother always seemed
an old mother. The remembrance they keep of her is,
if not more dear, at least more sacred, and that veneration
which old age has is added to the august dignity which
motherhood has."

Thus Coppée had reason to be grateful for the home of
his youth. It was a home made sacred by hard work, a
home where all was guided by religion; in a word, a truly
Christian home. Even when he knew it not the association
with these wonderful parents of his was exercising an
eternal influence on his life. He needed such influence.
Of a frail and delicate constitution, of a nervous energy,
and made to learn very early both physical and moral suffering, compelled to face the sorrows and disappointments
of life, he needed the faith of those loved ones—even
though for years that was but an unconscious power in his
life—to enable him to accomplish the work which has
brought lasting glory to himself and to those who were
content to be known as the humble Coppées.

Coppée was never a brilliant student at school. When
it came time for him to begin his education in earnest he
was sent to the Hortus, and afterwards, when he was fourteen, to the St. Louis Lyceum. But the father remained

his mentor still. Under his eyes François studied his lessons, at times rewarded with a story or a song from his father, while the proud mother sat nearby sewing, and the two elder sisters read, or worked at the restoration of old paintings. Those days of family life are described in his book *Toute Une Jeunesse*—which he says is no more an autobiography—and we would like to say, no less— than "David Copperfield." He was perfectly happy at home, preferring the company of his mother and three sisters to that of boys of his own age. Even then the poetic instinct was strong, though at the time he knew nothing of the making of verses. School had little attraction. He liked rather to walk the streets, to visit the museums, to read real books, to lounge in the gardens of the Luxembourg, reveling in the flowers and the sunsets.

So the schools days passed till the close of the third year at the Lyceum. The elder Coppée's health began to fail, due to an affection of the brain, and it was necessary to put him in a sanitarium. It meant the end of school to François. He saw his duty clear, to go out into the world and become the breadwinner of the family. He got a clerkship in an architect's office, and at once showed himself so efficient that his employer urged him to prepare for admission to the school of Fine Arts. At the same time during his leisure he drew plans for contractors, and in this way added to the small income of the family. It was a time of trial, but the experience was of lasting benefit. One thing it did for the youth was to make him appreciate the education he had been obliged to give up. He became more studious out of school than he had been as a student. He became more interested in literature, read a great deal, and night after night when his work was done he would be found in the library of Ste. Geneviéve pursuing his interrupted classics. Architectural work was not pleasing to the young poet, for he was then expressing his soul in verse, though nothing had as yet been published by him. He gave up his intention of preparing for the school of Fine Arts and got a position in the War Department, where he remained for two years, while spending his leisure as formerly in study and in making verses.

Evidently, Coppée's youth was not a glad one. During those six years there was sorrow in the home, due to the condition of his father, who finally succumbed to his affliction of paralysis of the brain and ended his Christian life among his loved ones, carefully and lovingly attended through the trying years by the devoted wife.

François, twenty years of age, was now actually the head of the family. It was his to shoulder the burden. One sister had married, another had died at the age of twenty-two. There remained the old mother and his sister Annette, who never married but was her brother's companion to the end, his devoted admirer, sympathizer and adviser. She died but a few days before him.

It was shortly after the death of his father that the amateur versifier had the good luck to meet Catulle Mendes, the poet, in 1863. Mendes thus describes him as he was in those days: "Very young, thin enough, pale, a refined air, timid eyes which looked around him; a scanty coat, new, however, and very up to date; he had the air of a commercial clerk or a clerk in the ministry, and at the same time the elegance of his features, the ironic grace of his smile with something sweet and a bit sad in it, Parisian in all his bearing, would make one notice him."

Mendes did not know then that his new acquaintance wrote poetry. One day Coppée got the courage to bring to him the manuscript of verses which he had called *Les Fleurs Mortelles*. Mendes thought the verses remarkable for a beginner and asked Coppée to bring to him all that he had written. Delighted, the budding poet brought his reams of verse, and Mendes had the patience to read all. His decision to Coppée was that the whole of it was ex-

ecrable and that the author did not know the first prin-
ciples of his trade.

"All right," said Coppée, "you teach me then"; and
in all humility he threw into the fire the fruit of his
years of toil.

And Mendes did teach him. He was a good mentor for
the aspiring poet. It was a time of poetic revival in
France, the days of the Parnassus, a group of young poets
bound together by ties of friendship but severe in the
criticism of one another's work. They used to meet at
the home of Mendes. There one would see José Maria
de Heredia, Léon Dierx, Albert Glatigny, Léon Cladel,
Villiers de l'Isle—Adam, Albert Mérat, Léon Valade,
Georges Lafenestre, E. des Essarts, and sometimes Sully
Prudhomme. Later on this group united with another
which included Paul Verlaine. Helped by this school
of writers, and especially by Mendes, Coppée published
in 1866 at his own expense his first volume—*Le Reliquaire,* and in the year following *Les Intimités.* At once
he was recognized by literary people as a true poet with
a charm of his own. But it was a local, a limited fame.
It was only when he tried his hand at dramatic poetry
that he succeeded in becoming a celebrity. This was with
his play, *Le Passant,* produced in 1869 at the Odeon,
beautiful verse, indeed, but in no small way helped to
success by the wonderful talents of the actresses, Agar and
Bernhardt. In his usual humility the author gave most
of the credit to them, but, whatever the case, Coppée woke
up one morning to find himself famous. He was regarded
as a genius. At last his life was to be made easier. Théo-
phile Gautier presented him to Princess Mathilde, the
"good princess" as she was called, who received him in
her salon with the poets and other great men of the day.
She also rendered him a more practical service in obtaining for him a position in the library of the Senate, for
which he received a good salary, which provided for the

needs of those at home and gave him leisure for the development of his poetic talents.

Surely there was joy in the heart of the old mother at this beginning of success. Anatole France writes: "We know that Madame Coppée saw the first glimmers of the celebrity of her son. The friends of that good time recall, in the modest and flower-filled home of the Rue Rousselet on the morning following the *Passant,* the joy that illumined the countenance of that brave woman."

But the joy did not last long. For six weeks the young poet, now a figure in Paris, enjoyed his new fame. Then with scarcely a warning he became seriously ill, suffering from fever and bronchitis and threatened with consumption. Life that had been so sweet was now so bitter! Yesterday fame, today the approach of death to end it all; for Coppée was ordered away for the winter, and he himself, as all his friends, thought that the end was near.

It was, though he knew it not, a grace from God, but at this time he rejected the grace. For the young poet, as he himself confesses later on with tears, was in those, his days of success, a sinner. He was a victim of impurity, had been such from his early youth, and had even given evidence of it in some of his early poems. Long ago he had lost his innocence, and with his innocence had gone his faith. The first evil step taken, and unconfessed, the slippery path was easy to follow. Immorality was but a necessary experience of life; the consorting with evil women but a help to the singing of love! The loss of faith as a consequence of immorality is thus described by him in the preface to *La Bonne Souffrance*:

"I was brought up," he writes, "in a Christian manner, and after my first Communion I fulfilled my religious duties for several years with a fresh fervor. It was, I say it frankly, the crisis of adolescence and the shame to make certain avowals which made me give up my practices of piety. Many men who are in the same case will agree, if they are sincere, that that which first separates them from religion is the hard rule which it imposes on all in regard to the senses, and that later on they only ask from reason and science the metaphysical arguments which permit them to free themselves of all restraint. For me at least such was the case. I ceased to practice my religion from shame, and all my evil came from this first fault against humility, which seems to me decidedly the most necessary of all the virtues. This step taken, I did not fail to read on the way many books, to hear many words, and to see many examples destined to convince me that nothing is more legitimate for man than to obey his pride and sensuality; and quickly I became almost indifferent to all religious feeling. My case, you see, is a very vulgar one. It was the cheap desertion of the soldier from discipline. I did not, surely, hate the banner under which I had served; I had fled from it and forgotten it, that was all."

During that first illness grace was trying to enter the heart of the impure, bad Catholic. He tells us that always the thought of dying without the priest was terrible to him. But he turned his mind to poetry even in his illness and gave no heed to the affairs of his soul. In the April of 1870 he met with a second great success in the theatre with the production of his *Deux Douleurs,* a success which doubtless contributed no little to the restoration of his health. Then came the War of 1870, and we find him shouldering the gun of the national guard, while at the same time he gave his best talents to the production of patriotic poetry which brought him new popularity. A new success in the theatre gave him an assured position among the dramatists, and he also proved by his *Une Idylle Pendant Le Siège* and in subsequent books that he was a master of prose as well as of poetry. But Coppée's true fame came to him in 1872 with the publication of *Les Humbles,* poetry of the people and for the people. It gave him his name of "Poet of the Humble," and sealed him as a true poet.

Surely the poet's father would have rejoiced could he have foreseen what fruit would be born by his lessons in love for the lowly. But he would have grieved, too, had he seen how far this fame would take his child away from God. For Coppée restored to health, and become a popular idol, was again the Coppée whose life was such that he was afraid to go to confession. Back he went to his mistresses and his sins. There was little thought then of the terrible misfortune of dying unshriven. Even the death of his idolized mother in 1874, while it almost drove him to despair, did not shock him out of his immoralities. "I have been," he wrote, "the witness of this simple and noble life, and it is, I am sure, because I have grown up near this admirable woman who had all strength and gentleness, that the flower of sensibility blooms in my heart and in my imagination, and that I have become a poet."

Rather a pagan memorial, one would say, but it was the memorial of one who had lost touch with grace. Later on, when he came back to the faith which had made his mother truly great, he wrote thus with all the sensibility of the true Catholic soul:

"When she died she was seventy-one years old and I was thirty-three. I was then a man—a man who had lived, worked, had pleasure, suffered, gone through the flame of passions many times, a man who doubtless had been faithful to his principal duties, but guilty of many faults, alas, and without innocence. Certainly my mother knew it. She had known how to encourage my efforts, how to excuse my weaknesses; she had her share in my joys, and counseled me in the hours of distress. But if, woman of manly intelligence, and of a judgment high and sure, she spoke to me as to a man when I asked her advice, I became to her—adorable illusion! her child, her poor little child

when I had need only of her love." "How many sufferings," he writes again, "how many sorrows I have caused
her, that adorable woman. Not that she could ever doubt
for a single instant my respect and my love, God forbid!
But one is young, one falls foul of life driven by the fierce
wind of desire, and one forgets that there is at the family
hearth, and all too often abandoned, a poor old mother—
full of indulgence, indeed, who scarcely dares to address
to her big son a timid reproach, but who is alarmed at the
dangers he courts, who suffers at seeing him lose his white-
ness, his purity—and who weeps. May this page fall
under the eyes of some young man and stop him at the edge
of a serious fall! If he knew what bitterness it is for the
soul later on, toward the end of life, to think that though
he has not been a bad man, though he may have nothing
serious to reproach himself with, yet he has made his
mother weep!"

But it was only afterwards that Coppée reproached himself for the pain he had given his mother by his life of sin
and lack of faith. It was not to religion he turned for
solace at her death, but to poetry. His heart was far from
conversion. He worked hard with his pen and produced
many important works which in 1876 won for him the
cross of the Legion of Honor. That same year he gave to
the stage of the Comédie Française *le Luthier De Cré-
mone* which was a great success then and still holds an honored place in the repertoire of that institution. That same
year, too, the poet fell in love with a girl of seventeen
whom he had met at Geneva. He sought to marry her, but
the girl's mother, a widow who had fancied that the famous
poet had been smitten with herself, was indignant at the
proposal and hurried her daughter off from what she was
now pleased to regard the contaminating presence of this
man. How deep the attachment was it is hard to say now,
even though the poet's biographers see in his subsequent
poetry the results of his pure and unrequited love. It

furnished him with an ideal—in poetry; it did not turn him to the task of cleaning out his defiled soul.

One need not go into the details of those mature years of Coppée's genius. New books of poems, new plays, so many and so successful that he seemed to have devoted himself entirely to the theatre, and then the masterly critiques of the drama which from 1880 he contributed to *Patrie* at the time he was librarian-archivist of the Comédie, a position he resigned later on account of a falling out with the actor Coquélin. His excellent literary work caused him to be elected a member of the French Academy in 1884. The honor only spurred him on to new zeal in writing. His productivity was marvelous. He wrote everything and adorned everything he touched—comedy, drama, lyric, poetry, descriptive poetry, elegy, lieder, romance, short story, novel, critique, articles, prefaces; the entire field of literature was his, and when in 1892 he was made commander of the Legion of Honor, his readers, innumerable truly, for he was the poet of all social classes, agreed that he well deserved the distinction.

In a worldly sense this was the crowning of the poet of the humble. But the most glorious event in the life of Coppée was the spiritual victory which he won over himself and which led him back to God. He himself calls the memorable year of 1897 the time of his return to God. "Oh, it was cruel to me that year 1897! Is it not, I ask myself, the worst of my life? No, no, O my God, it is the best." Surely the best for his soul, for in that year he refound his Catholic faith. In the preface to *La Bonne Souffrance,* that beautiful book which was the result of his conversion, he relates the experiences of his soul. After telling how he had lost the faith by his immorality he proceeds to give the account of its refinding: "Today when I have refound the faith I ask myself if I had ever absolutely lost it. One will meet in my writings some rare pages which I disown and detest, where I have spoken of religious things with a foolish lightness, sometimes even with the most culpable boldness; one will seek in vain for a blasphemy. When by chance I entered a church, respect met me on the threshold and accompanied me to the altar. Always the ceremonies of the worship moved me by their venerable character of antiquity, their harmonious pomp, their solemn and penetrating poetry. Never did I put my finger in the cold water of the holy water stoup without trembling with a strange shiver which was perhaps that of remorse." A little of the Christian faith, he thinks, always slept at the bottom of his heart, as evident in the resignation with which he met the disappointments of life, its poverty and misery, which never drew from him a cry of rebellion.

"This conversion, as it is fitting to call it," he writes, "was rapid without a doubt, but not quite sudden nor accompanied by extraordinary circumstances. Yet I ought to attribute it to Divine grace; for when I compare my moral state of other days to that in which I have found myself for some months now, I am astounded before such a change and it seems to me miraculous. The benefit which I have gathered is within the reach of all. To obtain it, it is sufficient to demand it with a humble and submissive heart."

Often in the days when Coppée had withdrawn himself from the presence of God he was tormented by the problems of life and death, of pain and tears. None of the solutions offered by men had satisfied him; he had thought it absurd to think that good or evil done in this life would have consequences only in this life. Thus he always felt the need of God. "My conscience," he says, "especially for some years, became more exacting. Every time that I happened to think of my last end, to judge myself as one day God would judge me, I was not content with myself. When I reviewed my past I often had to blush, and I felt weighing me down the heavy burden of my sins. By weakness, by cowardice, I did not reform my conduct; but it is necessary to believe, I repeat, that there was in me a foundation of Christianity, for often in thought I made a sort of act of contrition; and that there was also a foundation of Catholicism, for every death seemed terrible to me which was not preceded by a confession and an absolution."

How the conversion came about is best described in Coppée's own words. "The God of indulgence and of goodness," he writes, "reserved for me something better than a hasty and trembling repentance *in extremis*. In the month of January, 1897, during a sojourn at Pau where, suffering for several months, I had fled the winter, I suddenly had to summon my surgeon from Paris and submit to a serious operation. I then made myself perfectly understand the danger which threatened me, and I prayed the excellent Dominican Sister who watched at my bedside— and to whom I have given a remembrance in this book— to go and get a confessor in case my condition became worse. But my friend, Doctor Duchastelet, saved my life that first time, and I thought no more of anything but the speedy and complete cure which was promised me. The warning was clear to me, but it was not heeded, and I blush today in recalling my culpable indifference and my foolish levity. . . . The improvement in my physical condition was of short duration. At the beginning of the month of June a new attack more severe than the first set me again at the threshold of death. This relapse condemned me to keep a suffering immovability for many days. The sufferings were terrible. Then only did my soul turn to graver thoughts. Judging myself with a scrupulous severity, I was disgusted with myself, I was horrified at myself, and this time the priest came, he to whom this book is dedicated. I had known him a long time, but not intimately. In meeting him at the house of friends I had been charmed only by his exquisite gentleness and his rare

distinction of soul. He is now one of the men whom I
love most in the world, my dear counselor, the intimate
visitor of my soul, and my father in Jesus Christ. I confessed to him in tears of the most sincere repentance, I
received absolution with an ineffable comfort. But when
the priest spoke of bringing Holy Communion to me, I
hesitated, full of trouble, not feeling myself worthy of
the sacrament. The danger of death was not imminent. The
man of God did not insist. 'Pray only,' said he, 'and read
the Gospel.' During the weeks and months passed in
bed and in my room, I have lived with the Gospel; and
little by little each line of the holy book has become living
for me and has convinced me that it speaks the truth. Yes,
in all the words of the Gospel I have seen the truth shine
as a star, I have felt it beat as a heart. How disbelieve
henceforth in miracles and mysteries when there was accomplished in me a transformation so deep and so mysterious? For my soul was blind to the light of faith, and
now it sees it in all its splendor; it was deaf to the word
of God, and today it hears it in its persuasive softness;
it was paralyzed by indifference, and now it lifts itself to
the heavens with all its power of flight; and the impure
demons that troubled it and possessed it are forever put
to flight. You shrug your shoulders, proud ones swelled
up with vain learning. What difference to me? I will
not even ask you to explain to me how the word of a humble workman of Galilee confided by him to some poor
people with the command to teach it to all nations, re-
sounds victoriously yet after nineteen centuries wherever
man is no more a barbarian. All that I know is that this
same word, heard and understood by me in cruel hours,
had that prodigious virtue to make me love my sufferings.
I go forth from trial physically weak and destined to submit probably to the end to the slavery of an infirmity very
painful. But because I have read and meditated on the
Gospel my heart is not only resigned but full of calm and

courage. Not two years ago, having still some health, but experiencing already the first attacks of age, I saw with terror old age coming, solitary old age, with its cortège of sadness, disgust and regrets. Today let it come upon me prematurely; I embrace it with firmness, let me say almost with joy, for if I do not ask for sufferings and death, at least I do not fear them, having learned in the Gospel the art of suffering and dying."

When Coppée did submit it was an entire submission, the submission of a little child ready to be told what to do. "A compelling desire," he says, "pushed me towards God. I did not resist. I let myself be led; in a word, I have obeyed, and today I taste the delights of obedience."

Answering those who used to say to him that nothing in him seemed changed since his conversion, he writes: "They only prove in this way how impenetrable man is to man; for I myself know very well that I have become another man. It is clear that the fact of saying my prayers morning and night, of going to church on Sundays and holy days and fulfilling my religious duties has not sensibly modified my apparent life. Clearly one does not read on my forehead either the reforms which I have been able to effect in my actions and my thoughts, or the resistance which now I oppose to the temptations to which formerly I would have succumbed. It is, nevertheless, the exact truth. That they do not find me changed—I am not astonished at that after all; for my progress in the Christian life, that is to say towards moral perfection, is still very weak. However, I have become as severe as possible with myself; those whom I loved I love better and otherwise than formerly, and make constant efforts to become more charitable, better. Yet, notwithstanding the too numerous defects in my conduct, and that of which I accuse myself with more sorrow—in spite of some last attacks of doubt and dryness of heart, I displease myself less than formerly, and very often when I think of the saddened days which remain for me to live and the death that approaches I experience a sentiment of sweetness which surprises myself. This peace of soul is obtained only by the admirable discipline of religion, by the examination of the conscience and by prayer. Thus I have no better moments than those wherein I address myself to God, in offering to Him the repentance for my past sins and all my good will for the future, and wherein I ask of Him that peace which He has promised to us in the next life and of which His grace gives us in this world the delightful presentiment. Yes, there is nothing so truly beautiful as the hour when one prays, when one puts himself in the presence of God. A hundred times, then, be the suffering blessed which has brought me back to Him. For I know Him now, the Unknowable! The Gospel has revealed Him to me. He is the Father, He is *my* Father."

It was not strange that this new peace of soul began to find expression in the weekly articles which for some time he had been contributing to the *Journal*. It was thus that the essays, "sublime in their simplicity," later on collected under the title *La Bonne Souffrance,* were written, scribbled in pencil as he lay "bound with bandages like a mummy of ancient Egypt," as he describes it, his feverish head against the pillow. In one of those papers he wrote, referring to his mother: "Never did I so often call forth the memory of my mother as during this sickness and this long convalescence which has inspired me with so many serious meditations. It is in stammering after so many years the prayers my mother taught me in my infancy that my soul has sought to lift itself to God. It is in the hope of seeing my mother once more that I wish to believe in life eternal. Oh, how I thought of my mother that day when to merit the reward of finding her again in Heaven I promised that the time left me to live would be filled with dreams more pure and actions more worthy."

Another memento of that wonderful year was the little

essay *Au-Dessus Du Nuage,* wherein Coppée likened his
struggle towards the faith to the climbing of the mountain:
"Scarcely had I taken the first step when already the mist
of pride and impurity which hid from me the good
way disappeared. Higher still, my soul! Always higher!
Above all that we see of the sky! What memories have
I called up all at once! On the mountain I climbed only
toward the sun. Today I lift myself towards a brightness incomparably more dazzling; for according to the
beautiful saying of Michael Angelo—the sun is only the
shadow of God."

If Coppée had done no more than this little book of his
confessions, or expression of his faith in the Catholic
Church, he would still be a classic. Excellent, the articles
were considered as they appeared from week to week, but
it was only when they came out in book form with the
wonderful preface, which may be called the apologia of his
conversion, that their true beauty, their spiritual unity
was discovered. It is this book which makes Coppée deserve to be studied as a great apologist, a great convert.
It is a soul-study, valuable in itself apart from the literary
genius of the popular poet. He had thought the articles
ephemeral things, but—"Some persons," he writes, "whose
advice is very precious to me, counsel me today to gather
these pages wherein I have confessed to my readers my
return to God. Hence this little book wherein one will
find neither plan nor composition, for it is only a collection of newspaper articles, but which will awaken, I hope,
a little sympathy in Christian souls, and will not be useless
to those—they are many—who having let scatter the beliefs of their young years regret them towards the end of
their life without having, however, the courage to ask
God to give them that interior strength. It is especially
with a view to these troubled souls, for whom doubt is the
soft pillow of which Montaigne speaks, and who stop, so
to speak, at the edge of faith, that I place at the beginning

of this book the simple narrative of the moral revolution which happened in me. Long have I been as they, and I have suffered from the same disease. I offer them the remedy which has cured me."

Not only in *La Bonne Souffrance* did Coppée give expression to his deep sense of sin, his regret for the past years of forgetfulness of God. It was eminently fitting that his last volume of poems—*Dans la Prière and Dans la Lutte*—should express in beautiful poetry what he had already expressed in prose. Thus in *Le Devoir Nouveau* he chants his hymn of repentance: "Then in the sufferings of age, when God with pity for me showed to my soul, before the shipwreck, the lighthouse of faith, my companions have seen me change my life and, converted by suffering, become in repentance less impure, wiser and better. And more than one no doubt has envied me, Christian full of serene hope, traveler finishing my journey in the sweet peace of a beautiful evening; poet whose last work would show to an astonished world the grateful prayer of a poor, pardoned sinner; and an old man whose head bends low, seeing in the field of rest a divine brightness shine among the tombstones."

It is a similar thought that is expressed in this wonderfully beautiful poem—*L'Etable,* wherein he describes in matchless verse the mystery of Christmas night. " 'Dreams, fancies,' said the laughing sceptic; 'a fabulous legend, a tale of the Orient.' Ah, I have denied as he. Pardon, veritable God! My soul was then the corrupt and dark stable open to Thy parents, the poor travelers. For, alas, in the least culpable sinner there is in desire and thought only secret shame and heaped up refuse. In my soul dwelt a common, low vice, like to a vile animal wallowing on his dunghill. And in the unwholesome darkness, filled with miasma, remorse, a monstrous spider, waited for me. But Jesus to whom now I pray on my knees was born in a place not less defiled. If the least thrill of repentance penetrates into a heart saturated with evil, God can be born there. I knew this hope and this truth one blessed day when sorrow visited me. I prayed, asking pardon for my sins. Humbly I reopened to the God of my childhood my soul, that dwelling impure and dark. He deigned to descend thither, and, generous master, who gives even to the late worker a reward, today He reigns there, perfumes it and brightens it. Prayers, Sacraments, O ineffable blessings! As the stable to the eyes of the dazzled shepherds shone with a wonderful and sudden brightness, so my soul shines now that God dwells there. On the blue night where sounds the Christmas hymn, the dark roof opens which had hid the heavens from me; and hideous remorse, the spider in his net, shines suddenly and becomes a star." So, too, the poem, *Dans Une Eglise de Village*. It is a prayer for faith, a prayer of faith. It is one of the most beautiful things Coppée ever wrote, this prayer of "the soul of an old sinner, late converted."

The conversion of Coppée was not a passing experience. There had been, as he says, a moral revolution in his soul. He was never done after that giving thanks to God for His goodness to him in opening his eyes to the terrible condition of his soul. Henceforth there never left his singing the strain of the penitential psalm. He was seeking to redeem the time, showing himself thoroughly Catholic in all things, proud to confess the faith to which he had been so long indifferent. He had been a sinner; his wish now was to be a true penitent. He found at hand the way to atone. God Himself chose the discipline for him. Those last years were years of bitter suffering. But there was no rebellion. Suffering was sweet. He had learned to kiss the cross. At the end of his life he could write in truth:

> I have conquered my old pride and unbelief,
> And all in tears, extending my hands to the cross,
> I dare to say, My God, I love you, I believe.

A few weeks before his death he was asked by the director of the *Mercure de France* what his conception of religion was. In his letter he answered: "This one word—Credo."

To believe, to love, to suffer, to repent: that was the secret of life discovered by the poet on his bed of pain. That secret he would share with all the world in his zeal to let men know what a folly sin is.

"I have been like to you," he wrote, "poor sinner of the troubled soul, O my brother. As you, I was then very miserable and I sought by instinct a confidant full of clemency and tenderness. I found Him. Do as I have done. Open your Gospels, and return to the Cross."

J. K. HUYSMANS

A STRANGE being was Huysmans. A lashing critic, with a tongue like a two-edged sword even after his conversion, a man who had plumbed the depths of iniquity and who afterwards aimed at the peaks of sanctity, who consorted with demons and then with mystics, and at last biting the dust in penitence gave his body a willing victim to the most excruciating pain—no wonder this most individual man, even apart from his literary genius, is still regarded as an enigma. One can understand how the disciples of the world regard his life as a puzzle; it is hard, however, to see how Catholics, many of them, still look on him as a suspect. For to study the man is to come face to face with sincerity if ever there was such a thing. One of Huysmans' biographers says that the Church has not failed to make a great racket about his conversion. Not such a racket as might have been made, as should have been made; for Huysmans, strange apologist though he is, is nevertheless one of the greatest of modern apologists. Full of faults he is, with many a line in his apologetics that might well have been eliminated; but there is no use complaining about that, you must take Huysmans as he is. A petty critic he is at times; your convert is very apt to be hypercritical. These are but flimsy clouds before the sun. And underneath all one finds the burning heart of the great penitent who with Augustine could cry out—"Too late have I loved Thee, O Beauty, so ancient and so new."

George Joris Karl Huysmans—he dropped the name George at the publication of his first book and afterwards was known merely as J. K. Huysmans—was born at Paris February 5, 1848. The Huysmans were a family of artists. Everybody in the family, said Huysmans, from father to son, painted. We find at least four of these Flemish painters of the name in Antwerp in the seventeenth century. The most noted of these ancestors was Cornelius, some of whose pictures are in the Louvre, a very facile painter whose canvases were widely scattered. One of J. K.'s uncles was for a time professor at the academies of Breda and of Tilburg. The artist blood thinned out the nearer it came to J. K., for his father, Gotfried, who came from Breda in Holland to Paris, was but an illuminator of missals, and the like small work. Still, if J. K. did not inherit the ancestral technique he was at heart an artist. There never was a better critic, a more honest critic. And as has been often said, if he did not paint pictures he was at least one of the greatest word-painters in all literature. The inherited artistry was but manifested in another way. One thing he did inherit from his father was a generous supply of bile. Gotfried was discontented with his lot in life; it explains somewhat the pessimistic strain in his son. There was another ancestral strain which in due time had its influence upon him. Strange to say, it was the strain of piety. Gotfried's sisters were nuns in Holland. When Huysmans came to try to explain his conversion he did not omit reference to the ancestral piety which was somehow in the blood even during the long years that he regarded religion as a poor, foolish thing.

Whatever borrowed glory there was on the paternal side, there was none on the maternal. His mother, whose name was Badin, belonged to the bourgeosie, a self-reliant woman who after the death of her husband in 1856, when J. K. was eight years old, supported herself by sewing and soon had a workshop of her own.

The youth of Huysmans was not that of the precocious

literary genius. Neither at the Hortus, the boarding school
to which he first went, nor later at the St. Louis Lyceum,
did he amaze his professors with his talent. He was far
from being a brilliant scholar—just enough to get his
B. A. in his graduation from the Lyceum in 1866 at the
age of eighteen.

Even then Huysmans did not know what he wanted to
do in life. He enrolled himself in the Law School, and
passed the examinations. But that did not appeal to
him, and he gave up the law to enter the ministry of the
Interior; but he cared little for that and only constrained
himself to take up the work on the principle that of two
evils one should choose the less. So Huysmans himself
described his entrance into the ministry of the Interior,
led thither by the advice of his maternal grandfather
who was cashier there. He was then much of the dilettante frequenting the Latin Quarter, reading a great deal,
wondering what his life should be, leading a hermit's life
and having his fling at the pleasures of the world. There
was nothing to keep the youth straight; he had been
brought up with no religion whatever and, as he says
later in the preface to *A Rebours,* it seemed entirely natural to him to satisfy the senses. The Latin Quarter of
those days besides its moral dangers had its political ones,
too. There were gathered the young political firebrands
who conspired for the overthrow of the Empire. But
these had little appeal for J. K.; in fact he was always
indifferent to politics, considering that government the
best which harmed nobody.

Huysmans had been working in the ministry two years
when the Franco-Prussian war broke out. He joined the
Sixth Battalion of guards of the Seine, but did not serve
long. He was taken sick and sent to Evreux where he
remained for a time convalescing, and where he resigned
as a soldier. He returned to the ministry of the Interior
at the time of the Commune at Versailles, and returned

with it to Paris in 1871. The only thing he got out of
his service as a soldier was a bad stomach to which may
be ascribed some of the pessimism of the future critic.
Huysmans never liked the work in the ministry, but,
strange to say—and it is a tribute to the man's capacity
for application and hard work—he remained at the work
for thirty years and was always regarded as a model
employee; so much so that when in 1893 he was given the
Cross of the Legion of Honor the mark of respect was
more for his work as an employee of the government than
for his great literary renown. It was he, too, who had con-
ceived the justice of admitting to the Legion the faithful
old employees of the government. Huysmans was at heart
a traditionalist, though it may seem hard to make that
statement agree with many of the things in his books.
That he was nevertheless, and it helps, apart from the
great explanation—the grace of God—to explain the steps
to his conversion. One example of his traditionalism is
seen in his love for the left side of the Seine. He would
live no place else in Paris. He called the right side the
demoniacal side where resided all that he hated; the men
of prey, the theatrical crew, the feverish life, expense and
luxury. A queer criticism coming from the naturalist
Huysmans.

Committed to this quasi-hermit existence—marriage
never had any appeal for him even in the flush of youth—
he sought enjoyment in writing. He loved the poetry of
Villon best of all and spent his leisure making verses in
imitation of his. He had no ambition then to be a writer;
or if he did it was in the far distance. At any rate he
learned how to use his tools before he sought to exhibit
his handiwork to the public. If any man ever wrote for
the love of writing it was Huysmans, especially in the
beginning. The hours of practise finally led to the production of some poems in prose which he collected under
the title of *Le Drageoir à Épices*—The Box of Spices.

He submitted the manuscript to the publisher Hetzel, with whom his mother had business relations, but Hetzel was disgusted with the work and refused to publish it, sarcastically asking Huysmans if he was trying to arouse a rebellion against the French language and start another Commune. Evidently the vivid word painting, of which Huysmans even then showed himself the master, was lost on Hetzel.

Nothing daunted by this rejection, Huysmans thought of going to Belgium and submitting the book to publishers there, but chafing under that delay which seems interminable to the author with his first book he brought it out at his own expense in Paris in 1874. The little masterpiece was well received; for masterpiece it was, something new in the French perfection of literature, a perfection ready to become decadent. Theodore de Banville called the book "a jewel of a master goldsmith, chiselled with a hand firm and light."

The success spurred him to further effort. In 1876 he went to Brussels and remained there a month seeking a publisher for his first novel, *Marthe, Histoire d'une Fille.* He succeeded in having it published there, but later republished it in Paris in 1879, where it was suppressed by the police. By this book the comparatively unknown writer entered the school of the naturalists, Balzac, Flaubert, Zola. Zola was not then the chief of that school—he was to become so with *L'Assomoir.* Huysmans, indeed, in those days, outdid Zola in realism, even though he may be called the first disciple of Zola. One thing about Huysmans in distinction from Zola is that in all his naturalistic writings he never insulted the Church; one other reason, no doubt, why he was able to submit to that same Church. But through many books he was the staunch naturalist. When in 1879 appeared his *Les Soeurs Vatard* it was dedicated to Zola, and being condemned by many of the anti-naturalists Zola rushed to its defence, a defence which was one for Huysmans and two for himself. The defence was necessary, for Zola was being eclipsed by Baudelaire who was already exercising a great influence upon Huysmans. In fact, Baudelaire became the idol of Huysmans, and he was never done talking his praises. One can explain Huysmans' bent to naturalism by the fact that he was naturally an insurgent. He must be original or nothing, even though, explain it as you will, he was fundamentally a traditionalist. He was, anyway, in letters an insurgent. The classics, like Corneille, Racine, Molière, had no appeal for him; he could not, would not read them. So he continued his realism. In 1880 appeared the *Soirées de Medan,* a collection of young writers, as DeMaupassant, Henrique and Paul Alexis, all under the patronage of Zola. To the series Huysmans gave his *Sac au Dos* which had already been published in a Belgian review, reminiscences of his short military career which added nothing to his literary reputation.

Love of art was strong in Huysmans. A master now of French prose, he could give expression to his ideas as to what great art should be, and as a result he published *Les Croquis Parisiens*—Parisian Sketches—a critique of the pictures exhibited in the salons of 1870, 1880, 1881, 1882. At once he was recognized as a great art critic, an honest critic, who was no cringing adorer of the past, a critic who did not hesitate to praise the unknown artist, and who took delight in coming to the defence of the painters who had been unjustly set aside. These critiques established Huysmans as one of the great masters of French prose.

The year 1881 was a prolific one for Huysmans. He published *Nana, Pot-Bouille,* and finally *En Menage. En Menage* was a glorification of naturalism at a time when naturalism, or as it might be called, nakedness, nakedness physical and moral, was the pursuit of so many writers. Huysmans in 1885 could call this his chosen book—which would show how far from the thought of conversion to God he then was. During those years there was nothing worth while to him but naturalism. In 1882 he published at Brussels *A Vau-l'Eau* which is called his *chef d'oeuvre* of naturalism. It is Huysmans in his most pessimistic strain. He sought therein to show life as unredeemably bad, the thesis being that "the life of man oscillates as a pendulum between pain and ennui." The hero, Folantin is a type, the Huysmans type which goes through all the subsequent books of the author, whether as the Des Esseintes of *A Rebours* or the Durtal of *La Bas* and *En Route*.

A Rebours appeared in 1884. The conversion of Huysmans did not take place till some eight years after that. But it is not too far fetched to find the beginnings of the return to God in this book which marks his break with naturalism and the school of Zola. Baudelaire was having a subtle influence on Huysmans the naturalist. After having reached the summit of naturalism, or rather the depths, in *A Vau-l'Eau* he discovered, as he says, that naturalism ends in a cul-de-sac. He was saturated with realism. He was sick of it. The dilettante Des Esseintes in *A Rebours* tried everything under the sun. He had come to the limits of physical and moral degeneracy. It was the same old theme of pessimism, the heart seeking its solace in sin and finding it not. Huysmans looked for something besides this naturalism. He did not know what he wanted. He knew only that he had gone into the blind alley and wanted to turn around and come to liberty. At any rate he was done with naturalism—in literature; not in his own life of the satisfaction of the passions. Zola was displeased at losing his pupil. "You strike a terrible blow at naturalism," he said bitterly. It was evident in *A Rebours* that Huysmans was seeking something. What it was even he did not know. At that time Jules Le-Maître wrote: "After the *'Fleurs du Mal'* I said to Baudelaire, 'There is left for you now logically nothing

but the mouth of a pistol or the foot of the Cross.' Baudelaire chose the foot of the Cross; but the author of *A
Rebours,* will he choose it?"

Huysmans, too, chose the foot of the Cross, but eight
years passed before he made his final decision. *A Rebours*
had ended in pessimism, almost. But the final words
were the heart cry of one who prayed to be delivered from
the total despair which seemed ready to engulf him.
"Lord," cried out Des Esseintes, "have pity on the Christian who doubts, on the unbelieving who would believe,
on the galley slave who embarks alone in the night under
a firmament which the consoling beacons of old hope no
longer brighten."

In the preface to a later edition of this book Huysmans
seeks to explain this religious appeal on the lips of one
who scarcely knew what it meant. "I was not brought up
in the religious schools," he writes, "but in a lyceum. I
was not pious in youth, and that side of the remembrance
of youth, of first Communion, of the education which so
often holds a large place in a conversion, held none in
mine. And what complicates the difficulty more, and
disconcerts all analysis, is that when I wrote *A Rebours*
I had not put a foot in a church, I knew not a practical
Catholic, or any priest. I did not experience any divine
touch inciting me to direct me to the Church; I lived in
my trough, tranquil. It seemed to me entirely natural
to satisfy the senses, and the thought did not even come
to me that this kind of tournament was forbidden. *A
Rebours* appeared in 1884 and I went to be converted at
La Trappe in 1892—nearly eight years passed before the
seeds of this book had risen; let us place two years, three
even, of a work of grace, heavy, stubborn, sometimes sensible; there remain less than five years during which I do
not remember to have felt any Catholic inclination, any
regret of the life I led, any desire to reform it. Why then
have I in a night been goaded on to a road that had been

lost for me? I am absolutely powerless to say; nothing, unless the prayers of nunneries and cloisters, prayers of the fervent Holland family which I otherwise scarcely knew, will explain the perfect unconsciousness of the last cry, the religious appeal of the last page of *A Rebours.*"

En Rade appeared in 1887, a book that need not be considered in the soul study of its author.

It is only in 1891 that we can begin to trace the real conversion of Huysmans. And strange to say it begins with that truly terrible book *La Bas.* Interesting as a study of the depths to which man can descend—if one need such a study—and explanatory of much of the psychology of Huysmans—the world would be none the poorer if he had never written it. For one thing, even while it is not autobiographical in the strict sense of the word, it gives a hint of what the private life of Huysmans was during those years of darkness. Huysmans was Parisian to the core and he intended to enjoy all the pleasures that Paris could give him.

He did enjoy them, for he tells us that his conversion let him escape from "a filthy time." Perhaps it is necessary to stress that point—of the animal existence of the man for so many years—in order to understand the long, hard way he had to travel when the grace of God came to him and set his face in the direction of home. *La Bas* still stands badly in need of expurgation. Yet this horrible book, this study in Satanism, by convincing him of the existence of spirits superior to man, was, strange to say, his first step to God. That book of 1891 was but the prelude to the conversion of 1892.

How describe that conversion? It is quite impossible to put in words the psychology of it, for Huysmans himself could not do so even in regard to his own soul and with his analytical mind. "Providence was merciful to me, and the Virgin was good," he wrote. "I was content not to oppose them when they declared their intentions.

I have simply obeyed. I have been led by what is called 'extraordinary ways.' "

Yet even from the human point of view it was too great an experience for the realist not to make a book out of it. Thus in 1895 was given to the world that truly remarkable book, *En Route,* in which Huysmans traces the steps of his conversion to God in the character of Durtal who had figured so ignominiously in *La Bas.* There is no doubt that Huysmans wished to have himself regarded as described in the character of Durtal even though it is not wholly autobiographical, especially in the scenes of *La Bas.*

During the octave of All Souls Durtal, who, with no religion to keep him back, had plumbed the depths of iniquity, entered the church of St. Sulpice while the office of the dead was being chanted. The plain-chant took possession of his soul. "That which seemed to him superior to the most vaunted works of theatrical or worldly music was the old plain-chant, that melody plain and naked, at the same time aerial and of the tomb." No one has written so beautifully of the music of the Church as Huysmans. The art to which the Church has given birth made an appeal to his soul. "Ah," he cries out, "the true proof of Catholicism is this art which it has founded, this art which nothing has ever surpassed. In painting and sculpture it was the Primitives; the mystics in poetry and the sequences; in music the plain-chant; in architecture, the Roman and the Gothic."

The sermon ended, Durtal was brought back to earth again. "I should have tried to pray," he said; "that would have been of more avail than to be lost there in my chair of empty reveries; but pray? I have no desire for it. I am haunted by Catholicism, intoxicated with its atmosphere of incense and wax. I roam around it, touched to tears by its prayers, impressed to the very marrows by its psalmody and its chants. I am very weary

of my life, very tired of myself, but it is another thing to
lead another existence. And then—if I am disturbed in
the churches, I become unmoved and dry as soon as I come
out. At the bottom I have a heart hardened and burned
by sensual indulgence. I am good for nothing."

And this irreligious sensualist suddenly became a believer.

How? Durtal asked himself. And he answered: "I
do not know; all that I know is that after having been for
years an unbeliever, suddenly I believe." "I have heard,"
he continued, "of the sudden and violent upheaval of soul,
of the clap of thunder, of the Faith making at the end
an explosion in the ground which is slowly and learnedly
mined. It is very evident that conversions can be effected
according to one or other of these two methods, for God
acts as seems good to Him, but there should be a third
method which is doubtless the most ordinary, that which
the Saviour used for me. And that consists in I know
not what; it is somewhat analogous to the digestion of
the stomach which works without one being sensible of it.
There has been no Damascus road, no events which determined a crisis; nothing supervened, yet one fine morning
one wakes and without knowing how or why the thing is
done. . . . The only thing which seems sure to me is
that there was in my case divine premotion—grace. I seek
in vain to retrace my steps by which I have gone; doubtless I can discover on the route gone over some marking
posts here and there; love of art, heredity, disgust with
life; I can even recall forgotten sensations of childhood,
little underground paths of ideas resurrected by my visits
to the churches; but what I cannot do is to bind together
these threads, to group them in a bundle; what I cannot
understand is the sudden and silent explosion of light
which has taken place in me. When I try to explain to
myself how, an unbeliever in the evening, I have become
without knowing it a believer in one night, I can indeed

discover nothing, for the heavenly action has disappeared without leaving any traces."

"It is very certain," he says again, "that it is the Virgin who acts in these cases on us; it is She who kneads you and puts you into the Hands of Her Son; but her fingers are so light, so soft, so caressing, that the soul which they have refreshed has felt nothing.

Nevertheless Durtal can find certain motives, or inclinations to a revival of faith. Piety was in the blood, it was ancestral; there were nuns in the family. It will be recalled that the sisters of his father were nuns in Holland.

The second motive was the disgust with life, driving him to look for solace he knew not where, but knowing that irreligion and lust had brought no satisfaction. The third motive was the passion for art, for music, architecture, for all those beauties which the Church has cherished in her worship.

The faith had come, but the struggle with sin had not ceased. Durtal believed, but Durtal's morals were the morals of *La Bas* and *A Rebours*. He relapsed into sin again and again. He was disgusted with himself after the sin, but he seemed powerless to resist the attractions of the old life. It was impossible for him to be continent! How reminiscent it is of the beginnings of the conversion of another great penitent—St. Augustine.

Durtal had confided his secrets of soul to the Abbé Gévresin, who is none other than the real Abbé Mugnier, a curate at the church of St. Thomas d'Aquin, who was his dear friend and director. The abbé finally succeeded in prevailing upon Durtal, not without hard work, to make a retreat in a Trappist monastery. It was so that Huysmans, on the advice of Abbé Mugnier, went to little Trappe of Notre Dame d'Igny. It is a touching avowal which Durtal makes to his God before setting out for his retreat. "My soul is a bad place; it is sordid and of bad character; up to now it has loved only perversion; it has exacted of my miserable body the tithe of illicit delights and undue joys; it is not worth much, it is worth nothing; and yet, down there near You, if You will help me, I know well that I will make something of it; but my body, if it is sick I cannot force it to obey me! that is worse than all, that! I am helpless if You do not come to my aid."

But God did come to the aid of the penitent who was so distrustful of his own weakness. Anyway, decided Durtal, "There are many who go to Barèges or to Vichy to cure their bodies, why should not I go to cure my soul in a Trappist monastery?"

The description of the state of soul of Durtal during that retreat, his struggle with himself, with the powers of darkness, with old memories, the awful agony of his general confession, make a soul study that cannot be surpassed. It is realism at its height. No *résumé* of *En Route* can be given; one might as well try to give a synopsis of the *Imitation*. Durtal made his confession and found peace for his soul. In the same way Huysmans made his confession and found peace. Confession always was to him one of the most opportune and beneficial institutions. Somewhere in *En Route* he says: "Confession is an admirable Godsend, for it is the most sensible touchstone there could be for souls, the most intolerable act which the Church has imposed on the vanity of man." Once a friend of his, a man of letters who was obsessed by certain scruples before he submitted to the faith, came to him with his difficulties. "You believe," said Huysmans, "that the priest before whom you kneel to tell your sins holds the place of our Saviour Jesus Christ, and that he will pardon you in His Name? You also believe that in the Mass the priest immolates Jesus Christ and that the Host with which he communicates you is Jesus Christ

Himself ?" "Yes," answered the other, "I believe that."
"Very well, then," said Huysmans, "go to confession
and Communion and all will arrange itself."

Huysmans had taken the great step. He had humbled
his soul and thus had found that his only strength was in
God. "If anyone," he once said, "could have the certi-
tude of the nothingness he would be without the aid of
God, it would be I." That lesson of his own nothingness he had learned in his sojourn at the monastery.
The monks made a great impression upon him and he
might have become one had his health permitted. But
God had other work for him to do.

Huysmans was forty-four years of age at the time of
his conversion. Up to then his life had been spent far
from God. It had been a wasted, criminal life. Not only
had he befouled his own soul with immoralities, but in
describing them in his shockingly naturalistic books he had
brought harm to other souls. He could not cast aside now
the talent which he had misused; he must use it for the
good of souls and seek to undo some of the harm he had
done. He must redeem the time.

Leaving his retreat and returning to Paris he placed
himself under the direction of Abbé Feret of St. Sulpice,
to who *La Cathédrale* is dedicated. Under his guidance
Huysmans undertook to retrace the steps of his conversion
in the epoch-making *En Route*. The book appeared in
1895. No book ever caused greater discussion. It was
bitterly attacked and as bitterly defended. Frankly, it
had scandalized many Catholics. It was too free in its
criticisms, hypercritical criticisms many of them; it was
too harsh, and too free in its dealing with sacred things.
Huysmans could not get rid of naturalism, even though in
his converted state the realism was spiritualized. It was
declared by Catholics as well as by the freethinkers who
sought to make light of the great conversion that Huysmans was still the grand poser, that he was not sincere

in his return to religion but had merely turned to mysticism because he had exhausted every other subject. In plain words it was said that he was a hypocrite, the worst kind of hypocrite, he who pretends to religion to make capital of it. He was even compared to Leo Taxil with the miserable Diana Vaughan hoax. All this deeply pained the heart of the convert, for if any man ever was sincere it was Huysmans. The pain was all the greater as he realized that some of the most violent attacks came from the Catholics whom he sought to serve. The Abbé Belleville went so far as to write a book—*Le Conversion de M. Huysmans*—in which he made bold to express his doubts as to the sincere conversion of the writer, his argument being that if he had been sincere he would have destroyed his former scandalous books instead of continuing to make money out of them. Another argument was that Huysmans dealt with sacred things in a repugnant manner. The argument was not without foundation. It is going too far, however, to accuse Huysmans of making money out of his evil books. That never entered his mind. Perhaps it was quite an impossible task to correct the books that were so widespread. Rest assured that Huysmans had given the matter serious consideration and only after viewing it from every angle had decided to let things as they were.

A certain ecclesiastic, a friend of his—Huysmans had many sincere friends among the priests—suggested to him that certain passages in *En Route* should be eliminated. "Perhaps today," answered Huysmans, "I would hesitate to write them. But I must avow it would be a mistake to eliminate them. They testify to the truth of the book. It is because it is true that it has a religious influence on souls." It was an action different from that of another great convert, Paul Féval, who had burned or corrected the books of his unregenerate life. Huysmans, in a word, left his untouched as a history of his state of soul. It goes without saying that *En Route* made many conversions, still makes them. It was the realization of this that cleared the mind of Abbé Ferret. He heard so many attacks made on the book, by good men even, that he, too, great as was his confidence in Huysmans, began to doubt. One day, however, a sinner came to him to confession. It was a striking conversion, and the Abbé asked what had led the man back to God. The answer was that conversion had come after reading *En Route*. This with other cases of conversion effected by reading of the soul struggles of the great realist, convinced the Abbé that in spite of some evident shortcomings the "confessions" of Huysmans were designed to do in modern times what the confessions of St. Augustine had been doing for many centuries.

Today we know that there should have been no suspicion of his conversion. He was not a merely literary convert, merely drawn to religion as to an unexplored field. He had become a practical Catholic, living the Christian life with ever new zeal, delighting to visit the churches of Paris, praying in the old shrines of the faith so wonderful to him, reading the mystics, listening to the plain chant of the Church as to the music of Heaven, visiting the monasteries which he loved so much that he would have wished to become a monk had he not been advised by his spiritual directors that he should serve God with his pen. What his life was in those days is seen in a letter of his to Gustave Coquiot, one of his biographers. Coquiot had written to him in 1896 asking him to express his views on literature and society. Huysmans answered: "My joys of the present—to follow the canonical hours in a cloister, to ignore that which passes at Paris, to read books on liturgy and mysticism, iconography and symbolism. To see as little as possible of men of letters and as much as possible of monks. . . . I feel myself removed from active life, and my books appear to me now as those of others—vain."

Huysmans, the convert, showed the literary world that in leaving the world of fleshy naturalism he had lost none of his wonderful talent; indeed, his genius is more evident in the books he made after he had seen the light of faith. It was said that he had discovered that he had the whole of Heaven to plumb. . Nothing now appealed to him but that same Heaven. The three years following the publication of *En Route* were spent in putting together the documents he had gathered about the Cathedral of Chartres. It was a true labor of love. He never thought that the book would find many readers. But when *La Cathédrale* appeared in 1898 it found as many readers as *En Route*. In the same way, too, it was attacked and defended. Even then the doubts as to his conversion persisted. Lucien Descaves, who has written so sympathetically of his friend, relates that many people asked him, knowing that he was one of the few who had the entrée to the home of the popular writer, if Huysmans was really sincere or if his conversion was not just a caprice of art. It was hard to kill the old slander. Descaves was indignant. He called the suspicion a gratuitous affront done to an honest man, to a man the least capable of deception he had ever known. His loyalty, said Descaves, actually shone. Today at any rate *La Cathédrale*, this example of naturalism spiritualized, has its sure place as a classic. If Huysmans had done nothing but this he would deserve the lasting gratitude of his fellow Catholics.

In the same year Huysmans received a pension from the government on account of his services in the ministry. This removed many of his financial worries and gave him more time to devote to his religious books. He was now particularly interested in the study of liturgy which was to be the basis of the last book of a trilogy. *En Route* had dealt with mysticism, *La Cathédrale* with symbolism. To allow himself to become saturated with liturgy he decided to make his residence in the vicinity of the abbey of

Liguge near Vienne. With some friends of his he bought a lot of land there and had a house built after his own designs, which he called Maison Notre Dame. Once established there he set about getting ready to make his profession as Oblate. His literary work consisted in the preparation of the life of St. Lydwine and he made a short trip to Schiedam to get the locale of his story and to make certain investigations. But it was not all literary work. His chief work in those days was to sanctify his soul. The cloister appealed to him, and again he would have sought to be admitted, but the necessity that would follow of being obliged to submit his writing to censure deterred him; he felt that he would be able to do greater good as a free lance in literature. Every morning he assisted at the High Mass, no matter how great the heat or the cold, and prayed there full of faith, lost in deep meditation, so earnest and simple in his religion that the religious as well as the peasants were edified by him. He would leave the church only when the monks left. He mingled with the monks a great deal, not letting a day pass without seeing them, learning all that he could from them, especially in the matter of liturgy which now greatly occupied his attention. Descaves who visited him there tells of watching him across the fields, his head bowed, his prayer book under his arm, the bells of the old abbey calling him away from the literary work which was interrupted only by the need of assisting at the offices. After Mass he would return to the house and talk with his friends of other things than those which really interested him. Descaves says that the spirit of proselytism was seen only in his books, not in his conversation with his friends.

It seemed to be an ideal life for Huysmans, but at last he tired of it. He was homesick for Paris, for he was Parisian to the core always and it was hard for him to live elsewhere. He never liked the country, he had a kind of inbred aversion for the peasants. He was never a lover of nature, and even the sun exasperated him, due no doubt to the growing affection of his eyes.

In February, 1901, he published *Sainte Lydwine de Schiedam*. That, too, was a labor of love for his heart had been touched by the life of this woman who for thirty-eight years had lain on her bed of pain, with scarcely any nourishment but that of Holy Communion, scarcely any sleep. She was a victim for others, a victim of expiation. The idea of expiation had appealed to Huysmans even in the days when he was writing *En Route*. This book on Sainte Lydwine is a compelling one. It is Huysmans' epic on suffering. His Way of the Cross henceforth was to be that of patient suffering. How beautifully he writes of it. "The truth is that Jesus commences by making one suffer and that He explains afterwards. The important thing then is to submit in the beginning and to stop complaining instantly. He is the greatest Mendicant that the heavens and the earth have ever had, the terrible Mendicant of Love. The wounds of His hands are the purses always empty, and He holds them out for each one to fill them with the little money of his sufferings and griefs. There is then only one thing to do—to give to Him. Consolation, peace of soul, the means to use and transmute at length his torments into joys can be obtained only at this price. The receipt for this Divine alchemy of sorrow is abnegation and sacrifice. After the period of necessary incubation the great work is accomplished; out of the brazier of the soul comes the gold, that is to say, Love which consumes the sorrows and tears; the true philosopher's stone is there."

Huysmans afterwards called his sojourn at Liguge the most beautiful time of his life. Homesick though he was at times, it is very likely that he would have remained there were it not for the exile of the Congregation. The law of Associations had taken away the parish church from the monks and had placed a secular priest in charge.

At the end of September of that year the monks went to live in Belgium. Huysmans who was deeply afflicted by the dispersion had no longer any reason to remain there after them, and immediately he came back to Paris, happy no doubt to be home again.

But he did not relax his pious practices. He was a familiar figure in the churches, assisting at the offices, his favorite place being the foot of Our Lady's altar, for he had a wonderful, childlike devotion to the Mother of God. He still felt an attraction to the monasteries and went to make his dwelling with the Benedictines of the Blessed Sacrament. He remained there, however, only a year and then took apartments. Huysmans was not too easy to get on with; he was too individual to be happy in community life. He could live anywhere so long as he was lost in literary work, but once the book was finished he began to be restless again. The story of his sojourn at Liguge is told in *L'Oblat* which appeared at this time. It was the end of the trilogy which he had set out to write, and was received with as much acclaim as *En Route* and *La Cathédrale*. From a literary standpoint Huysmans had lost nothing by his conversion. His books sold, even though financial success had little appeal to him. But one must live, and his resources had never been any too great. Those resources had been helped a great deal when in 1900 he was made president of the Academie Goncourt of which he had been one of the founders. It gave him the necessary leisure for his subsequent books. In 1903 in company with his friend Abbé Mugnier he visited different cities, and he described the journey in *Trois Primitifs* which appeared in 1905. In the following year, 1906, he published *Les Foules de Lourdes,* a tribute to her to whom he had such great devotion, an answer as it was to the iniquitous book on the same subject by his former master, Zola.

Huysmans was coming near the end of his literary

work. But his life is not entirely seen in his books. He would have been a great man, worthy of study as a Christian, even if he had never published a line. He was a great penitent, an atoner by suffering. Shortly after the publication of *Les Foules de Lourdes* began the trouble with his throat which was at last to cause his death. The affliction was cancer of the palate. He began to decline, reduced to nothing but skin and bone by months of torture. His whole body, indeed, was a prey to suffering. His teeth gave him constant pain, he suffered from neuralgia, from pains in the chest, and from dyspepsia. Added to that was an affection of the eyes, so great that the light became unbearable to him and it was finally necessary to sew his eyelids shut and compel him to pass months in darkness. Through it all he never complained; religion gave him courage. At length, by what he believed to be a miracle, his sight was restored. But the other ills from which he suffered continued. He did not repine—he who once had been such a victim of ennui. His only comment was, "The good God sends me this sickness for the good of my soul." It was not merely resignation; it was joyful conformity, a delight in being asked to suffer. He had hoped to be cured by Easter, but not with any great longing, and he was not disappointed when Easter passed and left him still in pain.

"I ask neither to be cured nor to die," he said; "God is the Master. Suffering has its work to do in my soul. When that is finished death will have only to come."

There was little else to write about—there were no more subjects—but there was always his soul to sanctify. It was Huysmans humbled. He loved the humble. He made money, but he hated it; he would touch only what was necessary for his few wants. The soul of Huysmans was, when all is said, a humble one. Not that he disdained praise; he knew his own talents, knew all that was said about him, and wanted to know, even when the criticisms were far from being palatable. He had no ill will for anybody. He was simple of soul, childlike especially in his faith. He had tried the wisdom of the world and had discovered its real folly. Learning as an aid to religion he did not value much. It was vain, said he, to seek to make converts by philosophical discussion. "It is the humbling of our intelligence before God which is necessary for us."

He humbled himself. Like Baudelaire he chose the foot of the Cross. That was the only thing in life worth while. He had known sin; he knew how to sympathize with others who were struggling against it. There is nothing more truly sympathetic than his defence of the relapsing Paul Verlaine in the preface he wrote for the collection of the poet's religious verses. He was hard on nobody but himself. As to himself he felt that he deserved all the suffering that could be heaped upon his head. His was the motto of St. Teresa—"to suffer or to die." "It was necessary that I should suffer like this," he said to a friend a few days before his death, "in order that those who read my works might know that I had not only made literature; it was necessary that I should suffer my work." His friends admired his strength of soul. "He lives," said they, "his most beautiful pages on suffering." Suffering was his penance for sin. It was why the penitential orders appealed to him; he calls them somewhere the lightning-conductors of the world. "Hospitals," said he, "are necessary things in life." And again, "One must rejoice in having the chance to expiate one's sins so."

The conversion of Huysmans had made a special appeal to that other great convert, François Coppée. He devotes several pages in *La Bonne Souffrance* to him apropos of *La Cathédrale,* which he calls a book "infinitely interesting" and "profoundly sincere." "If as the proverb says," he writes, "a proverb which finds here its just application, all roads lead to Rome, Huysmans has certainly taken the longest. Some years ago an unhealthy attraction brought him to study the mysterious abominations of Satanism; and to read one after the other, *La Bas* and *En Route,* one could believe—if one did not know that the first of these two stories is quite imaginary —why Durtal, that is to say, Huysmans, ran to take refuge at La Trappe on coming forth from a black Mass. That which is true is that this scornful and incorrigible man, so hard to satisfy in all things, in matters of style as in cooking, came one day to be disgusted with himself. This sentiment which he has often expressed with the most energetic frankness had to take finally in a scrupulous conscience the form of repentance. Whoever repents finds the need of being pardoned; and, there is only one tribunal where indulgence is infinite and absolution perfect, the confessional. Durtal then rushed upon penance; you will find in *En Route,* on this crisis of soul, pages of a singular and penetrating emotion—and he was henceforth a Christian."

"Where Huysmans moves me," continues Coppée, "is when he is human; it is when newly converted, having lived to a ripe age almost entirely according to the senses, and having employed his thought scarcely for anything but the painful but amusing gymnastics of letters, he suffers in having so much difficulty to create in himself an interior life; it is when he deplores, with accents of poignant sincerity, the little ardor of his piety and the dryness of his heart in prayer. I recall then the frightful words, 'God vomits the tepid.' For I know like sufferings, the just punishment of those who are not frightened till late at the emptiness of their soul, and seek then with anguish to collect with care some ruins of faith and hope. Alas! from the first hour we have been separated from the Cross; during the heat of the day we have lived far from it, and it is only towards evening that its shadow lengthens and touches us. The moment, no doubt, is propitious, for all else is going to fail us. We return then towards the protecting Cross, we embrace it with a gesture of distress, and we try to pray. But not with impunity have we passed long years in indifference to eternal things, and it seems to us that the sweet prayers of our infancy wither in passing our impure lips. Courage, however. . . . Let us pray then without doubting His inexhaustible mercy. Let our prayers be as dry as they may, they have nevertheless their virtue. Are not we already rid of much of our baseness and the temptations which obsessed us? Do we not feel less unjust, more resigned, more humble, and especially more charitable?" Yes, Huysmans might have answered. Penance had done its work in his soul. Religion was easy to him now. "Everything," said he, "becomes easy when one has once said *Fiat* from his heart. It is no merit to me to believe in the supernatural. Ever since the day of my conversion I have touched it, felt it."

The end was nearing. The sufferings increased, but so great a value did he set on their purifying influence that he would not let himself be robbed of any of them. They wanted to give him morphine to lessen the pain, but he refused it. He knew that the day of death was not far off. He made his will, burned his worthless papers, forbade the publishing of his letters and unedited manuscripts, so great a horror did he have of "confidences" and "souvenirs," and made arrangements for the publication of *Trois Églises,* his last work, one that was deeply religious. There was no sentiment about the end; it was all religiously businesslike. One April day, a few weeks before his death, he was standing on a ladder in his library when his friend de Caldain entered. "What are you doing?" he was asked. "I am looking for the Pontifical," answered Huysmans; "I'm waiting for the priest to give me Extreme Unction."

At last the suffering body was worn out. Huysmans died May 12, 1907. He had asked to be buried in the robe of a Benedictine monk, and his friend the master of novices at Liguge, Father Dom Besse, who afterwards pronounced at Brussels a beautiful eulogy of the Oblate, sent him the habit, and thus he lay in death in the tunic and scapular, the hood on his head, the crucifix and relics on his breast. His hands were joined as in prayer, those hands which had written so much for which he had to do penance, but hands, too, that had written great apologies for faith and repentance.

Crowds came to see the great writer dead. Men of letters, people of the world, priests, religious, all entered the room which Dom Besse describes as the dwelling of "a man of the Middle Ages wandered into our times."

So passed one of the great figures of his day, one whom Havelock Ellis in his *Affirmations* calls "the greatest master of style and, within his own limits, the subtlest thinker and the acutest psychologist who in France today uses the medium of the novel." It is not, however, of Huysmans as a great writer that we love to think, but of Huysmans the sinner who had cleansed his soul by the tears of suffering and penance.

PAUL VERLAINE

THERE is a story somewhere of a man who after leading an honorable, even heroic, life for many years died. Admiring citizens erected a monument to his glory, and pointed with pride to one who had brought such renown to his native place. But in reality the man had not died; he had simply disappeared by that strange loss of memory which so many novelists have used as the center of their plots. One day he came back to his old town. The sight of the monument—a monument to him!—recalled the past. But alas, what was he now? No longer the upright citizen who did good to his fellows; but a poor derelict, a prey to every vice, a criminal with a price on his head. Yet there was the monument erected to him; to him but not to him; to his dead self, his nobler self, not to the miserable thing he now was. He could not, would not claim his due glory. Let his friends think kindly of him for what he once was. Never must they know that their hero had turned criminal. He let the underworld swallow him and left his dead youth in possession of its glory.

The mystery of the dual personality has always interested psychologists. But it is no great mystery after all. There is a Dr. Jekyll and a Mr. Hyde in every man. It is all very clear by the doctrine of original sin; otherwise it becomes inexplicable. How plainly St. Paul expressed it in his Epistle to the Romans (VII, 22, 23): "For I am delighted with the law of God, according to the inward man. But I see another law in my members fighting against the law of my mind, and captivating me

in the law of sin, that is in my members." It is the soul
struggling against the body, and the body struggling
against the soul.

There is in every man the making of a saint or the making of a devil. Men on the threshold of Heaven have
about-faced and walked into Hell; the cedars of Lebanon
have crashed from the heights into the ravines. Men, too,
just as the judgment of eternal damnation seemed ready
to be pronounced, have taken fright at their own wickedness and have risen over their dead selves till they found
a place somewhere among the canonized saints.

Somehow, when one reads the story of Paul Verlaine he
cannot get the thought of the mysterious dual personality
out of his head. Verlaine reached the heights of mystic
song; he fell to the depths of the obscene guffaw. One
day with the glorious seraphim; the next with the harpies
of Hell. Which is the true Verlaine? Psychologists
have tried to harmonize the two distinct beings he seemed
to be. They cannot be harmonized, for sin and virtue
cannot be harmonized. It is clear only in this: with the
grace of God one can do all things; but, too, it is possible
to lose that grace. Verlaine had his chance; he lost it.
He had his call to sanctity. How nobly he answered it
in the generosity, expressed as St. Francis himself might
express it, in the glorious religious poems by which, as
Huysmans, no mean critic and no mean mystic, says: "The
Church has had in him the greatest poet of whom she
can be proud since the Middle Ages." His was a call to
sanctity, and then the relapse into all that was low, cheap,
vile.

How then presume to place Verlaine among the "great
penitents", among those who from the moment of conversion fought their way back into the light? The degradation of his later life up to the very moment of his death
would seem to deny him a place among good penitents
just as for years he was denied a place among good men,

his name a byword, synonymous with sins which even bad
men hesitate to name. But Verlaine was at one time,
however short or long a time his change of heart lasted,
a great penitent. He is moreover the classic poet of penitence, far more so even than his friend Coppée. When
all his other work is forgotten, his penitent cries will still
be heard. Men will no longer remember that he so often
abused his gift of song; his corrupt verses will be of interest only to antiquarians, but his religious poetry will
be a part of the eternal classics. As time goes on these
penitential poems, so personal to him when he wrote them,
will lose a great deal of that personal touch and will be
used to voice the sentiments of any singer, just as the
psalms which David wrote to express his own personal
afflictions have become the impersonal, yet for that reason
all the more personal, voice of mankind.

Verlaine was the great penitent—ruined. He found his
soul once in prison. Did he lose it again? God knows.
Not for us to judge. Max Nordau who had made a study
of Verlaine dismissed him as a degenerate. Huysmans
commenting upon Nordau's statement, that Verlaine
"struggled sadly against his bad instincts," says: "Yes,
he did struggle; he was for the most of the time conquered;
and after? Who is the Catholic who would believe he
has the right to cast the first stone?" Who, indeed, will
set a limit to the mercy of God, and for one especially who
once served Him loyally, wholeheartedly, and in tears?

Paul Marie Verlaine was born March 30, 1844 at Metz,
in Lorraine when that province was still French territory
before it came under the heel of the German conqueror.
His parents, associated with the military profession, could
not call any abode their permanent home. This may explain somewhat the tendency of their child to the life of
vagabondage.

Nicholas Auguste Verlaine, the poet's father, was born
at Bertrix, then on French territory but ceded to Luxem-

bourg by the treaty of 1815. Nicholas, the son of a no-
tary, could claim an old and good ancestry. At the age
of sixteen he was in the army of Napoleon during the last
campaign of 1814-1815. He went through all the grades
of promotion, and at the time he resigned, a few years
after the birth of Paul, dissatisfied, thinking he had been
treated unjustly, he was captain in the second regiment of
engineers, a Chevalier of the Legion of Honor, and also
of St. Ferdinand of Spain. His colonel, Niel, afterwards
Marshal, had great admiration for Captain Verlaine and
urged him to withdraw his resignation, but the captain was
headstrong and followed his bent. Like father like son;
Paul Verlaine, especially when drinking, was the essence
of stubbornness. The captain was forty-six years of age
when his only child was born, and happened to be stationed
at Metz. There the family lived, with short intervals of
change of garrison to other places, during the first six or
seven years of the boy's life.

Paul Verlaine always loved his birthplace. He was always filled with patriotic and even militaristic sentiments
for Metz and France, and after the conquest of Lorraine
always spoke of it with the deepest emotion—"O town
where laughed my infancy." He can well be called a
great patriotic poet, quite as much as Coppée. No wonder. He had a fine example in his father, whom he always loved and admired. What a great hero he must have
been to the little lad, this especially tall soldier, of superb
carriage, with a face so martial yet so gentle. Useless
now to talk of what might have been had Captain Verlaine
remained in the army. But, as we have said, he resigned,
and at once moved his family to Paris, where he took
apartments in the Quartier des Batignolles, sacred now
as the place where the poet lies buried with his father and
mother. Paul, who was then seven, was placed in a small
institution, where as a day scholar he learned to read and
write and figure. There he soon fell ill of a fever, and

was tenderly nursed back to health by his devoted mother. That mother of Verlaine! She began early her ministrations of love to the wayward son and never ceased them till her death. Paul Verlaine's mother will live as long as Paul Verlaine himself.

Madame Verlaine was Elisa Julie Josephe Stephanie Dehée, and was born at Fampoux in Pas-de-Calais, in French Flanders. She belonged to an old family of landowners, cultivators, sugarmakers, and was an heiress of considerable importance, having at the time of her marriage a fortune of some four hundred thousand francs, a great deal of which was afterwards lost through the bad speculations of her husband. She was thirty-six at the time of Paul's birth. She was an excellent woman, tall, straight, dignified, always dressed in black, cold and calm —God knows she had need to be calm with such a son—a woman of very few words, saving, somewhat ceremonious in manner. And whereas her husband was indifferent in matters of religion, though always respectful to the Church, she was particularly pious. There is room here for psychological digression in the immediate antecedents of Paul Verlaine and the pre-natal effects on him of the wandering military life, the religious indifference of the father, the deep piety of the mother. But such digressions are beyond our point. Verlaine's fate was in himself. He had what would seem to be a guarded youth in his home and in his schools, yet in spite of this protection sin came into his life very early. The Captain adored his boy, nevertheless he sought to treat him with a certain discipline, and when he was sent to the *Institution Landry,* a large boarding-school, he used to come daily to inquire about the lad's health, bring him dainties and often take him out to dinner.

Paul remained at the Institution several years. He said afterwards that he had been a poor student, but in this, as in many other things, he exaggerated. It was there he made his First Communion, preceded by a general "scrupulous" confession. He writes in his *"Confessions"*; "And my First Communion was 'good.' I felt then for the first time that thing almost physical which all who partake of the Eucharist feel of the Presence, absolutely real, in a sincere approach to the Sacrament. One is invested. God is there in our flesh and in our blood. The sceptics say that it is faith alone which produces that in the imagination. And the indifference of the impious, the coldness of the unbelieving, when by derision they absorb the Sacred Species, is the effect even of their sin, the temporal punishment of sacrilege." He had sinned much when in 1895 these words were written. As a boy he was assiduous enough in his religious exercises, but it was not long before he became acquainted with vice. Precocious in talent, he was also precocious in vice. His boyhood was filled with impurity; indeed, he was little more than fifteen when he began to frequent the company of bad women. Taken all in all there were very few months in his life when his tendency was not to animal passions. Evil companionship had helped to that end, especially the evil companionship of bad books. Verlaine could scarcely remember the time when he had been pure.

While still boarding at the *Institution Landry* he entered the courses of the *Lycée Bonaparte* where he studied from 1853 to 1862. Though of limited faculties, especially as to sciences, he had a certain success in his studies, chiefly in rhetoric and Latin, won several prizes, and succeeded in getting his Bachelor degree, which was sufficiently hard to win. When he left the *Lycée* he was a youth of eighteen, with absolutely no morals, and less faith. Impure books, rationalistic books, read clandestinely, had done their work.

As soon as his school days were finished he went with his parents to visit his mother's relatives in Artois. Subsequently he made many visits there, for he loved that country, and, although never what may be called a poet of nature, he loved nature. During that vacation he walked in the woods, fished and hunted. Hunting was his favorite sport. He made himself one of the country people, dressed like them, lived like them, and soon drank like them. It was here he got his passion for strong drink, which was eventually to be the cause of all his misfortunes. Verlaine was at heart always a northerner; he hated the sun. This happy-go-lucky life was just what appealed to him. It was after all the fundamental weakness of his character—instability. He was essentially a dreamer. His parents were already planning his future—they wanted him to take up law—but he was the least concerned of all.

There was no need to worry about finances, and the hunting was good. Verlaine then as always was a great reader. He read with avidity all that came under his hand, history, romance, poetry. We find him even in those days expressing delight over a life of St. Teresa he was reading. Why, it is hard to say, for as we have said, even in those young days his faith had gone with his morals. He occasionally visited the churches, as one of his friends assures us, but it was merely to satisfy his artistic curiosity. He would follow a sermon of Père Monsabre or some other great preacher, but merely for the sake of the oratory. It brought no spiritual message to his soul, so young yet so corrupt. It was so manly to be an unbeliever at eighteen! In one of his letters to a school chum he writes that he has been reading the "Ramayana," by Indra! He exclaims, "How fine it is! and how it disgusts you with the Bible, the Gospel and the Fathers of the Church." Poor silly youth, how wise it is!

On the return to Paris Verlaine undertook to study law, but it was evident at once that he had no aptitude for it. Most of his time was then spent in the drinking

places of the Latin Quarter. The military father sensed
the impending ruin. He was anxious to place the youth
away from the danger of idleness, and finally got him a
position with an insurance company. To qualify himself
for the work Paul went to a commercial school. Once in
this position everything looked bright for a while. He
was forced to be sober, and as he was allowed little spending money he led a rather decent life. He even saved
some money from his wages, and gave some to his parents.
They must have breathed a sigh of relief when they saw
him so industrious, spending his leisure with books and
paintings and not, as formerly, in the cabarets. It was
but a temporary relief, however, for he gradually contracted the drinking habit again, a habit that he further
developed during the days of the Siege, and which finally
bound him body and soul.

From the insurance office he passed in 1864, when he
was twenty, to a position in one of the city departments.
But his heart was not in that work either. As soon as
his day's work was over, he would hurry to the Café du
Gaz, then the rendezvous of literary and artistic folk,
where he would delight in taking part in the discussions
on poetry and other matters, a discussion that was punc-
tuated by much drinking. As an employee he had no
ambition. He never had ambition. He was the type of
the care-free poet; for Verlaine even then was a budding
poet. Far back as the time when he was but fifteen or
sixteen he had begun to write verses, without, however,
any thought of publication.

Captain Verlaine died December 30, 1865. Paul
grieved over his death. It was a loss in more ways than
one, for the hand of the father had had some restraining
influence on the boy so inclined to waywardness and so
easily led.

A few months later Paul Verlaine made his début in
the literary world with the publication of his first book,

Poèmes Saturniens. The famous literary group, so many of whom attained fame, known as *La Parnasse,* began with Louis Xavier de Ricard, who had gathered at his mother's house the young men just beginning to write. There were seen Catulle Mendès, Coppée, Anatole France, Sully Prudhomme, de Heredia, the de Goncourt brothers, and others. *La Parnasse Contemporaine,* devoted for several months, week after week, to the publication of the verses of new poets, caused a stir in the literary world, and also brought upon the writers, unjustly, a great deal of ridicule. Alphonse Lemerre, who up to that time had specialized in pious books, agreed to publish the works of the budding poets at their own expense. Thus the *Poèmes Saturniens* appeared, on the same day, by the way, as *La Reliquaire* of Coppée and a book of de Ricard. Needless to say, the new book of a contemporary, comparatively unknown poet created no sensation. His friends of course flattered him upon it, and even estimable critics, like Saint Beuve, recognized in the youth of twenty-two a real poet, but the reading public ignored the book, and the press, as was to be expected, was quite silent about it. It did not meet the success of Coppée's first book. Verlaine's verses were impersonal. He was then but a carefree boy who scarcely knew that he had a soul; anyway he did not put that soul into his poems until the day when the hand of God afflicted him. The same thing may be said of his next book—*Fêtes Galantes*—which appeared in 1869. It was barely noticed outside the salon of the strange Nina de Callias where the Parnassian group used to congregate.

The real tragedy of Verlaine's life began with his marriage. One day he called upon his friend Charles de Sivry. By chance de Sivry's half sister, Mathilde de Mauté, entered the room. She had seen Verlaine in an amateur play in which he had had great success as a comedian. Introduced to the young poet of a certain literary, though limited fame, she told him how much she appreciated his verses. It was a case of love at first sight. The young girl—she was only sixteen—was pleased to have a poet make much of her, and Verlaine, so intensely ugly as to his personal appearance that he himself knew it and delighted in drawing caricatures of himself, a man, too, who was timid in the presence of women, in spite of his sinful youth, felt flattered that he whose ugliness ordinarily repelled women seemed to hold the attention of this charming girl. She was a girl of good common sense, with no romantic notions, and was worshipped in her own family. Verlaine, beside himself with this first love, went north to think the matter over, and almost immediately wrote to de Sivry asking for the hand of his sister. It was an extraordinary way to propose, but de Sivry pleaded his friend's cause. There was little need of pleading, however. Nobody was opposed to the marriage. Verlaine was considered quite a good catch. He had a good position in City Hall, his mother was known to have a good amount of money which eventually would come to him, and—perhaps the deciding factor with Mathilde's parents —he was willing to take the girl without a dowry. Verlaine's mother, too, was pleased, thinking that marriage would make him settle down and make a man of him. She was always the doting mother. She adored her boy, she spoiled him with her ready indulgence, and she cried all too late. No matter what his transgressions she quickly pardoned him. When he came home drunk, she put him to bed, took care of him, and then went to her room to weep over his misfortunes. The next day she would kill him with kindness, find excuses for him, and blame everybody else for his faults. She was very proud of his talents, even though she was not literary, and perhaps never read one of his books.

For a time it seemed that she was right about the marriage. Love, and it was a great love, sobered the man.

He stayed away from the saloons and wrote poetry. It was at this period when he was longing for his wedding day that he wrote *La Bonne Chanson,* poems in praise of the girl who was to be his wife, the volume appearing in 1870 during the war. The marriage at last took place in the Church of Notre Dame de Clignancourt in the time of the Commune.

It is useless to discuss whether or not Verlaine ever should have married. He was a bundle of nerves, excitable to fury when he drank. Whether this lot would have been different with another wife, it is also useless to discuss. It is folly to talk of what might have been. The times were, indeed, strenuous. Shortly after the honeymoon came the Siege, then the Commune. Verlaine might have escaped the service had he wished, but, the true son of his soldier father, he was a good patriot and, filled with zeal, joined the national guard. He did not last long as a military man. He had the soul of a hero, but the body of a coward. An attack of bronchitis not only weakened him, but it impelled him to drink in spite of his resolution at the time of his marriage never again to touch the stuff. The army anyway had its special temptations to drink. Dispensed from service through illness, he never took up his gun again, though in reality while being classed among the Communards he never took an active part. He was back at work in the City Hall where his task was to clip from the papers all that was favorable or unfavorable to the Commune. And all the while he was writing poetry to the sound of the cannon.

The honeymoon, meanwhile, had not lasted long. Scarcely six months had passed when one day he came home drunk. The young wife was so surprised and disgusted that she left him and returned to her parents. She at last acceded to his importunities, trusting in his good resolves, and came back to him. But it was only a temporary reconciliation. The rift in the lute was widened

by his idleness.   He refused to go back to the bureau after the defeat of the Commune, being afraid that his former activity in the cause, small though that activity was,
would militate against him.   In reality he was glad to be
rid of the prosaic job.   It was a misfortune, but a greater
one was his going to live with his wife's people.   Idle
now, he had more time to drink, and he drank heavily.
He went north with his wife and spent the summer there,
returning to Paris in September.   He afterwards regretted that he had not kept his position; years afterwards he
tried in vain to get it back.   But that was long afterwards.
At first the idleness did not worry him a bit, though it
was the beginning of his many misfortunes.   When sober
Paul Verlaine was of fine disposition, agreeable.   When
drunk he was disagreeable, violent, unbearable.   Even
the birth of his son, George, did not wake him up.   He
was living in a fool's paradise.   His faults were great
enough, but they were greater when seen through the mag-
nifying eyes of his people-in-law.   Had his wife been of
strong character—like her parents she had little religion—
she might have reclaimed him, for he loved her devotedly.
But one must not be too hard on her.   She suffered much
at the hands of her poet husband.

The growing ill-will came to a climax through the youth
who was Verlaine's evil genius, Arthur Rimbaud, a boy
of sixteen, precocious, intelligent, anarchistic, even athe-
istic, who could drink strong drink like water.   He had
run away to Paris from his home in the Ardennes—Verlaine's own country.   A poet himself, he had read Verlaine's verses and had liked them.   He affected to despise
the classics.   He sent one of his poems to Verlaine who,
flattered by the tribute, wrote at once to the youth offering
him the hospitality of the house where he himself was only
a guest, and quite an unwelcome one at that.   The Mauté
family did not share Verlaine's enthusiasm for the precocious poet and they soon dismissed him, much to Ver-

laine's chagrin. Rimbaud lodged here, there and every-where. He imposed himself wherever he could. But Paul was his great friend, taking him about with him, proud to show him off to all the literary circles. Rimbaud was a vain youth. He had a real talent, an original one, and a monument has been erected to him in his native town of Charleville. But he was unbearable. Addicted to drink and drugs he was forever quarreling, insulting even his hosts, so that after a while no one wanted him. Verlaine's feelings were hurt by this rejection of his pro-tége and he broke with his old friends out of loyalty for this *"enfant Shakespeare,"* as Victor Hugo—cynically no doubt—called Rimbaud. The strange association was the cause of daily quarrels in the Verlaine home. The vilest insinuations even were made as to the nature of the friend-ship, but Verlaine clung to Rimbaud in preference to his wife. Thinking himself a martyr, an abused husband, he decided to leave home. His wife was quite indifferent. She had ceased to care for him, ceased to respect him. His mother, as usual hoping for the best, gave him the means to support himself on his uncertain journey. It was a poor service to him.

The queer pair set out that July day of 1872 for Arras. From Belgium they went to London. Scarcely had they left Paris when Verlaine's wife entered her appeal for a separation from him. It was an evil period in the life of the poet, no matter how charitably we may be inclined to him. It was a period of drink and lust. That was evident from the book of poems he sent back to Paris to be printed, and which on its publication was confiscated by the police.

Rimbaud's friendship did not last long. He found Lon-don useful inasmuch as he was able to learn English there, but he soon returned to Belgium. Verlaine was incon-solable. He became ill, and telegraphed for his wife and mother to come to him. The poor doting mother came, of

course. The wife ignored the request. She was done
with Paul Verlaine. When his mother returned to Paris
he refused to go with her, although she pleaded with him.
Instead he went to Belgium in the spring of 1873, where
he remained a while with his relations. All the while
he hoped, vainly, that his wife would become reconciled to
him.

Meanwhile he had been writing poetry. He had completed *Les Romances Sans Paroles,* but was unable, owing
to unsettled conditions in politics, to get a publisher. He
heard then that his wife had been granted a decree of
separation, and at once he wrote for Rimbaud to come
back. The return meant another drunken debauch, as
they wandered first in the Ardennes and then back to
London again, where they tried to gain a living by giving
lessons in French. But the chief means of support was
the money that came from the poor, foolish mother.

The strange friendship lasted for two years and a half.
Then one June day, 1873, the poets quarreled, Verlaine
going off in a huff to Anvers without telling Rimbaud, and
without leaving him any money, for it was considered
Verlaine's privilege to pay all the bills. Verlaine was
morbid; he even thought of suicide. He wanted his wife;
he loved her, and he cursed her. He met his mother at
Brussels, and she brought the final word that his wife
would have nothing more to do with him. He sought
solace in drink, and more drink, and again he sent for
Rimbaud. Rimbaud came, not for the sake of his friend,
but to seek to bleed him and get enough money to take
him to Paris. He even tried to extort money from
Madame Verlaine. A quarrel ensued between him and
Paul. Rimbaud started to leave, and Verlaine, drawing
the revolver, fired at him. The shot went wild. The
mother, shocked at the vulgar quarrel that had almost
ended in murder, gave Rimbaud the money he wanted
and sent him on his way. Paul insisted on accompanying

him to the train and walked out with him, when Rimbaud,
fearing that he was going to shoot again, called the police
and had his friend arrested. He then took the train for
home, breathing a sigh of relief that he had escaped with
his life.

Verlaine was immediately brought to the prison of
Petits Carmes, where he was detained until an investiga-
tion into his character was made in Paris. The report
that came back was bad, and he was sentenced to two years
in prison and a fine of two hundred francs, August 8,
1873. The poor mother did her best to get him released.
Other friends aided her, but all to no purpose. Verlaine
was doomed to remain in prison. He tried to make the
best of it. He bore it well, and was as patient as could
be expected under the circumstances. In the February of
1874 *Les Romances Sans Paroles* was published. Copies
were sent to those designated by him, to papers for review,
but in vain. Nobody wanted the book. Paul Verlaine
was dead to his world; he was a disgraced, a dishonored
man, a convict. But at that very moment of his rejection
by his friends he was about to receive a wonderful grace.
God was preparing to do a great work in his soul. And
what a soul it was! the idle vagabond, the drunkard, the
brawler, the impure and foul-mouthed man, the free-
thinker without a shred of faith. Men do not fall much
lower than Verlaine had fallen up to the time of his imprisonment.

In his book, *Mes Prisons,* published in 1893, he tells
the story of his sudden, his wonderful conversion back to
God and to decent living. No one can question the sincerity of it even though the poor weakling relapsed into
sin after a long hard struggle to be true to his nobler self.
Read in the light of his after degradation the conversion
of Verlaine moves one to tears.

In that prison of Mons, he did not curse his lot. He
confesses that he knew that he really deserved the scaffold.

He tried to make the best of it and amused himself by reading and by playing simple games which he invented. He worked, read poetry, projected plays, read Shakespeare especially in order to perfect his English, and made plans for the translation of contemporary English books. We find him reading among other books Cardinal Wiseman's *Fabiola*.

But at last the great day dawned. He writes:

"Jesus, how did you come to take me? Ah, one morning the good director himself entered my cell. 'My good friend,' he said to me, 'I bring you bad news. Courage! Read.' It was a sheet of crested paper, the copy of the separation (from his wife), so merited, but so hard to bear. I fell in tears on my poor back on my poor bed." An hour or two later he asked that the chaplain be sent to him. When he came Verlaine asked him for a catechism, and the chaplain brought him a copy of Abbé Gaume's *Catechism of Perseverance*. "I am a literateur," he writes, "I enjoy correctness, subtility, all the art of style, as of law, order, etc. But in spite of a deplorable art in point of writing, and of painful syntax, Abbé Gaume was for me—so rotten with pride, with syntax and Parisian foolishness—an apostle." "The proofs," he continues, "mediocre enough, given by Abbé Gaume in favor of the existence of God and of the immortality of the soul, pleased me but little and convinced me not at all, I admit, in spite of the efforts of the chaplain to corroborate them with his better and more cordial commentaries. It was then he thought of a supreme idea and said to me, 'Skip the chapters and pass at once to the Sacrament of the Eucharist.' I do not know if those pages constitute a *chef d'oeuvre*. I even doubt it. But in the state of soul in which I found myself, the profound ennui in which I was plunged, the despair at not being free, the shame at being in prison, determined one certain June morning, after what a bitter sweet night of meditation on the Real

Presence and the multiplicity without number of hosts figured in the holy Gospels by the multiplication of the loaves and the fishes—all that, I say, determined in me truly an extraordinary resolution."

There hung in his cell above a little brass crucifix a picture of the Sacred Heart, a lithograph that was far from being a work of art. His eyes rested upon that picture.

"I do not know," he says, "what or Who suddenly raised me. I threw myself out of my bed without taking time to dress myself, and I prostrated myself in tears and sobs at the foot of the crucifix and of the picture evocative of the strangest, but to my eyes the most sublime devotion of modern times in the Catholic Church. Only the hour of rising two hours or less after this veritable small—or great?—moral miracle, made me get up from my knees. I went about the care of my cell, according to the rules, making my bed, sweeping the room, when the day-guard entered, and addressed me in the conventional, 'All goes well?' I said to him at once, 'Tell the chaplain to come.' "

The chaplain entered the cell a few moments afterwards, and Verlaine told him about his conversion. "I believe," he said, "I saw, it seemed to me that I knew; I was illuminated."

The chaplain was persuaded of the prisoner's sincerity. Priests are never surprised at the workings of the grace of God. He calmed the penitent, and upon Verlaine's expressing a desire to go to confession at once, the good priest prevailed upon him to wait for a while. Verlaine meanwhile prayed—"Praying through my tears, through my smiles, as a child, as a redeemed criminal, praying on my knees, with my hands, 'with all my heart, with all my soul, with all my strength' according to the words of my revived catechism."

"How much I reflected on the essence and evolution even of the thing which had taken place in me. Why?

How? How good I was, how simple, how childish, and how ignorant. *Domine, noverim Te.* What candor of a childish heart, what gentleness of an old—and young—then converted sinner, the proud humbling himself, the violent man become a lamb." As a sign of his conversion he gave up all profane reading, Shakespeare included. He plunged into de Maître and Auguste Nicolas, eager to learn all he could about his renewed faith, the chaplain explaining whatever difficulties he had.

At length the great day of confession arrived. It was long, detailed, the first since the day he had renewed his First Communion years before. There were shameful things to tell, for the soul of Verlaine had been, indeed, a leprous one. But when it was ended and the words of absolution pronounced on that glad Assumption day, a new peace came into his soul, a peace which remained till the day of his liberation from prison, and indeed long afterwards.

Verlaine was a true convert, and burned with zeal to share his good fortune with others. He desired to convert his old school chum, Lepelletier, and wrote to him, advising him to get a copy of Gaume. "All that I am going to tell you now," he wrote, "is that I experience in a great, an immense degree, that which one feels when, the first difficulties surmounted, he perceives a science, an art, a new language, and also that inexpressible feeling of having escaped a great danger. I implore you to tell no one what I write to you. If anyone asks of you news of me, say that you know I am well, that I am better, that I am absolutely converted to the Catholic religion, after ripe reflection, in full possession of my moral liberty and my good sense."

Lepelletier, his biographer, does not wish to grant that the conversion was sincere. He calls it "an impulsive act." Verlaine, he says, in his youth despised religion, had read materialistic books, and had lost faith in the supernatural, getting instead, "a rational and intelligent atheism!" He seeks to explain the psychology of it in a natural way. The habits of the man had changed, he had become sober by force, and hence less nervous, less excitable; he was less the boy now, and had become more serious; he stopped swearing, blushed for his past, examined his conscience and asked himself what he had done with his youth; from that there came a moral depression, and he got the idea that he must do penance; then the religious idea awoke, and he invoked the Lord for help. This mere natural explanation is unjust to Verlaine.

There is no doubt that the man's heart was converted to God. His one thought during those days was to atone for his sins. Piety occupied his mind to the exclusion of everything else. Worldliness had left even his poetry. "I am making canticles to Mary," he writes, "after the system and the prayers of the primitive Church." It may be noted that henceforth Verlaine's poetry sounded the personal note.

His reading, too, had changed. He wrote that he wanted to translate "a remarkable book of Lady Fullerton—*Ellen Middleton.*" Strange that that book, written before Lady Fullerton entered the Catholic Church, stressed the need of man to confess his sins. Verlaine had already decided that when he was liberated he would make his living by translating. One gets an idea of his change of heart in a letter he wrote to Lepelletier, September 8, 1874:

"It is necessary to have passed through all that I have suffered for three years, humiliations, disdain, insults, to feel all that is admirably consoling, reasonable, logical, in this religion, so terrible and so sweet. Oh, terrible! Yes! But man is so bad, so truly fallen, and punished by his birth alone. And I do not speak of proofs, historic, scientific and other, which are blinding when one has this immense goodness to be drawn from this society, abominable, rotten, old, foolish, proud, damnable." The prison, through the religion which it brought to the soul of the sinner, regenerated Paul Verlaine. It was under that wonderful influence that he wrote in prison most of the great religious poems of *Sagesse,* which Verhaeren calls, "the white crown of his work," though the book was not published till 1881, several years after he had been released from prison. *Sagesse* is wonderfully beautiful; every line of it could be quoted to show how Verlaine had remade his soul through tears of repentance. One example must suffice, one of the most glorious lyrics ever written. We give the fine translation made by Ashmore Wingate.

> My God, but Thou hast wounded me in love,
> And quivers still the wound that Thou hast made:
> My God, but Thou hast wounded me in love.
>
> My God, but with Thy dread Thou'st stricken me,
> Thy blast, which thunders yet I feel anear:
> My God, but with Thy dread Thou'st stricken me.
>
> My God, I have discovered all is vile,
> Now that in me Thy glory is installed:
> My God, I have discovered all is vile.
>
> Submerge my soul in flood-waves of Thy Wine,
> And from Thy table's Bread upbuild my life:
> Submerge my soul in flood-waves of Thy Wine.
>
> Behold my blood, which I have never shed;
> Behold my flesh, unworthy to feel pain:
> Behold my blood which I have never shed.
>
> Behold my forehead, which can only blush,
> For footstool of Thy feet adorable:
> Behold my forehead, which can only blush.

Behold my hands, which have no labour done,
For burning embers and for incense rare:
Behold my hands which have no labour done.

Behold my heart, which hath but beat in vain,
To throb upon the briers of Calvary:
Behold my heart, which hath but beat in vain.

Behold my feet, these frivolous voyagers,
To hasten to the summons of Thy grace:
Behold my feet, these frivolous voyagers.

Behold my voice, a sullen, lying sound,
For the reproaches made by Penitence:
Behold my voice, a sullen, lying sound.

Behold mine eyes, lights which with error shine,
To be extinguished in the tearful prayer:
Behold mine eyes, lights which with error shine.

Ah, God of offering and forgiveness,
What is the depth of my ingratitude?
Ah, God of offering and forgiveness.

Oh! God of terror and of sanctity,
Behold the black abysm of my sin:
Oh! God of terror and of sanctity.

Thou God of peace, of joy, of goodness, too,
All these my fears, all this mine ignorance:
Thou God of peace, of joy, of goodness, too.

Thou knowest, yea, all this Thou knowest well,
And how I am most poor of all that live:
Thou knowest, yea, all this Thou knowest well.

Yet, Lord, that which I am, to Thee I give.

Verlaine was released from prison January 16, 1875. The faithful old mother was waiting for him at the door. They were escorted to the French borders by the police, and the mother brought him to her relations to rest a while before taking up his life again. She alone was faithful. Verlaine was dead to society, buried alive, and not even his name was mentioned, a fact that must be taken into account when there is consideration of his relapses and his final degradation.

How sincere his conversion was is evident from the fact that he did not drink for five years after his conversion. Had he been given a helping hand in those first days of fervor, things might have been different towards the end. But he was received coldly even by his relatives. There was the taint of the jail upon him. But he was still dominated by his conversion. He was a sincere penitent; he sought to arrange his life so as to avoid the temptations of the past. He had to look for some way to earn a living, for his mother's fortune had dwindled to almost nothing. He thought of taking up farming, but wisely put away the idea. Literature, his *métier,* offered no financial prospects, and he had no bent to journalism. Anyway, he did not wish to return to Paris, where his name was a byword, and where, moreover, there were so many dangers for his soul. The vagabond life, the cabarets, all Paris was full of temptations. No better proof of his sincere repentance is wanted than his manly, even heroic efforts to lead a new life. So he decided to teach Latin, French and English in some school where he could live and there find forgetfulness of the past in honorable work. He advertised in the papers and soon got a position in the Grammar School of a Mr. Andrews, in Stickney, near Boston, England. There he taught French, Latin and drawing, and made his dwelling with the family of Mr. Andrews, a charming, learned man. Verlaine led a very happy existence there for a year and a half, leading a laborious, regular life, working hard at learning English and finding solace for his soul in the open fields of the beautiful English country. He wrote little or no poetry in those days, but he read a great many books. He writes from Stickney, November 19, 1875, that he has been reading theology and the mystics—The *Summa* of St. Thomas, and the works of St. Teresa!

Anxious to see his mother, he left the school and came to Arras, and remained there for a time, writing poetry and studying English. He finally came to Boston, England, and tried to make a living by giving private lessons in French but failing in that he got a position in an institution at Bournemouth, directed by a Mr. Remington. Here he wrote several of the poems of *Sagesse,* "masses of verse," as he said. But the homesickness was upon him, and he returned to Paris where he remained for a while, though unknown. Through his friend Ernest Delehaye, then a professor in the Catholic College of Notre Dame at Rethel, he got a position teaching literature, history, geography and English. Most of his fellow professors were priests *"gens cordiaux,"* as he calls them. He found there in this "Thebaid" peace and calm. The priests did not know the history of the man till long after he had left them. They had found him uncommunicative, but faithful to duty, regular in his religious exercises. They never suspected that in the quiet of his room he was writing some of the greatest religious poetry of all time, his recreation after correcting the themes of his pupils. He was a modest, simple, pious man. Verlaine always kept the most pleasant remembrances of the college. And the college reciprocated. It was proud of him. In 1897 the alumni gave a banquet at Paris in memory and in honor of their late professor.

It is said by some of his biographers that at Rethel the old temptation to drink came upon him, and that being reprimanded for it he left. Whatever the reason he resigned. He wanted to reclaim his position in society, to get a place in the world.

One of his students was Lucien Letinois, a farmer's son, a pious youth whom Verlaine loved much. He went with the lad to the farm and lived there for a time. He persuaded his mother to come and buy a farm in the vicinity. Poor business man that Verlaine was, he had the place bought in the name of the elder Letinois. The dreamy poet was never meant to be a practical farmer, and the undertaking was a miserable failure. He gave it up; old Letinois sold the farm and pocketed the money, and Verlaine with the wanderlust again in his soul set out with the boy for London. They remained there but a short time, for they had no money, and back to Paris they came to his mother, with whom he remained from 1881 to 1883. He tried in vain to get back his position in the bureau. It was in this period of uncertainty, of mental suffering that he brought out his greatest book, the immortal *Sagesse*, 1881. It had been a hard struggle to place it. No one wanted poetry, especially pious poetry. It was a Catholic publisher, Victor Palmé, who finally accepted it.

Needless to say it passed unnoticed. Even the Catholics did not buy it. The book was dedicated to his mother. It is interesting to read the original preface, suppressed in later editions, since it gives an insight into the spiritual condition of the poet at that time, long after the first fervor of his conversion.

"The author of this book has not always thought as he thinks today. For a long time he wandered in contemporary corruption, taking his part there through ignorance. Griefs, well merited, have since then warned him, and God has given him the grace to heed the warning. He is prostrated before the altar, so long unknown, he adores the All Good and invokes the All Powerful, a humble child of the Church, the least in merits but full of good will. The knowledge of his weakness and the memory of his

falls have guided him in the elaboration of this work, which
is his first act of public faith after a long literary silence;
one will not find anything here, he hopes, contrary to this
charity which the author, hereafter Christian, owes to
sinners, whose odious morals he formerly and almost up
to the present has practised. . . . The author published when very young, that is to say a dozen years ago,
verses sceptical and sadly light. He dares to think that
in these here there is no dissonance to shock the delicacy
of the Catholic ear; that there is no such fault would be
his dearest glory as it is his proudest hope."

Oh, the pity that in time these good resolves disappeared
and the poet gave to the world not only light verses but
verses rankly obscene.

Verlaine was now at the edge of the precipice. Lucien
Letinois had died of typhoid. Verlaine was inconsolable
at the loss of the youth whom he loved as a son. He wept
in agony as he went to bury him. In time he found resignation, beautifully expressed in his book—*Amour*—
written in memory of the youth. We can date the beginning of Verlaine's new decline, moral and intellectual,
from the passing out of his life of the good influence of
Lucien Letinois.

For a while Verlaine got work on the *Reveil* (which
afterwards became the *Echo de Paris*), contributing short
essays such as constituted later his books—*Les Memoires
d'un Veuf* and *Quinze Jours en Hollande* and *Les Poétes
Maudits*. He wrote other prose at the same time and a
new volume of verse *Jadis et Naguere*. In 1883 he returned to Belgium and made another attempt at the farmer's life. His mother went with him. But it was the
same old story. The ennui drove him to drink. He quarreled with her, fell into bad company and became so objectionable that she left him and went back to Paris,
where he followed her. They returned again to the country. But he drank again in spite of his good promises,

and in one of his fits of drunkenness raised his hand against this old woman of seventy-five years whose only fault was that she loved him too well. For this offense he was imprisoned for a month. After his release he sold the farm, at a loss of course, and came back to Paris. He was ill, weak, breaking up from his debauches. He that once had been so near sanctity!

The last years of Verlaine are a distressing study. His mother died in January, 1886. It was a black day for him and he was never any good after that. His life thereafter was one of bad company, misery, sickness. With no money, he lodged in deplorable conditions, in the poorest district, sometimes in hovels where there was not even a floor. His wife remarried in 1886. In August, 1887, we find him writing that he did not have a sou.

The life of poverty, of heavy drinking, of immorality soon broke down his body, naturally robust. Time and again he had to go to the hospitals, his only refuge. There he was forced to be sober, there he could work; there, too, he could weep over his past sins. "All the maladies I have," he wrote in humility, "I have well deserved. I am able to say my *mea culpa*. I have burned my life, and so much the worse for me." The doctor who attended his death bed said that Verlaine had eight or ten mortal diseases.

In the hospital he was contented for a while, but after a couple of weeks the ennui would seize him and he would go back to the hovels of the Latin Quarter. He was always the big irresponsible child. It was this, perhaps, that drew so many friends to him. There was a certain fascination about him and no one could be angry with him for long. Even the police had orders not to arrest him no matter what his vagaries. Bad women preyed upon him, exploited him, made him support them.

The last years, 1892 to 1896, were lamentable. He lived here, there, everywhere, drinking, carousing, a life of vulgar lust, even prostituting his wonderful poetic talent for a few pence in the writing of poems some of which were so positively indecent that they could not be published openly. He had lectured with much acclaim in Holland, in Belgium and in London, and had this late in life tasted the joys of popularity. But it was too late to redeem him. He had gone back to the vomit. Still there was something of the old faith when he wrote in his *Confessions* (1895), "To conclude, as the Christian I have tried to be and who is not perhaps quite submerged, ought I not repeat, speaking of my past, with that other great self-confessor, the adorable Bishop of Hippo—*Domine, noverim Te—Lord, That I might know Thee!*"

The last days of the poet were tranquil enough. He had given up drinking and was assiduous at his work. About Christmas, 1895, he was taken ill and was obliged to keep to his room. Strange, his last poem was on *Death.* He was ill several days, neglected by the woman who preyed upon him. When help did come it was too late. He fell into a coma. The priest was sent for, but Verlaine was unconscious when he arrived. The poet died January 8, 1896, "fortified by the Sacraments of the Church," the funeral notice read.

When the news was spread about everybody in the world of letters came, a tribute to the genius of the man. Among those who came was Huysmans, also Coppée, who wept for his friend. Coppée was not far from that day that was to mark his own great conversion. The hour for the funeral had been set for two o'clock, but through the influence of Coppée, sorry that no one had thought of having a Mass said for the poor soul, the hour was set for ten o'clock. Letters of condolence came from all parts of the world, the humble room was filled with flowers, and all Paris thronged to the funeral Mass at the Church of St. Etienne du Mont, Verlaine's parish church. Fifteen pages of a register were filled with the names of visitors to the home of the dead poet. He was buried in the cemetery of Batignolles with his father and mother. The great writers of the day, such as Mendès and Coppée, pronounced his eulogy. Coppée's tribute is a classic.

So passed one who, as Maurice Barrès says, "was the victim of his own genius."

In *Mes Prisons* (1891) Verlaine tells us that after his conversion he persevered for several years, and that relaxation followed little by little, and then new falls; and he writes: "Irremediable? Perhaps not, for God is merciful and has sent me afflictions, ruin in truly the most humble circumstances, deceptions, treasons from my scandalized neighbors. Oh, the catechism of Abbé Gaume! Oh, not to be able to read it again, not to want to read it again, perhaps, and this time to keep it! God, nevertheless, is merciful, and hope is a theological virtue which departs more willingly. Lord, have pity on us!"

Verlaine must remain always something of an enigma. But one thing is sure, he was at one time of his life a great penitent, near to God, even though his later relapse is all too plain. His friend, Lepelletier, will not admit his real conversion. He calls it, "a sort of religious conversion," a "theatrical religiosity, external and bookish." But we prefer to have the opinion of Huysmans. Verlaine loved Huysmans. Apropos of one of the books of Huysmans— *La Bas*—some one asked Verlaine if he had ever attended a Black Mass. The question irritated him. "Do you think me," he replied with vehemence, "so cockney or so sick as to give myself to those mummeries so infamous, so repugnant in themselves, so truly repugnant to the Catholic faith which I have always professed sincerely, notwithstanding all my weaknesses, all my errors?"

In Verlaine there was the struggle between the senses and the soul, and no one knew it better than himself. He sinned; then he was ashamed of his sins. But his faith was never shaken. All, Catholics and unbelievers, recognized him as a great Catholic poet, though many Catholics, and justly, too, suspected him on account of the life he was leading. Huysmans in 1904 wrote the Preface to the collection of the religious poems of Verlaine. He comes to the defence of the dead poet. He seeks, he says, to dissipate the misunderstanding which exists between Verlaine and the faithful, distrustful of his person and his books, to make them understand that he was not the impenitent sinner they suppose. "Unique, in effect, across the ages, he has recovered those accents of humility and candor, those prayers grieving and benumbed, that joyfulness of the little child, forgotten since that return to the pride of paganism which the Renaissance was."

Huysmans, big convert as he himself was, knew the human heart, the weakness of human nature. It was not for him to throw stones at a sinner. He expresses his faith in the reality of Verlaine's break with sin. "The conversion of Verlaine was then entire. He lived then in his cell the new existence of sins wiped away by repentance and absolved by pardon; he was no longer the prisoner discontented with men, but the captive enamoured of God; he experienced the sweetness of the St. Martin's summer of the soul which the Lord reserves for the rejuvenated old age of His own; there were for weeks the pouring out of prayers, joys softened by tears; as all penitents he was fondled (spoiled) by the Virgin, rolled in the swaddling-clothes of tenderness; he had an advance of his inheritance of the joys of Heaven, and he ended by thinking the punishment of his imprisonment too short. So one can affirm that his resolve henceforth to live right was sincere." Verlaine, says he, was a big child whose will would not hold with conscientiousness when he drank; the absinthe "uncaged in him, alas, an evil beast delivered without defence to the Spirit of Evil. He deplored it, swore never to drink again, and he drank." He lived, unavoidably, in the midst of wicked men and women, who were always a temptation. Some of his friends tried to redeem him from them, but in drink Verlaine was indocile, headstrong. "What he needed," says Huysmans, "was some priest to lead him, but God did not send him one. Hence," he adds, "Verlaine was more to be pitied than blamed, the more so that he had awakenings of conscience, of remorse, in this wretched existence." Ah, be assured, that he was not in his lucid moments the haughty, the light-hearted one; he wept with disgust at himself; perhaps he even drank then, as so many others, to forget. Safe from temptations in the hospital he could write mystic poems, he could pour out his heart to her he loved so much, the "Réfuge of Sinners"; he could write then "the most beautiful poems of repentance and the most beautiful rhymed supplications that exist."

So also Coppée. Addressing Huysmans in *La Bonne Souffrance*, he says: "A wind has passed—*spiritus flat ubi vult*—and religious words have been spoken by mouths whence one would not expect to hear them. The poor Verlaine began it. You recall the admirable plaints of penitence in *Sagesse*."

Many affected to despise Verlaine. There was, indeed, much about him that was ignoble. But to such poets and penitents as Huysmans and Coppée he was always "Poor Verlaine." Perhaps that is what will remain of him, the memory not of the old man, old before his time, drunk with absinthe, frequenting low dives, the companion of loose, scheming women, the relapsed sinner who was the weakest of mortals, but the weeping sinner, crushed to earth in his prison cell, rising from his knees to chant through his tears some of the most beautiful penitential psalms ever written. Poor Verlaine!

A LITANY OF PENITENTS

SAINT TERESA always had a special devotion to those saints who once had been great sinners. She found comfort in thinking of their conversion, praying that through their intercession God would forgive her as He had forgiven them. She had devotion in particular to St. Mary Magdalen and to St. Augustine.

For that very reason the life of the great penitent makes an appeal to all of us. God forgave him; the realization of that fact induces us to hope that He will also forgive us. More than that, the true penitent is always a living testimony to the truth of religion. Men do not leave the pleasures of sin, do not afflict their bodies with the scourging rod and the hair-shirt for a mere whim. Hardly. It is because they are convinced that their true happiness, their eternal happiness, can be had but at the price of tears shed over the evil they have done. It is their personal testimony to the belief in the necessity of penance. To them penitence is a plain statement of fact; there is nothing heroic in their eyes in their own suffering for sin, in their turning away from the allurements of the world to follow God. It is just a plain need; if they want Heaven they know they must do penance, for there is no Heaven for the man in sin. We might call that the common sense of religion, even though it is a common sense very much derided in these days when there are so many who affect to believe that Hell and the punishment of sin is just a sorry little joke on the part of God. Just plain common sense we could call it, for it is a strange fact that there is no people, no religion which does not profess at

least to believe that to obtain from its god or gods the re-
mission of sins committed it is necessary to have a sincere
regret for past faults and a firm purpose to sin no more;
while most of them agree that every bad action requires a
real, a corporal expiation. So, with the Egyptians, the
Greeks, the Syrians, the Romans, with nearly all the peo-
ples of antiquity this expiation of sin was a religious truth;
there could be no initiation into the mysteries without such
expiation. It was, too, a fundamental dogma of the
Brahmins, the Buddhists, the negroes of Africa, the In-
dians of America. In this universally surviving truth
there is seen, of course, the remnant of primitive revela-
tion and the history of the primal fall.

Needless to quote the numberless passages in Sacred
Scripture wherein God requires the sinner, if he would be
saved, to do penance. The Old Testament is one continual appeal to penance. The penitential psalms are the
classics of the poems of repentance. The history of King
David is the example that never stales of the folly of sin
and of the wisdom of coming back to God in humble regret at ever having left Him. As Saint Ambrose says:
"David seems to have sinned that he might at once become
an example of penitence."

In the New Testament the teaching of the necessity of
penance is more insistent still. "Do penance, for the
Kingdom of Heaven is at hand." So declares the Lord
(St. Matthew IV, 17). "Amen, I say to you, unless you
do penance you shall not enter into the Kingdom of
Heaven" (St. Matthew, XVIII, 3). "Unless you do penance, you shall all likewise perish" (St. Luke, XIII, 5).
And, indeed, how lovingly the inspired writers tell the
story of the first great penitents of the New Law, Magdalen, Peter, the Good Thief. Jesus was the "friend" of
sinners. We read in an old book that when a zealous pas-
tor named Carpus was weary in trying to reclaim an ob-
stinate sinner in vain, Christ in a vision rebuked him, tell-

ing him He was ready to die a second time for the salvation of sinners.

What the Master taught, so also taught His apostles. Their great message is, "Do penance; be converted to God." How St. Paul must have wept and prayed for the soul of the slave Onesimus—Onesimus, the thief, who had robbed his master, Philemon, and then run away for fear. By the grace of God he met Paul, then a prisoner at Rome, and the great Apostle of the Gentiles converted the poor slave to God, sent him back to his master, and obtained his deliverance. Not only from material bondage was Onesimus freed but from the greater bondage of sin. He is one of the first great penitents of the Church. More striking is the beautiful story we read in the life of St. John the Evangelist. On one of his visitations while he was preaching he was very much attracted to a handsome youth in the congregation. Won to the lad, he brought him to the bishop of the city and said to him, "In the presence of Christ and before this congregation, I earnestly recommend this young man to your care."

The bishop took the trust, educated the lad, baptized and confirmed him. Soon the boy fell into wickedness and ended by becoming the leader of a band of highway robbers. Some time after that St. John returned to the city and asked the bishop for the trust he had committed to him. What a surprise and grief was his when he learned the terrible truth. He wept bitterly. "Oh," said he, "what a guardian have I provided to watch over a brother's soul!" Off he rode to the mountains and, being seized by the robbers, asked to be led to their leader. When the youth saw his old friend, he was covered with confusion and sought to run away from him. But St. John pursued him, crying out, "My son, have compassion on me. There is room for repentance; your salvation is not irrevocable. I will answer for you to Jesus Christ." The robber dropped his weapons and burst into tears. He was henceforth a true penitent, reclaimed by him whose one sermon in his old age was, "Little children, love one another."

That message of repentance the Church has continued to repeat. Sorrow for sin is to be a new baptism, "the baptism of tears," as St. Cyprian calls it. Hence the Church in her practices, her law of Lent, her laws about fasting and abstinence, but gives the expression of her belief that sin once done must be atoned for. It is the law of satisfaction. To the Church sin is always the only evil. She never minimizes that evil; and it is because she knows how great an evil it is that when she succeeds in putting her own conviction into the hearts of her children that she falls to rejoicing, in imitation of her Divine Founder, the Good Shepherd, Who rejoiced over the sheep that had been lost and now was found again. Rejoice she does over the return of the sinner but, true Mother that she is, she is not the doting mother that would spoil with too much kindness the wayward one. She would welcome home the sinner, but her love indicates that there is something else to be done besides the mere wish to return. The sinner has to prove himself. Hence the system of public penance which, so long in vogue in the early Church, strikes terror into our weak souls today because of its severity. To read the penitential canons of the past with the years of penance assigned to various sins, five years for this, twenty-five for that, is to make us tremble at the little penances at which we grumble.

It was in the second century and at the beginning of the third that the penitential discipline of the Church was most severe. It was then, as it were, a great concession to a man who had sinned grievously to be allowed even to begin his penance. Penance was a painful operation necessary for the lasting cure of the sin-diseased soul. Not only was the Church's concern for the sinner himself, but the example of the penances he was made to endure was to keep others from falling by striking terror into them at the sight of the penalties which sin exacted. Hence permission to do penance and so become reconciled to the Church was given only to those who showed unmistakably that they were in earnest. There was to be no dilly dally-ing with sin; it must be cast aside absolutely. The sinner must beg to be allowed to come back home, and until he had obtained that permission, he must be an outcast from the faith, not even allowed to take part in the public offices of the Church he had so disgraced. When he was granted permission to begin his penitential life he came on the first Wednesday in Lent and had the bishop and the clergy im-pose hands on him as they prayed. He was barefoot, his hair clipped, ashes upon his head, and his clothing was of the poorest kind. He prostrated himself on the ground and then the sentence according to the laws of the Church was pronounced upon him. He was told how many years he must do penance, the practices of austerity he must submit to, and urged piously to humility and to a spirit of true mortification.

There were generally four states of penance; the first was for the penitent to remain outside the Church and beg all the faithful who entered to plead his case with God and with the bishop. After he had finished that course of pen-ance he was permitted to stand in the portico of the Church and be present at the prayers before the Mass. His real penance began with the third step when he was allowed to enter the nave of the Church and assist at the Mass of the Catechumens. He left the Church with them before the Mass of the Faithful. Before he advanced to the fourth step he had the hands of the bishop again im-posed upon him and heard the prayers offered up for him. And finally he came to the fourth step when he was al-lowed to participate in all the prayers and celebrations of the Church and to assist at the Holy Sacrifice, being al-lowed, however, to receive Communion only after the solemn declaration of the bishop that the penance was completed. After such a penance there was little danger of relapse. Drastic the remedy was, but effective, as the Church well knew. Well could she be proud of her work of reclamation through such trials and tears.

Seeing that the solicitude of the Church for the sinner is so great, it is not surprising that the penitent has always been a noted figure. He is always the prodigal welcomed home; he is the experienced traveler who assures us on his life that what God said was true, that there was no real happiness in sin, that it was folly to cast aside innocence of heart for the husks of pleasure, that the only real wisdom of life is to love God and serve Him alone. For that reason the study of the lives of great penitents is one of the most salutary; useful not only to the sinner as showing him his miserable folly, convincing him by example of the eagerness of God to welcome him home, but also to the man who has never sinned grievously, as telling him that the life of sin which sometimes seems so alluring is, after all, not worth while; that in the end it has to be regretted; and what sense is there in doing what one will have to regret?

The example of penance has always been cherished in Christian literature. One could make a litany of penitents out of the lives of the Fathers of the Desert. What penitents they were even though in most of them there never had been any grievous sin! It was the example of these terrific penances that drew thousands away from the world, that made the desert bloom with the innumerable flowers of holiness, watered by the tears of the penitents. Those were the ages of penance *par excellence*. But in all ages there have been great penitents: "His mercy is from generation to generation to them that fear Him." The Church has always provided for those who are weary of serving the world and wish to return to God. One sees that in the many penitential orders, as they are

called, wherein the members of these orders take the obliga-
tion upon themselves to do extraordinary works of penance,
or provide for others the means of atoning for great sins.
The same spirit is seen in the confraternities of penitents
who publish to the world even by their manner of dress
that they are poor sinners anxious to atone for their sins.
"To bring forth fruits worthy of penance;" so entreated
the Baptist.   That has been the aim of all who have sought
holiness.   Even in the lives where there has been no great
sin we see extraordinary penance.   Sometimes the grief of
the saints over their petty faults would seem to us almost
an exaggeration, but their yearning for perfection, their
burning love for God, made even the venial sin seem to
them an extraordinary crime of ingratitude.   So we read
of the grief of some of the saints over what we of untender
consciences would dismiss almost as a joke.

We are told that when St. Thomas, Bishop of Hereford,
was young and studying philosophy at Paris he took the
prop of a vine from another man's vineyard in order to hold
up his window.   And so great was his remorse afterwards
for the petty theft that he did severe penance for it sev-
en longs years. So, too, we read in the life of St. Philip
Neri that once when he was a little boy he pushed away his
little sister who was teasing him while he was reading the
psalter; all his life he bewailed this as a great fault.   St.
Ephrem would always bewail the little fits of anger he had
against his playmates in the days before his baptism.
St. Macarius the Elder, a wonderful penitent, had stolen
some figs as a child and had eaten one of them.   From the
day of his conversion to the day of his death be bemoaned
that sin.   St. Walston, Bishop of Worcester, was once
tempted to a sinful thought.   It was only a temptation but
it so disturbed his conscience that he threw himself into a
thicket and there bewailed his fault.   Yet the same man
was always so tender with penitents that he would weep

over them. The great St. Anselm would cry over the petty faults which to his pure eyes seemed great. In the life of St. Conrad of Piacenza we read that one day he ordered one of his servants to set fire to some brushwood. The fire got beyond control and a conflagration was the result. A poor beggar was accused of the crime and was sentenced to death. Conrad at once assumed the blame and even sold all his property in order to make up the losses which his innocent action had caused. So filled was he with penance that he retired to a hermitage, while his wife entered the Poor Clares. For thirty years he led a life of austere penance.

It was because their souls were so tender that they wept over even these little faults. To them tears were sweet so long as they were shed for God. Penance was their love; it was such a very little thing to bear great sorrow so long as the pain brought them to eternal life. Thus when St. Peter of Alcantara appeared to St. Teresa, he said, "O happy penance, which hath obtained me so great a reward!" What mattered the sufferings of the body while the spirit was dwelling with the angels. That was why Saint Francis of Asissi called his body "Brother Ass"—because it was to carry burdens, to be beaten, and to eat little and coarsely.

The litany of penitents is as cosmopolitan as the litany of the saints. From every age and country and station in life their cry of sorrow ascends to Heaven. A litany could be made even of the names of the penitents "that are in the houses of kings." High station in the world may be nothing to brag about, but there is always a specially striking lesson in the conversion of the high and mighty. Surely it takes a great grace from God to make the king or the gay courtier humble himself in the dust. St. Ignatius, St. Francis Borgia are all the more convincing in that they sacrificed much that the world holds dear in order to walk the way of the Cross. It is not easy for the ruler of men to put off his soft purple and fine linen for the hair-shirt and the ashes. But it is not an isolated story in the history of penitents. Not in vain had King David given the example of bitter tears. One loves to be told that the doughty Richard Cœur de Lion died showing signs of sincere repentance and so won his greatest battle, that over himself. It was the same spirit that converted the French King, Dagobert I, from a dissolute life to one of holiness on the occasion of the birth of his son who was to be the great St. Sigebert II. What a cheap bauble was the crown to the man who knew himself to be a miserable sinner.

In all history there is no more striking example of humbled royalty than that of the great Emperor Theodosius. A general of great probity and valor, he had triumphed over the barbarians in Britain and Africa. The Emperor Gratian had such respect for him that he finally made him his colleague, and emperor of the East, in 379. St. Ambrose in 390 was holding a council at Milan when the news was brought that a dreadful massacre had been committed at Thessalonica. A charioteer had been imprisoned for an offense he had committed, and the people were so enraged because the authorities would not release him in order that he might perform in the circus that some of the officers were stoned to death and their bodies dragged through the streets. Theodosius when he heard of the affair was very angry, but Ambrose and the other bishops finally prevailed upon him to overlook the crime. Other advisers, however, urged him to put down the insolence of the public, and at last orders were given to send the soldiers against the city. While the people were in the circus the soldiers surrounded them and a slaughter took place which lasted three hours; seventeen thousand were massacred. Ambrose and the other bishops were filled with horror at the terrible crime. When Theodosius returned to Milan, Ambrose left the city and sent a letter to him telling him that he must do penance and that until he did he would not celebrate Mass before him.

When Ambrose returned, Theodosius as usual came to church. But Ambrose faced him at the door. "It seems to me, sir," said the fearless bishop, "that you do not yet rightly apprehend the enormity of the massacre lately committed. Let not the splendor of your purple robes hinder you from being acquainted with the infirmities of that body which they cover. You are of the same mould with those subjects which you govern; and there is one common Lord and Emperor of the world. With what eyes will you behold His temple? With what feet will you tread His sanctuary? How will you lift up to Him in prayer those hands which are still stained with blood unjustly spilt? Depart, therefore, and attempt not by a second offence to aggravate your former crime, but quietly take the yoke upon you which the Lord has appointed for you. It is sharp, but it is medicinal, and conducive to your health." The emperor tried to defend himself by suggesting that David, too, had sinned. But Ambrose replied: "Him whom you have followed in sinning follow also in his repentance." Theodosius returned home, humbled. For eight months he did penance, clad in penitential weeds, and weeping abundantly over his sin. Rufinus, the master of the offices, tried to soothe him by telling him that there was no need of such grief inasmuch as he had only punished criminals. "Rufinus," replied the emperor, "thou dost but make sport and mock me. Thou little knowest the anguish and trouble I feel. I weep and wail my miserable condition. The Church of God is open to beggars and slaves; but the church doors, and consequently the gates of Heaven, too, are shut against me. For our Lord has peremptorily declared that whatever you shall bind on earth shall be bound in Heaven."

When the emperor finally begged Ambrose to absolve

him, the great bishop ordered him to take his place with the public penitents. Theodosius obeyed; he knelt at the church door among the penitents repeating David's cries of sorrow. He beat his breast, tore his hair, and confessed his sin while the people wept with him. What an edifying sight to see the great emperor humbled in the dust! Ambrose absolved him. It was love for the sinner that closed his eyes to the worldly grandeur of the emperor. It was the greatest blessing that could come to Theodosius. Every day till the day of his death he continued to do penance for his sin. He had the happiness to die in the arms of the bishop who had withstood him. It was Ambrose, too, that preached his funeral sermon.

One of the most thrilling stories of penance is that of St. James of Persia (A. D. 421). He was a nobleman of the highest rank, a man of fine talent, and a great favorite of the king. He was a Christian but apparently only a nominal one, for when the king proclaimed war against Christianity, James lacked the courage to confess himself a member of the hated religion, and denied his God. It was so hard to give up his place in the world for a mere matter of conscience! His wife and his mother, who were devout Christians, were heartbroken at his defection, and they wrote him a letter taunting him with his cringing before a mortal man and threatening him with the Divine justice he must one day face. James was moved by the fearless letter, and began to think of his terrible sin of apostasy. He left the court which had been the cause of his downfall and bewailed in tears his denial of the faith. The king was told of his favorite's penance and sending for him reproached him with ingratitude. But James did not heed the reproaches of the earthly monarch; he saw himself as a wretched sinner, an ingrate to his God. The end of it all was that the gay young courtier was called upon to do penance in his blood for the sin he had committed. He was hacked to pieces. He did not flinch.

He knew that all the agony that could be inflicted upon him was little enough to atone for his crime of apostasy.

That is one thing about the great penitents; they set no bounds to what they wish to endure in atonement. It was so with another nobleman, St. Bavo, the patron saint of Ghent, who lived in the seventh century. For years he had led a life of sin, when one day, some time after the death of his wife, he listened to a sermon preached by St. Amand. So deeply was his heart touched that on the instant he was converted from his wickedness. He followed the preacher and threw himself in tears at the feet of the holy man. Weeping bitterly, he confessed himself the lowest of sinners, and begged to be directed how to atone for his past. Amand was not too tender with the convert; he knew that here was a great sinner who needed to do great penance. The saints while tender with sinners never minimize the horror of sin. Bavo made his confession. He was done with the world now; he sold all his property and gave the proceeds to the poor, one of the hardest penances for any man to do. In time he became a hermit, building for himself a cell and living all the rest of his days on herbs and water, thinking all suffering but small in comparison with the goal to which it led. We read in his life that so great was the example of his penance that sixty other noblemen left the world to lead a life of the most austere penance. Taken from these ages long gone by, these penitents may seem but as mere names, but we must not forget that they were all men like ourselves, to whom pleasure was just as sweet, the smell of life just as attractive, and the practice of self-denial just as repellent. For that reason every one of them must be a hero to us poor weaklings.

The story of St. Hubert has always been a popular one in art and poetry. Hubert was a worldling if ever there was one. The gay court was his world; he thought little of the things of the spirit. One thing to which he was especially devoted was hunting. The legend goes that one Good Friday when everybody else was at the solemn services of the Church, he went forth to hunt. A magnificent stag came across his path and at once he gave chase to it. Suddenly the animal turned. Hubert saw a crucifix between the antlers, and heard a voice which said to him: "Hubert, unless thou turnest to the Lord and leadest a holy life, thou shalt quickly go down into Hell." The huntsman prostrated himself upon the ground and cried out, "Lord, what wouldst Thou have me do?" Henceforth his life was one of rigorous penance, of devotion to the service of God as first bishop of Liège and as apostle of the Ardennes. So earnest was he in his penitence that he longed to wipe out his sins by the blood of martyrdom. But God had other work for him to do, and Hubert lived his saintly life giving to the world he had left the example of sorrow for sin (727).

One likes to linger over the story of Blessed Gunther of Bohemia. He was of a noble family, was related to St. Stephen, King of Hungary, and had the world at his feet. The court was his life; its pleasures filled his mind, and his one thought was to rise in the world. He was fifty years of age when the call to conversion came. Thenceforth his life was one of mortification in atonement for his sins. For thirty-four years he led the life of a hermit, a life of tears and pain, yet considered it all cheap in comparison with the joys of Heaven for which he labored (1045).

A contemporary of his was St. Romuald, founder of the order of the Camaldolese. He belonged to the family of the dukes of Ravenna, and was a thorough worldling, a slave to his sinful passions. The occasion of his conversion was a strange one. His father Sergius slew his adversary in a duel. Romuald, then twenty years of age, was a witness of the crime, and so shocked was he by it that he thought it necessary for him to expiate the crime of his father in a monastery. There he went through a course of rigorous penance for forty days. The penance won his soul to God; from doing penance for the sins of his father he saw the need of doing penance for his own sins. From that day till his death at seventy, through hard labors for the Church, through terrible temptations in the memory of the luxuries of the court he had quitted, he atoned for the sins of his youth (1027).

How often in the history of the saints we see repeated the manner of the conversion of St. Paul, struck to the ground by a blow from Heaven. That was the case with St. John Gualbert. His parents were of the nobility, with an abundance of wealth. Young John had a great future in the world. He lived as a great lord, was full of family pride, a law unto himself. Very poor material, indeed, for a saint; and no one would have laughed as heartily as the young courtier himself had any one suggested that he would ever exchange his fine silks and satins for the ugly hair-shirt.

One day his brother Hugo was murdered and John determined to have revenge. To this he was incited by his father, for the honor of the family demanded that blood should be paid for by blood. As in the case of St. Hubert the conversion took place on Good Friday. John was riding home with his attendant when in a very narrow passage he came face to face with his enemy. He drew his sword to execute his vengeance, when the other threw himself from his horse, fell on his knees and with his arms extended in the form of a cross begged John by the Passion of Christ to spare him. The bloodthirsty John felt the heart within him melt. "I can refuse nothing," he said, "that is asked of me for the sake of Jesus Christ. I not only give you your life, but also my friendship forever. Pray for me that God may pardon my sin." The two former enemies embraced and parted. John came to a monastery and entering the Church prayed before the

Crucifix and in tears begged God to forgive him his sins. The story goes that in answer to his appeal and as a reward for his heroic act of forgiveness the Crucifix bowed to him. A thorough conversion was effected in the heart of the man. He threw himself at the feet of the abbot and asked to be received into the monastery. The abbot was afraid of the anger of John's father, but he permitted him to live there in his secular habit. That would not do John, however; he cut his own hair and borrowed a religious habit. When the father came, angrily protesting against such a course, John finally prevailed upon him to allow him to remain and follow the will of God which had been manifested so clearly to him. The rest of life was for the penitent an austere one. From a hot, impulsive youth he became meek and humble. Yet with that continual penance there went great service for the Church. At the time of his death he had founded twelve monasteries. So great was his practical charity to the poor that often he would empty the granaries of the monasteries to feed them. As in the case of all the other saints, the greater the penance the greater the charity. Sometimes we are given an idea of penitents as poor useless beings wasting their time in idle grief; nothing is further from the truth. St. Peter could weep penitent tears till his cheeks were furrowed, but who was ever more active? So with all these other men of God; the more they realized their own sins, the greater their zeal for the souls of others. Your great penitent is never a man of selfishness.

The description of the penance and the tears of St. Norbert (1134) is one of the most edifying stories we have in the lives of the saints. He belonged to the world of the nobility, loved the life of ease and pleasure which was his birthright and went on his way singing. One day he was thrown from his horse in the midst of a terrific thunder storm. "Lord," he cried in fright, "what wilt Thou have me do?" The answer came: "Turn away from evil and do good; seek after peace and pursue it." It was in the ways of penance he sought and found that peace. Through a long life of penance he never ceased to meditate on the mercy of God, which had given him a chance when so many others had been thrown into Hell.

The desire to do penance impelled the saints to heroism. St. John Capistran had the world at his feet, and then he kicked it away from him. To him there seemed nothing worth while in life but to do penance. He had not been what we would call a great sinner, nevertheless he was a great penitent. When he sought admission into a Franciscan monastery, the guardian, who knew the nobleman's history, and how much he had loved the world, in order to try him out, ordered him to don a ridiculous dress and ride on an ass through the streets of Perugia, with a paper cap on his head on which the names of many grievous sins were written in capital letters. It was a severe trial to the rich young man, once the nice dandy, but he did not shirk it. He was willing to be considered a fool for the sake of Christ. Henceforth his life was a terrible penance. It was that same spirit of sorrow for sin that gave such power to his sermons. One sermon he preached on death and judgment in Bohemia moved one hundred and twenty young men to enter religious orders. There never was absent from him the thought of his sins. He often declared that God treated him with too much leniency. The old man of seventy-one died on the floor, a humble penitent.

Then, too, there was St. Ennodius, of one of the great families of France, related to all the great lords of his day. The world was bright to him; he was married to a rich and noble woman, he was talented, devoted to eloquence and poetry. But he had sinned. One day the grace of God touched his heart and he was moved to weep bitterly over his sins. With the consent of his wife, who embraced a life of continency, he took orders and thenceforth gave his life, his literary talents, to the service of the

Church, in which he attained a high position as Bishop of
Pavia. He endured many things for the faith, but gave
great lustre to the See he so well served. One thinks of
him, however, not as the great bishop but rather as the
poor penitent who had tasted of the sweets of sin yet saw
how all turned to ashes on the lips.

It was not always the man of the world that was the
penitent. Sometimes we find the virtue wonderfully exem-
plified in the lives of the young. Such a one was St.
Andrew Corsini. The Corsini family was one of the most
illustrious in Florence. Andrew, the child of pious
parents, the result, indeed, of prayer, and consecrated to
God before his birth, fell into wickedness as a mere boy.
One day his pious mother, like another Monica grieving
over the dead soul of her child, reproached him for his evil
life. So touched was the boy that he went to the Church of
the Carmelites to pray and think the matter over. There
came to him then a resolution never to go back home again,
but to leave the world and do penance for his youthful
wickedness. From that time till the day of his death at
the age of seventy-one he never lost his first fervor. It
was a life of stern penance, with his hair-shirt, his iron
girdle and his humble bed of pine branches on the floor,
a life of perpetual prayer and tears that finally sanctified
the soul which once was on the edge of perdition. It was
a noble life of the service of God and His poor; but through
it all sounded the lamentations of one who had been a
sinner (1373).

So goes the litany from one age to another. The royal
courts, the palaces of the nobles have given all too many
examples of the service of the world, the flesh and
the devil; yet there is also the other side of the picture, of wonderful sanctity, of the garment of sackcloth underneath the fine linen. So much is said in mem-
oirs of the evil life of the Duchess de la Vallière, for instance; so little of such men as the Jesuit, Pére Ainèet,

who resigned his office as confessor to Louis XIV because that monarch would not give up his illicit attachment for the Duchess. We like to return again and again to the days of the Bourbons when the court of France was a battle ground where the spirit of sin and the spirit of penance were in continual conflict among mesdames and messieurs. "To die well, to die penitent," says Guizot, "was in those days a solicitude which never left the most worldly." The Prince of Conti died devout; even De Retz made his peace with God. Mazarin in the shadow of death saw the vanity of life. "I have misgivings," said he to his confessor, "about not being sufficiently afraid of death." Toward the end, when he was commiserated for his sufferings, he humbly said, "I shall have a great deal more to suffer." When Berulle brought the Carmelites from Spain to France the convent soon numbered among its penitents women of the highest rank in the world. It was there that Mme. de Longueville did penance for twenty-five years. "Now that I make not a single step which does not lead me to death," wrote the young favorite, Cinq Mars, to his mother, "I am more capable than anybody else of estimating the value of the things of the world." When he went forth to his death, wrote the Councillor of State, he "showed a never changing and very resolute firmness to death, together with admirable calmness and the constancy and devotion of a Christian." As his friend de Thou said to him as he marched to the scaffold, "Enough of this world; away to Paradise." It was thus that the two young courtiers recovered their faith in God there in the valley of the shadow of death; and both had been near to losing their souls at the royal court.

"Enough of this world; away to Paradise." Often the same sentiments have been expressed at the approach of death by those whose lives have been so scandalous that their return to God seemed impossible. Who would have expected a change of heart on the part of the licentious,

renegade Talleyrand. A persecutor of the Church whose
holy orders he had received, he was declared by his own
episcopal chapter as "deserving infamy in this world and
damnation in the next." He had reached the heights of
power as a statesman, he had attained the glory of the
world, but in the end it brought only affliction of spirit.
Every night Bishop de Quelen prayed for the conversion
of the notorious sinner: "O my God, I ask for the conversion of M. de Talleyrand. I offer my life to obtain it,
and I willingly consent never to hear of it if only I can
obtain it." The humble prayer was answered. Some time
before his death Talleyrand humbled himself by signing
an open retraction of his errors. He made his confession
and received the last Sacraments. His repentance was
earnest and he died fervently praying to the Mother of
God, for whom he had always had a sentiment of devotion.
Talleyrand then saw that his wisdom which he had thought
so great was but the folly of the heedless prodigal. It
was only by a great grace from God that a Talleyrand
could humble himself to admit that he had been a fool.

Not the least prominent position in the litany of great
penitents is held by those who once had been great soldiers.
It is hard to exaggerate the part played by the warriors in
the early ages of Christianity in helping to propagate the
faith. A great army could be numbered out of the fighting
men whose military career finally led them to martyrdom
in the arena. Some of them had served the world all too
well, had led lives of wickedness in the camp till the grace
of God humbled them into weeping penitents.

Such a one was St. Joannicius, once a driver of hogs,
then a soldier in the Guards of the Emperor Constantine.
A big, robust fellow he was, fearless, who had won fame
by many brilliant military exploits. His life, however,
was one of moral rottenness, and in addition to that as an
Iconoclast he took part in the persecution of the Church.
By the grace of God he was at last converted after a con-

versation with a holy monk. From that time on no penance was too great for him to atone for his past wickedness. During the six years that he remained in the army
after that his whole life seemed to be made of tears, fasting
and prayer. At the age of forty he left the army and
became a monk; and from that day till the day of his
death at the great age of one hundred and sixteen he was
one of the greatest penitents the Church ever had. It is a
great line, that of the soldier penitents, with such wonderful heroes as St. Ignatius Loyola, St. John Camillus,
St. John of God, and in our own day the young Italian
soldier, Giosue Borsi, great sinner, great penitent, great
ascetic, great patriot, a man whose literary testament, "A
Soldier's Confidences with God," is destined to become
one of the great books of the ages.

From every walk of life, indeed, there goes the procession
of sin-weary penitents into the vale of tears. God's grace
softens the hardest hearts. Even the apostate doctor,
Pantaleon, who sacrificed his faith for worldly ambition,
was allowed to come back and atone for his sins by shed-
ding his blood as a martyr. Today the apostate Pantaleon,
tomorrow the great martyr, St. Pantaleon. What hope
there is to the sinner who reads the story of the "Seven
Robbers" who became the seven martyrs; in the story of
the outlaw, Talon, notorious in the Middle Ages, who after
having assisted at the execution of Aimé du Poncet became
a sincere penitent and willingly embraced death as a little
atonement for the evil life he had led. What an inspiration there is in the stories of the penitent women, from
Magdalen down! One could compile a litany of penitents
from the old stories of sorrowing women, of such heroines
of atonement as St. Mary of Egypt, St. Pelagia, St. Thais,
St. Margaret of Cortona, Blessed Angela of Foligno, who,
after having drunk the cup of shame to the bitter dregs,
braved the ridicule of the world they had so long served
and put off the soft garments for the sackcloth and ashes.

Over and over again it is the same story of Magdalen, the woman once a sinner now suffered to behold face to face her risen Master.

But the greatest victory for the spirit of penance was that won over the intellectuals. And how endless the list is. The proudest intellect of all, Augustine, became the model of lowliest penitence. It was the same spirit that led Prudentius to become an ardent penitent, fasting every day until night, using his literary talent to glorify God and to atone for the sins of his youth. It was the same spirit which made the penitent Chaucer disclaim those books of his which he thought "consonant with sin"; which turned the gallant, self-sufficient Racine into a lowly penitent. Several of Racine's daughters were nuns; it was no doubt by their prayers he came back to God. "He was loving towards God," said his son, "when he returned to Him." The life of all the penitents is summed up in these words. How edifying are the last days of La Fontaine. "O my dear friend," said he to one of his companions, "to die is nothing, but thinkest thou that I am about to appear before God? Thou knowest how I have lived." He had lived a life of sin, but for the last two years had done heroic penance. When they came to put him in his shroud they found that he had been wearing a hair-shirt. The maker of wise fables had given in his own last days the best lesson of true wisdom, that the only peace is in keeping the commandments of God. So Lamartine, who in his old age returned to the wisdom of the faith which in the days of his strength he had treated as foolishness. So Boileau who said at the end: "It is very shameful to be still busy-ing myself with rhymes and all these Parnassian trifles when I ought to be thinking of nothing but the account I am prepared to go and render to God." So with the great Manzoni, a wanderer far from God; his wife, who had been a Protestant became a Catholic and Manzoni followed her into the Church. From that time on he desired only to serve the faith which once he had derided. How good was God to them! He would not have them throw their souls away. As an old priest once said about Passaglia: "Never fear, he will die penitent. He has written too beautifully of the Mother of God to be allowed to perish." Passaglia, a true genius, eminent theologian, had written three volumes on the Immaculate Conception, and had had a leading part in preparing the definition of the dogma. Pride of intellect brought about his downfall and his excommunication. It seemed a hopeless case. But some days before his death he retracted his errors and was reconciled to the church.

It would be an endless task, indeed, to complete the litany of those who wandered far from God, who sought their joy in the cup of sin, and finding it all but vanity and affliction of soul came back to Him over the rugged road of the Cross to drink to the dregs the penitential cup of tears. It was thus they found their happiness. They would not have exchanged their hideous hair-shirt for the royal robes of kings. They knew that here, no matter how the world ridiculed their foolishness, was all wisdom. As the great dramatist says of Wolsey:

> His overthrow heap'd happiness upon him;
> For then, and not till then, he felt himself,
> And found the happiness of being little;
> And, to add greater honours to his age
> Than man could give him, he died fearing God.